Later Poems: Selected and New

Also by Adrienne Rich

Your Native Land, Your Life: Poems

Sources

A Wild Patience Has Taken Me This Far: Poems 1978–1981

On Lies, Secrets, and Silence: Selected Prose, 1966–1978

The Dream of a Common Language: Poems 1974–1977

Twenty-one Love Poems

Of Woman Born: Motherhood as Experience and Institution

Poems: Selected and New, 1950–1974

Diving into the Wreck: Poems 1971–1972

The Will to Change: Poems 1968–1970

Leaflets: Poems 1965–1968

Necessities of Life

Snapshots of a Daughter-in-Law: Poems 1954–1962

The Diamond Cutters and Other Poems

A Change of World

Later Poems:
Selected and New

1971–2012

ADRIENNE RICH

W. W. NORTON & COMPANY

New York · London

For information about permission to reproduce selections from this book, write to Permissions, W. W. Norton & Company, Inc., 500 Fifth Avenue, New York, NY 10110

For information about special discounts for bulk purchases, please contact W. W. Norton Special Sales at specialsales@wwnorton.com or 800-233-4830

Manufacturing by Courier Westford

Library of Congress Cataloging-in-Publication Data

Rich, Adrienne, 1929–2012.
[Poems. Selections]
Later poems : selected and new, 1971–2012 /
Adrienne Rich. — 1st ed.
    p. cm.
Includes bibliographical references and index.
Poems.
ISBN 978-0-393-08956-1
I. Title.
PS3535.I233A6 2012
811'.54—dc23
                          2012035461

W. W. Norton & Company, Inc.
500 Fifth Avenue, New York, N.Y. 10110
www.wwnorton.com

W. W. Norton & Company Ltd.
Castle House, 75/76 Wells Street, London W1T 3QT

1 2 3 4 5 6 7 8 9 0

Contents

A Wild Patience Has Taken Me This Far (1978–1981)

Your Native Land, Your Life (1981–1985)

Time's Power (1985–1988)

Telephone Ringing in the Labyrinth (2004–2006)

Tonight No Poetry Will Serve (2007–2010)

New and Unpublished Poems (2010–2012)

———•———

These selections were chosen by Adrienne Rich before her death. The volume was assembled by her editor, and in creating the collection some reformatting of pages was necessary.

Diving into the Wreck

Trying to Talk with a Man

Out in this desert we are testing bombs,

that's why we came here.

Sometimes I feel an underground river
forcing its way between deformed cliffs
an acute angle of understanding
moving itself like a locus of the sun
into this condemned scenery.

What we've had to give up to get here—
whole LP collections, films we starred in
playing in the neighborhoods, bakery windows
full of dry, chocolate-filled Jewish cookies,
the language of love-letters, of suicide notes,
afternoons on the riverbank
pretending to be children

Coming out to this desert
we meant to change the face of
driving among dull green succulents
walking at noon in the ghost town
surrounded by a silence

that sounds like the silence of the place
except that it came with us
and is familiar
and everything we were saying until now
was an effort to blot it out—
Coming out here we are up against it

Out here I feel more helpless
with you than without you
You mention the danger
and list the equipment
we talk of people caring for each other
in emergencies—laceration, thirst—
but you look at me like an emergency

Your dry heat feels like power
your eyes are stars of a different magnitude
they reflect lights that spell out: EXIT
when you get up and pace the floor

talking of the danger
as if it were not ourselves
as if we were testing anything else.

1971

When We Dead Awaken

(for E. Y.

1. Trying to tell you how
   the anatomy of the park
   through stained panes, the way
   guerrillas are advancing
   through minefields, the trash
   burning endlessly in the dump
   to return to heaven like a stain—
   everything outside our skins is an image
   of this affliction:
   stones on my table, carried by hand
   from scenes I trusted
   souvenirs of what I once described
   as happiness
   everything outside my skin
   speaks of the fault that sends me limping
   even the scars of my decisions
   even the sunblaze in the mica-vein
   even you, fellow-creature, sister,
   sitting across from me, dark with love,
   working like me to pick apart
   working with me to remake
   this trailing knitted thing, this cloth of darkness,
   this woman's garment, trying to save the skein.

2. The fact of being separate
   enters your livelihood like a piece of furniture
   —a chest of seventeenth-century wood
   from somewhere in the North.
   It has a huge lock shaped like a woman's head
   but the key has not been found.

In the compartments are other keys
to lost doors, an eye of glass.
Slowly you begin to add
things of your own.
You come and go reflected in its panels.
You give up keeping track of anniversaries,
you begin to write in your diaries
more honestly than ever.

3.   The lovely landscape of southern Ohio
betrayed by strip mining, the
thick gold band on the adulterer's finger
the blurred programs of the offshore pirate station
are causes for hesitation.
Here in the matrix of need and anger, the
disproof of what we thought possible
failures of medication
doubts of another's existence
—tell it over and over, the words
get thick with unmeaning—
yet never have we been closer to the truth
of the lies we were living, listen to me:
the faithfulness I can imagine would be a weed
flowering in tar, a blue energy piercing
the massed atoms of a bedrock disbelief.

1971

Incipience

1.   To live, to lie awake
under scarred plaster
while ice is forming over the earth
at an hour when nothing can be done
to further any decision

to know the composing of the thread
inside the spider's body
first atoms of the web
visible tomorrow

to feel the fiery future
of every matchstick in the kitchen

Nothing can be done
but by inches. I write out my life
hour by hour, word by word
gazing into the anger of old women on the bus
numbering the striations
of air inside the ice cube
imagining the existence
of something uncreated
this poem
our lives

2.   A man is asleep in the next room
        We are his dreams
        We have the heads and breasts of women
        the bodies of birds of prey
        Sometimes we turn into silver serpents
    While we sit up smoking and talking of how to live
    he turns on the bed and murmurs

A man is asleep in the next room
      A neurosurgeon enters his dream
      and begins to dissect his brain
      She does not look like a nurse
      she is absorbed in her work
      she has a stern, delicate face like Marie Curie
She is not/might be either of us

A man is asleep in the next room
      He has spent a whole day
      standing, throwing stones into the black pool
      which keeps its blackness
Outside the frame of his dream we are stumbling up the hill
      hand in hand, stumbling and guiding each other
      over the scarred volcanic rock

1971

The Mirror in Which Two Are Seen As One

1.

She is the one you call sister.
Her simplest act has glamor,
as when she scales a fish the knife
flashes in her long fingers
no motion wasted or when
rapidly talking of love
she steel-wool burnishes
the battered kettle

Love-apples cramp you sideways
with sudden emptiness
the cereals glutting you, the grains
ripe clusters picked by hand
Love: the refrigerator
with open door
the ripe steaks bleeding
their hearts out in plastic film
the whipped butter, the apricots
the sour leftovers

A crate is waiting in the orchard
for you to fill it
your hands are raw with scraping
the sharp bark, the thorns
of this succulent tree
Pick, pick, pick
this harvest is a failure
the juice runs down your cheekbones
like sweat or tears

2.

She is the one you call sister
you blaze like lightning about the room
flicker around her like fire
dazzle yourself in her wide eyes
listing her unfelt needs
thrusting the tenets of your life
into her hands

She moves through a world of India print
her body dappled
with softness, the paisley swells at her hip
walking the street in her cotton shift
buying fresh figs because you love them
photographing the ghetto because you took her there

Why are you crying dry up your tears
we are sisters
words fail you in the stare of her hunger
you hand her another book
scored by your pencil
you hand her a record
of two flutes in India reciting

3.

Late summer night the insects
fry in the yellowed lightglobe
your skin burns gold in its light
In this mirror, who are you? Dreams of the nunnery
with its discipline, the nursery
with its nurse, the hospital
where all the powerful ones are masked
the graveyard where you sit on the graves

of women who died in childbirth
and women who died at birth

Dreams of your sister's birth
your mother dying in childbirth over and over
not knowing how to stop
bearing you over and over

your mother dead and you unborn
your two hands grasping your head
drawing it down against the blade of life
your nerves the nerves of a midwife
learning her trade

1971

From the Prison House

Underneath my lids another eye has opened
it looks nakedly
at the light

that soaks in from the world of pain
even when I sleep

Steadily it regards
everything I am going through

and more

it sees the clubs and rifle-butts
rising and falling
it sees

detail not on TV

the fingers of the policewoman
searching the cunt of the young prostitute
it sees

the roaches dropping into the pan
where they cook the pork
in the House of D

it sees
the violence
embedded in silence

This eye
is not for weeping
its vision
must be unblurred

though tears are on my face

its intent is clarity
it must forget
nothing

September 1971

Diving into the Wreck

First having read the book of myths,
and loaded the camera,
and checked the edge of the knife-blade,
I put on
the body-armor of black rubber
the absurd flippers
the grave and awkward mask.
I am having to do this
not like Cousteau with his
assiduous team
aboard the sun-flooded schooner
but here alone.

There is a ladder.
The ladder is always there
hanging innocently
close to the side of the schooner.
We know what it is for,
we who have used it.
Otherwise
it's a piece of maritime floss
some sundry equipment.

I go down.
Rung after rung and still
the oxygen immerses me
the blue light
the clear atoms
of our human air.
I go down.
My flippers cripple me,

I crawl like an insect down the ladder
and there is no one
to tell me when the ocean
will begin.

First the air is blue and then
it is bluer and then green and then
black I am blacking out and yet
my mask is powerful
it pumps my blood with power
the sea is another story
the sea is not a question of power
I have to learn alone
to turn my body without force
in the deep element.

And now: it is easy to forget
what I came for
among so many who have always
lived here
swaying their crenellated fans
between the reefs
and besides
you breathe differently down here.

I came to explore the wreck.
The words are purposes.
The words are maps.
I came to see the damage that was done
and the treasures that prevail.
I stroke the beam of my lamp
slowly along the flank
of something more permanent
than fish or weed

the thing I came for:
the wreck and not the story of the wreck
the thing itself and not the myth
the drowned face always staring
toward the sun
the evidence of damage
worn by salt and sway into this threadbare beauty
the ribs of the disaster
curving their assertion
among the tentative haunters.

This is the place.
And I am here, the mermaid whose dark hair
streams black, the merman in his armored body
We circle silently
about the wreck
we dive into the hold.
I am she: I am he

whose drowned face sleeps with open eyes
whose breasts still bear the stress
whose silver, copper, vermeil cargo lies
obscurely inside barrels
half-wedged and left to rot
we are the half-destroyed instruments
that once held to a course
the water-eaten log
the fouled compass

We are, I am, you are
by cowardice or courage
the one who find our way
back to this scene
carrying a knife, a camera

a book of myths
in which
our names do not appear.

1972

The Phenomenology of Anger

1.   The freedom of the wholly mad
to smear & play with her madness
write with her fingers dipped in it
the length of a room

which is not, of course, the freedom
you have, walking on Broadway
to stop & turn back or go on
10 blocks; 20 blocks

but feels enviable maybe
to the compromised

curled in the placenta of the real
which was to feed & which is strangling her.

2.   Trying to light a log that's lain in the damp
as long as this house has stood:
even with dry sticks I can't get started
even with thorns.
I twist last year into a knot of old headlines
—this rose won't bloom.

How does a pile of rags the machinist wiped his hands on
feel in its cupboard, hour upon hour?
Each day during the heat-wave
they took the temperature of the haymow.
I huddled fugitive
in the warm sweet simmer of the hay

muttering: *Come.*

3.   Flat heartland of winter.
The moonmen come back from the moon
the firemen come out of the fire.
Time without a taste: time without decisions.
Self-hatred, a monotone in the mind.
The shallowness of a life lived in exile
even in the hot countries.
Cleaver, staring into a window full of knives.

4.   White light splits the room.
Table.   Window.   Lampshade.   You.
My hands, sticky in a new way.
Menstrual blood
seeming to leak from your side.
Will the judges try to tell me
which was the blood of whom?

5.   Madness.   Suicide.   Murder.
Is there no way out but these?
The enemy, always just out of sight
snowshoeing the next forest, shrouded
in a snowy blur, abominable snowman
—at once the most destructive
and the most elusive being
gunning down the babies at My Lai
vanishing in the face of confrontation.
The prince of air and darkness
computing body counts, masturbating
in the factory
of facts.

6.   Fantasies of murder: not enough:
to kill is to cut off from pain
but the killer goes on hurting
Not enough. When I dream of meeting

the enemy, this is my dream:
white acetylene
ripples from my body
effortlessly released
perfectly trained
on the true enemy

raking his body down to the thread
of existence
burning away his lie
leaving him in a new
world; a changed
man

7.   I suddenly see the world
as no longer viable:
you are out there burning the crops
with some new sublimate
This morning you left the bed
we still share
and went out to spread impotence
upon the world

I hate you.
I hate the mask you wear, your eyes
assuming a depth
they do not possess, drawing me
into the grotto of your skull
the landscape of bone
I hate your words
they make me think of fake
revolutionary bills
crisp imitation parchment
they sell at battlefields.

Last night, in this room, weeping
I asked you: *what are you feeling?*
do you feel anything?
Now in the torsion of your body
as you defoliate the fields we lived from
I have your answer.

8. Dogeared earth. Wormeaten moon.
A pale cross-hatching of silver
lies like a wire screen on the black
water. All these phenomena
are temporary.

I would have loved to live in a world
of women and men gaily
in collusion with green leaves, stalks,
building mineral cities, transparent domes,
little huts of woven grass
each with its own pattern—
a conspiracy to coexist
with the Crab Nebula, the exploding
universe, the Mind—

9. "The only real love I have ever felt
was for children and other women.
Everything else was lust, pity,
self-hatred, pity, lust."
This is a woman's confession.
Now, look again at the face
of Botticelli's Venus, Kali,
the Judith of Chartres
with her so-called smile.

10. how we are burning up our lives
testimony:
>   the subway
>   hurtling to Brooklyn
>   her head on her knees
>   asleep or drugged
la vía del tren subterráneo
es peligrosa
>   many sleep
>   the whole way
>   others sit
>   staring holes of fire into the air
>   others plan rebellion:
>   night after night
>   awake in prison, my mind
>   licked at the mattress like a flame
>   till the cellblock went up roaring
>   Thoreau setting fire to the woods
Every act of becoming conscious
(it says here in this book)
is an unnatural act

1972

For a Sister

*(Natalya Gorbanevskaya, two years incarcerated in a Soviet penal mental asylum
for her political activism; and others*

I trust none of them. Only my existence
thrown out in the world like a towchain
battered and twisted in many chance connections,
being pulled this way, pulling in that.

I have to steal the sense of dust on your floor,
milk souring in your pantry
after they came and took you.
I'm forced to guess at the look you threw backward.

A few paragraphs in the papers,
allowing for printers' errors, wilful omissions,
the trained violence of doctors.
I don't trust them, but I'm learning how to use them.

Little by little out of the blurred conjectures
your face clears, a sunken marble
slowly cranked up from underwater.
I feel the ropes straining under their load of despair.

They searched you for contraband, they made their notations.
A look of intelligence could get you twenty years.
Better to trace nonexistent circles with your finger,
try to imitate the smile of the permanently dulled.

My images. This metaphor for what happens.
A geranium in flames on a green cloth
becomes yours. You, coming home after years
to light the stove, get out the typewriter and begin again. Your story.

1972

For the Dead

I dreamed I called you on the telephone
to say: *Be kinder to yourself*
but you were sick and would not answer

The waste of my love goes on this way
trying to save you from yourself

I have always wondered about the leftover
energy, water rushing down a hill
long after the rains have stopped

or the fire you want to go to bed from
but cannot leave, burning-down but not burnt-down
the red coals more extreme, more curious
in their flashing and dying
than you wish they were
sitting there long after midnight

1972

Meditations for a Savage Child

(The prose passages are from J-M Itard's account of The Wild Boy of Aveyron, *as translated by G. and M. Humphrey)*

I

There was a profound indifference to the objects of our pleasures and of our fictitious needs; there was still . . . so intense a passion for the freedom of the fields . . . that he would certainly have escaped into the forest had not the most rigid precautions been taken . . .

In their own way, by their own lights
they tried to care for you
tried to teach you to care
for objects of their caring:

        glossed oak planks, glass
        whirled in a fire
        to impossible thinness

to teach you names
for things
you did not need

        muslin shirred against the sun
        linen on a sack of feathers
        locks, keys
        boxes with coins inside

they tried to make you feel
the importance of

        a piece of cowhide
        sewn around a bundle
        of leaves impressed with signs

to teach you language:
the thread their lives
were strung on

II

*When considered from a more general and philosophic point of view, these
scars bear witness . . . against the feebleness and insufficiency of man
when left entirely to himself, and in favor of the resources of nature which
. . . work openly to repair and conserve that which she tends secretly to
impair and destroy.*

I keep thinking about the lesson of the human ear
which stands for music, which stands for balance—
or the cat's ear which I can study better
the whorls and ridges exposed
It seems a hint dropped about the inside of the skull
which I cannot see
lobe, zone, that part of the brain
which is pure survival

The most primitive part
I go back into at night
pushing the leathern curtain
with naked fingers
then
with naked body

There where every wound is registered
as scar tissue

A cave of scars!
ancient, archaic wallpaper
built up, layer on layer
from the earliest, dream-white
to yesterday's, a red-black scrawl
a red mouth slowly closing

Go back so far there is another language
go back far enough the language
is no longer personal

these scars bear witness
but whether to repair
or to destruction
I no longer know

III

It is true that there is visible on the throat a very extended scar which
might throw some doubt upon the soundness of the underlying parts if one
were not reassured by the appearance of the scar . . .

When I try to speak
my throat is cut
and, it seems, by his hand

The sounds I make are prehuman, radical
the telephone is always
ripped-out

and he sleeps on
Yet always the tissue
grows over, white as silk

hardly a blemish
maybe a hieroglyph for scream

Child, no wonder you never wholly
trusted your keepers

IV

A hand with the will rather than the habit of crime had wished to make
an attempt on the life of this child . . . left for dead in the woods, he will
have owed the prompt recovery of his wound to the help of nature alone.

In the 18th century infanticide
reaches epidemic proportions:
old prints attest to it: starving mothers
smothering babies in sleep
abandoning newborns in sleet
on the poorhouse steps
gin-blurred, setting fire to the room

I keep thinking of the flights we used to take
on the grapevine across the gully
littered with beer-bottles where dragonflies flashed
we were 10, 11 years old
wild little girls with boyish bodies
flying over the moist
shadow-mottled earth
till they warned us to stay away from there

Later they pointed out
the venetian blinds
of the abortionist's house
we shivered

Men can do things to you
was all they said

V

And finally, my Lord, looking at this long experiment . . . whether it
be considered as the methodical education of a savage or as no more than
the physical and moral treatment of one of those creatures ill-favored by
nature, rejected by society and abandoned by medicine, the care that has
been taken and ought still to be taken of him, the changes that have taken
place, and those that can be hoped for, the voice of humanity, the interest
inspired by such a desertion and a destiny so strange—all these things
recommend this extraordinary young man to the attention of scientists, to
the solicitude of administrators, and to the protection of the government.

1.   The doctor in "Uncle Vanya":
     They will call us fools,
     blind, ignorant, they will
     despise us

     devourers of the forest
     leaving teeth of metal in every tree
     so the tree can neither grow
     nor be cut for lumber

     Does the primeval forest
     weep
     for its devourers

     does nature mourn
     our existence
     is the child with arms
     burnt to the flesh of its sides
     weeping eyelessly for man

2.   At the end of the distinguished doctor's
     lecture
     a young woman raises her hand:

You have the power
in your hands, you control our lives—
why do you want our pity too?
Why are men afraid
why do you pity yourselves
why do the administrators
lack solicitude, the government
refuse protection,
why should the wild child
weep for the scientists
why

The Dream of a
Common Language

Power

Living   in the earth-deposits   of our history

Today a backhoe divulged   out of a crumbling flank of earth
one bottle   amber   perfect   a hundred-year-old
cure for fever   or melancholy   a tonic
for living on this earth   in the winters of this climate

Today I was reading about Marie Curie:
she must have known she suffered   from radiation sickness
her body bombarded for years   by the element
she had purified
It seems she denied to the end
the source of the cataracts on her eyes
the cracked and suppurating skin   of her finger-ends
till she could no longer hold   a test-tube or a pencil

She died   a famous woman   denying
her wounds
denying
her wounds   came   from the same source as her power

1974

Origins and History of Consciousness

I

Night-life. Letters, journals, bourbon
sloshed in the glass. Poems crucified on the wall,
dissected, their bird-wings severed
like trophies. No one lives in this room
without living through some kind of crisis.

No one lives in this room
without confronting the whiteness of the wall
behind the poems, planks of books,
photographs of dead heroines.
Without contemplating last and late
the true nature of poetry. The drive
to connect. The dream of a common language.

Thinking of lovers, their blind faith, their
experienced crucifixions,
my envy is not simple. I have dreamed of going to bed
as walking into clear water ringed by a snowy wood
white as cold sheets, thinking, *I'll freeze in there.*
My bare feet are numbed already by the snow
but the water
is mild, I sink and float
like a warm amphibious animal
that has broken the net, has run
through fields of snow leaving no print;
this water washes off the scent—
You are clear now
of the hunter, the trapper
the wardens of the mind—

yet the warm animal dreams on
of another animal
swimming under the snow-flecked surface of the pool,
and wakes, and sleeps again.

No one sleeps in this room without
the dream of a common language.

II

It was simple to meet you, simple to take your eyes
into mine, saying: these are eyes I have known
from the first. . . . It was simple to touch you
against the hacked background, the grain of what we
had been, the choices, years. . . . It was even simple
to take each other's lives in our hands, as bodies.

What is not simple: to wake from drowning
from where the ocean beat inside us like an afterbirth
into this common, acute particularity
these two selves who walked half a lifetime untouching—
to wake to something deceptively simple: a glass
sweated with dew, a ring of the telephone, a scream
of someone beaten up far down in the street
causing each of us to listen to her own inward scream

knowing the mind of the mugger and the mugged
as any woman must who stands to survive this city,
this century, this life . . .
each of us having loved the flesh in its clenched or loosened beauty
better than trees or music (yet loving those too
as if they were flesh—and they are—but the flesh
of beings unfathomed as yet in our roughly literal life).

III

It's simple to wake from sleep with a stranger,
dress, go out, drink coffee,
enter a life again. It isn't simple
to wake from sleep into the neighborhood
of one neither strange nor familiar
whom we have chosen to trust. Trusting, untrusting,
we lowered ourselves into this, let ourselves
downward hand over hand as on a rope that quivered
over the unsearched. . . . We did this. Conceived
of each other, conceived each other in a darkness
which I remember as drenched in light.
                                    I want to call this, life.

But I can't call it life until we start to move
beyond this secret circle of fire
where our bodies are giant shadows flung on a wall
where the night becomes our inner darkness, and sleeps
like a dumb beast, head on her paws, in the corner.

1972–1974

Hunger

(for Audre Lorde)

1.

A fogged hill-scene on an enormous continent,
intimacy rigged with terrors,
a sequence of blurs the Chinese painter's ink-stick planned,
a scene of desolation comforted
by two human figures recklessly exposed,
leaning together in a sticklike boat
in the foreground. Maybe we look like this,
I don't know. I'm wondering
whether we even have what we think we have—
lighted windows signifying shelter,
a film of domesticity
over fragile roofs. I know I'm partly somewhere else—
huts strung across a drought-stretched land
not mine, dried breasts, mine and not mine, a mother
watching my children shrink with hunger.
I live in my Western skin,
my Western vision, torn
and flung to what I can't control or even fathom.
Quantify suffering, you could rule the world.

2.

They cán rule the world while they can persuade us
our pain belongs in some order.
Is death by famine worse than death by suicide,
than a life of famine and suicide, if a black lesbian dies,
if a white prostitute dies, if a woman genius
starves herself to feed others,

self-hatred battening on her body?
Something that kills us or leaves us half-alive
is raging under the name of an "act of god"
in Chad, in Niger, in the Upper Volta—
yes, that male god that acts on us and on our children,
that male State that acts on us and on our children
till our brains are blunted by malnutrition,
yet sharpened by the passion for survival,
our powers expended daily on the struggle
to hand a kind of life on to our children,
to change reality for our lovers
even in a single trembling drop of water.

3.

We can look at each other through both our lifetimes
like those two figures in the sticklike boat
flung together in the Chinese ink-scene;
even our intimacies are rigged with terror.
Quantify suffering? My guilt at least is open,
I stand convicted by all my convictions—
you, too. We shrink from touching
our power, we shrink away, we starve ourselves
and each other, we're scared shitless
of what it could be to take and use our love,
hose it on a city, on a world,
to wield and guide its spray, destroying
poisons, parasites, rats, viruses—
like the terrible mothers we long and dread to be.

4.

The decision to feed the world
is the real decision. No revolution
has chosen it. For that choice requires

that women shall be free.
I choke on the taste of bread in North America
but the taste of hunger in North America
is poisoning me. Yes, I'm alive to write these words,
to leaf through Kollwitz's women
huddling the stricken children into their stricken arms
the "mothers" drained of milk, the "survivors" driven
to self-abortion, self-starvation, to a vision
bitter, concrete, and wordless.
I'm alive to want more than life,
want it for others starving and unborn,
to name the deprivations boring
into my will, my affections, into the brains
of daughters, sisters, lovers caught in the crossfire
of terrorists of the mind.
In the black mirror of the subway window
hangs my own face, hollow with anger and desire.
Swathed in exhaustion, on the trampled newsprint,
a woman shields a dead child from the camera.
The passion to be inscribes her body.
Until we find each other, we are alone.

1974–1975

Cartographies of Silence

1.

A conversation begins
with a lie. And each

speaker of the so-called common language feels
the ice-floe split, the drift apart

as if powerless, as if up against
a force of nature

A poem can begin
with a lie. And be torn up.

A conversation has other laws
recharges itself with its own

false energy. Cannot be torn
up. Infiltrates our blood. Repeats itself.

Inscribes with its unreturning stylus
the isolation it denies.

2.

The classical music station
playing hour upon hour in the apartment

the picking up and picking up
and again picking up the telephone

The syllables uttering
the old script over and over

The loneliness of the liar
living in the formal network of the lie

twisting the dials to drown the terror
beneath the unsaid word

3.

The technology of silence
The rituals, etiquette

the blurring of terms
silence not absence

of words or music or even
raw sounds

Silence can be a plan
rigorously executed

the blueprint to a life

It is a presence
it has a history   a form

Do not confuse it
with any kind of absence

4.

How calm, how inoffensive these words
begin to seem to me

though begun in grief and anger
Can I break through this film of the abstract

without wounding myself or you
there is enough pain here

This is why the classical or the jazz music station plays?
to give a ground of meaning to our pain?

5.

The silence that strips bare:
In Dreyer's *Passion of Joan*

Falconetti's face, hair shorn, a great geography
mutely surveyed by the camera

If there were a poetry where this could happen
not as blank spaces or as words

stretched like a skin over meanings
but as silence falls at the end

of a night through which two people
have talked till dawn

6.

The scream
of an illegitimate voice

It has ceased to hear itself, therefore
it asks itself

How do I exist?

This was the silence I wanted to break in you
I had questions but you would not answer

I had answers but you could not use them
This is useless to you and perhaps to others

7.

It was an old theme even for me:
Language cannot do everything—

chalk it on the walls where the dead poets
lie in their mausoleums

If at the will of the poet the poem
could turn into a thing

a granite flank laid bare, a lifted head
alight with dew

If it could simply look you in the face
with naked eyeballs, not letting you turn

till you, and I who long to make this thing,
were finally clarified together in its stare

8.

No. Let me have this dust,
these pale clouds dourly lingering, these words

moving with ferocious accuracy
like the blind child's fingers

or the newborn infant's mouth
violent with hunger

No one can give me, I have long ago
taken this method

whether of bran pouring from the loose-woven sack
or of the bunsen-flame turned low and blue

If from time to time I envy
the pure annunciations to the eye

the *visio beatifica*
if from time to time I long to turn

like the Eleusinian hierophant
holding up a simple ear of grain

for return to the concrete and everlasting world
what in fact I keep choosing

are these words, these whispers, conversations
from which time after time the truth breaks moist and green.

1975

Twenty-one Love Poems

I

Wherever in this city, screens flicker
with pornography, with science-fiction vampires,
victimized hirelings bending to the lash,
we also have to walk . . . if simply as we walk
through the rainsoaked garbage, the tabloid cruelties
of our own neighborhoods.
We need to grasp our lives inseparable
from those rancid dreams, that blurt of metal, those disgraces,
and the red begonia perilously flashing
from a tenement sill six stories high,
or the long-legged young girls playing ball
in the junior highschool playground.
No one has imagined us. We want to live like trees,
sycamores blazing through the sulfuric air,
dappled with scars, still exuberantly budding,
our animal passion rooted in the city.

II

I wake up in your bed. I know I have been dreaming.
Much earlier, the alarm broke us from each other,
you've been at your desk for hours. I know what I dreamed:
our friend the poet comes into my room
where I've been writing for days,
drafts, carbons, poems are scattered everywhere,
and I want to show her one poem
which is the poem of my life. But I hesitate,
and wake. You've kissed my hair
to wake me. *I dreamed you were a poem,*
I say, *a poem I wanted to show someone . . .*

and I laugh and fall dreaming again
of the desire to show you to everyone I love,
to move openly together
in the pull of gravity, which is not simple,
which carries the feathered grass a long way down the upbreathing air.

III

Since we're not young, weeks have to do time
for years of missing each other. Yet only this odd warp
in time tells me we're not young.
Did I ever walk the morning streets at twenty,
my limbs streaming with a purer joy?
did I lean from any window over the city
listening for the future
as I listen here with nerves tuned for your ring?
And you, you move toward me with the same tempo.
Your eyes are everlasting, the green spark
of the blue-eyed grass of early summer,
the green-blue wild cress washed by the spring.
At twenty, yes: we thought we'd live forever.
At forty-five, I want to know even our limits.
I touch you knowing we weren't born tomorrow,
and somehow, each of us will help the other live,
and somewhere, each of us must help the other die.

IV

I come home from you through the early light of spring
flashing off ordinary walls, the Pez Dorado,
the Discount Wares, the shoe-store. . . . I'm lugging my sack
of groceries, I dash for the elevator
where a man, taut, elderly, carefully composed
lets the door almost close on me. —For *god's sake hold it!*
I croak at him. —*Hysterical,*— he breathes my way.
I let myself into the kitchen, unload my bundles,

make coffee, open the window, put on Nina Simone
singing *Here comes the sun.* . . . I open the mail,
drinking delicious coffee, delicious music,
my body still both light and heavy with you. The mail
lets fall a Xerox of something written by a man
aged 27, a hostage, tortured in prison:
My genitals have been the object of such a sadistic display
they keep me constantly awake with the pain . . .
Do whatever you can to survive.
You know, I think that men love wars . . .
And my incurable anger, my unmendable wounds
break open further with tears, I am crying helplessly,
and they still control the world, and you are not in my arms.

V

This apartment full of books could crack open
to the thick jaws, the bulging eyes
of monsters, easily: Once open the books, you have to face
the underside of everything you've loved—
the rack and pincers held in readiness, the gag
even the best voices have had to mumble through,
the silence burying unwanted children—
women, deviants, witnesses—in desert sand.
Kenneth tells me he's been arranging his books
so he can look at Blake and Kafka while he types;
yes; and we still have to reckon with Swift
loathing the woman's flesh while praising her mind,
Goethe's dread of the Mothers, Claudel vilifying Gide,
and the ghosts—their hands clasped for centuries—
of artists dying in childbirth, wise-women charred at the stake,
centuries of books unwritten piled behind these shelves;
and we still have to stare into the absence
of men who would not, women who could not, speak
to our life—this still unexcavated hole
called civilization, this act of translation, this half-world.

VI

Your small hands, precisely equal to my own—
only the thumb is larger, longer—in these hands
I could trust the world, or in many hands like these,
handling power-tools or steering-wheel
or touching a human face. . . . Such hands could turn
the unborn child rightways in the birth canal
or pilot the exploratory rescue-ship
through icebergs, or piece together
the fine, needle-like sherds of a great krater-cup
bearing on its sides
figures of ecstatic women striding
to the sibyl's den or the Eleusinian cave—
such hands might carry out an unavoidable violence
with such restraint, with such a grasp
of the range and limits of violence
that violence ever after would be obsolete.

VII

What kind of beast would turn its life into words?
What atonement is this all about?
—and yet, writing words like these, I'm also living.
Is all this close to the wolverines' howled signals,
that modulated cantata of the wild?
or, when away from you I try to create you in words,
am I simply using you, like a river or a war?
And how have I used rivers, how have I used wars
to escape writing of the worst thing of all—
not the crimes of others, not even our own death,
but the failure to want our freedom passionately enough
so that blighted elms, sick rivers, massacres would seem
mere emblems of that desecration of ourselves?

VIII

I can see myself years back at Sunion,
hurting with an infected foot, Philoctetes
in woman's form, limping the long path,
lying on a headland over the dark sea,
looking down the red rocks to where a soundless curl
of white told me a wave had struck,
imagining the pull of that water from that height,
knowing deliberate suicide wasn't my métier,
yet all the time nursing, measuring that wound.
Well, that's finished. The woman who cherished
her suffering is dead. I am her descendant.
I love the scar-tissue she handed on to me,
but I want to go on from here with you
fighting the temptation to make a career of pain.

IX

Your silence today is a pond where drowned things live
I want to see raised dripping and brought into the sun.
It's not my own face I see there, but other faces,
even your face at another age.
Whatever's lost there is needed by both of us—
a watch of old gold, a water-blurred fever chart,
a key. . . . Even the silt and pebbles of the bottom
deserve their glint of recognition. I fear this silence,
this inarticulate life. I'm waiting
for a wind that will gently open this sheeted water
for once, and show me what I can do
for you, who have often made the unnameable
nameable for others, even for me.

X

Your dog, tranquil and innocent, dozes through
our cries, our murmured dawn conspiracies
our telephone calls. She knows—what can she know?
If in my human arrogance I claim to read
her eyes, I find there only my own animal thoughts:
that creatures must find each other for bodily comfort,
that voices of the psyche drive through the flesh
further than the dense brain could have foretold,
that the planetary nights are growing cold for those
on the same journey who want to touch
one creature-traveler clear to the end;
that without tenderness, we are in hell.

XI

Every peak is a crater. This is the law of volcanoes,
making them eternally and visibly female.
No height without depth, without a burning core,
though our straw soles shred on the hardened lava.
I want to travel with you to every sacred mountain
smoking within like the sibyl stooped over her tripod,
I want to reach for your hand as we scale the path,
to feel your arteries glowing in my clasp,
never failing to note the small, jewel-like flower
unfamiliar to us, nameless till we rename her,
that clings to the slowly altering rock—
that detail outside ourselves that brings us to ourselves,
was here before us, knew we would come, and sees beyond us.

XII

Sleeping, turning in turn like planets
rotating in their midnight meadow:

a touch is enough to let us know
we're not alone in the universe, even in sleep:
the dream-ghosts of two worlds
walking their ghost-towns, almost address each other.
I've wakened to your muttered words
spoken light- or dark-years away
as if my own voice had spoken.
But we have different voices, even in sleep,
and our bodies, so alike, are yet so different
and the past echoing through our bloodstreams
is freighted with different language, different meanings—
though in any chronicle of the world we share
it could be written with new meaning
we were two lovers of one gender,
we were two women of one generation.

XIII

The rules break like a thermometer,
quicksilver spills across the charted systems,
we're out in a country that has no language
no laws, we're chasing the raven and the wren
through gorges unexplored since dawn
whatever we do together is pure invention
the maps they gave us were out of date
by years . . . we're driving through the desert
wondering if the water will hold out
the hallucinations turn to simple villages
the music on the radio comes clear—
neither *Rosenkavalier* nor *Götterdämmerung*
but a woman's voice singing old songs
with new words, with a quiet bass, a flute
plucked and fingered by women outside the law.

XIV

It was your vision of the pilot
confirmed my vision of you: you said, *He keeps*
on steering headlong into the waves, on purpose
while we crouched in the open hatchway
vomiting into plastic bags
for three hours between St. Pierre and Miquelon.
I never felt closer to you.
In the close cabin where the honeymoon couples
huddled in each other's laps and arms
I put my hand on your thigh
to comfort both of us, your hand came over mine,
we stayed that way, suffering together
in our bodies, as if all suffering
were physical, we touched so in the presence
of strangers who knew nothing and cared less
vomiting their private pain
as if all suffering were physical.

(THE FLOATING POEM, UNNUMBERED)

Whatever happens with us, your body
will haunt mine—tender, delicate
your lovemaking, like the half-curled frond
of the fiddlehead fern in forests
just washed by sun. Your traveled, generous thighs
between which my whole face has come and come—
the innocence and wisdom of the place my tongue has found
    there—
the live, insatiate dance of your nipples in my mouth—
your touch on me, firm, protective, searching
me out, your strong tongue and slender fingers
reaching where I had been waiting years for you
in my rose-wet cave—whatever happens, this is.

XV

If I lay on that beach with you
white, empty, pure green water warmed by the Gulf Stream
and lying on that beach we could not stay
because the wind drove fine sand against us
as if it were against us
if we tried to withstand it and we failed—
if we drove to another place
to sleep in each other's arms
and the beds were narrow like prisoners' cots
and we were tired and did not sleep together
and this was what we found, so this is what we did—
was the failure ours?
If I cling to circumstances I could feel
not responsible. Only she who says
she did not choose, is the loser in the end.

XVI

Across a city from you, I'm with you,
just as an August night
moony, inlet-warm, seabathed, I watched you sleep,
the scrubbed, sheenless wood of the dressing-table
cluttered with our brushes, books, vials in the moonlight—
or a salt-mist orchard, lying at your side
watching red sunset through the screendoor of the cabin,
G minor Mozart on the tape-recorder,
falling asleep to the music of the sea.
This island of Manhattan is wide enough
for both of us, and narrow:
I can hear your breath tonight, I know how your face
lies upturned, the halflight tracing
your generous, delicate mouth
where grief and laughter sleep together.

XVII

No one's fated or doomed to love anyone.
The accidents happen, we're not heroines,
they happen in our lives like car crashes,
books that change us, neighborhoods
we move into and come to love.
Tristan und Isolde is scarcely the story,
women at least should know the difference
between love and death. No poison cup,
no penance. Merely a notion that the tape-recorder
should have caught some ghost of us: that tape-recorder
not merely played but should have listened to us,
and could instruct those after us:
this we were, this is how we tried to love,
and these are the forces they had ranged against us,
and these are the forces we had ranged within us,
within us and against us, against us and within us.

XVIII

Rain on the West Side Highway,
red light at Riverside:
*the more I live the more I think
two people together is a miracle.*
You're telling the story of your life
for once, a tremor breaks the surface of your words.
The story of our lives becomes our lives.
Now you're in fugue across what some I'm sure
Victorian poet called the *salt estranging sea.*
Those are the words that come to mind.
I feel estrangement, yes. As I've felt dawn
pushing toward daybreak. Something: a cleft of light—?
Close between grief and anger, a space opens
where I am Adrienne alone. And growing colder.

XIX

Can it be growing colder when I begin
to touch myself again, adhesions pull away?
When slowly the naked face turns from staring backward
and looks into the present,
the eye of winter, city, anger, poverty, and death
and the lips part and say: *I mean to go on living?*
Am I speaking coldly when I tell you in a dream
or in this poem, *There are no miracles?*
(I told you from the first I wanted daily life,
this island of Manhattan was island enough for me.)
If I could let you know—
two women together is a work
nothing in civilization has made simple,
two people together is a work
heroic in its ordinariness,
the slow-picked, halting traverse of a pitch
where the fiercest attention becomes routine
—look at the faces of those who have chosen it.

XX

That conversation we were always on the edge
of having, runs on in my head,
at night the Hudson trembles in New Jersey light
polluted water yet reflecting even
sometimes the moon
and I discern a woman
I loved, drowning in secrets, fear wound round her throat
and choking her like hair. And this is she
with whom I tried to speak, whose hurt, expressive head
turning aside from pain, is dragged down deeper
where it cannot hear me,
and soon I shall know I was talking to my own soul.

XXI

The dark lintels, the blue and foreign stones
of the great round rippled by stone implements
the midsummer night light rising from beneath
the horizon—when I said "a cleft of light"
I meant this. And this is not Stonehenge
simply nor any place but the mind
casting back to where her solitude,
shared, could be chosen without loneliness,
not easily nor without pains to stake out
the circle, the heavy shadows, the great light.
I choose to be a figure in that light,
half-blotted by darkness, something moving
across that space, the color of stone
greeting the moon, yet more than stone:
a woman. I choose to walk here. And to draw this circle.

1974–1976

Upper Broadway

The leafbud straggles forth
toward the frigid light of the airshaft   this is faith
this pale extension of a day
when looking up   you know   something is changing
winter has turned   though the wind is colder
Three streets away   a roof collapses   onto people
who thought they still had time   Time out of mind

I have written so many words
wanting to live inside you
to be of use to you

Now I must write for myself   for this blind
woman scratching the pavement   with her wand of thought
this slippered crone   inching on icy streets
reaching into wire trashbaskets   pulling out
what was thrown away   and infinitely precious

I look at my hands and see   they are still unfinished
I look at the vine and see the leafbud
inching towards life

I look at my face in the glass   and see
a halfborn woman

1975

Paula Becker to Clara Westhoff

Paula Becker 1876–1907
Clara Westhoff 1878–1954

became friends at Worpswede, an artists' colony near Bremen, Germany, summer 1899. In January 1900, spent a half-year together in Paris, where Paula painted and Clara studied sculpture with Rodin. In August they returned to Worpswede, and spent the next winter together in Berlin. In 1901, Clara married the poet Rainer Maria Rilke; soon after, Paula married the painter Otto Modersohn. She died in a hemorrhage after childbirth, murmuring, What a pity!

The autumn feels slowed down,
summer still holds on here, even the light
seems to last longer than it should
or maybe I'm using it to the thin edge.
The moon rolls in the air. I didn't want this child.
You're the only one I've told.
I want a child maybe, someday, but not now.
Otto has a calm, complacent way
of following me with his eyes, as if to say
Soon you'll have your hands full!
And yes, I will; this child will be mine
not his, the failures, if I fail
will be all mine. We're not good, Clara,
at learning to prevent these things,
and once we have a child, it *is* ours.
But lately, I feel beyond Otto or anyone.
I know now the kind of work I have to do.
It takes such energy! I have the feeling I'm
moving somewhere, patiently, impatiently,
in my loneliness. I'm looking everywhere in nature
for new forms, old forms in new places,
the planes of an antique mouth, let's say, among the leaves.

I know and do not know
what I am searching for.
Remember those months in the studio together,
you up to your strong forearms in wet clay,
I trying to make something of the strange impressions
assailing me—the Japanese
flowers and birds on silk, the drunks
sheltering in the Louvre, that river-light,
those faces. . . . Did we know exactly
why we were there? Paris unnerved you,
you found it too much, yet you went on
with your work . . . and later we met there again,
both married then, and I thought you and Rilke
both seemed unnerved. I felt a kind of joylessness
between you. Of course he and I
have had our difficulties. Maybe I was jealous
of him, to begin with, taking you from me,
maybe I married Otto to fill up
my loneliness for you.
Rainer, of course, *knows* more than Otto knows,
he believes in women. But he feeds on us,
like all of them. His whole life, his art
is protected by women. Which of us could say that?
Which of us, Clara, hasn't had to take that leap
out beyond our being women
to save our work? or is it to save ourselves?
Marriage is lonelier than solitude.
Do you know: I was dreaming I had died
giving birth to the child.
I couldn't paint or speak or even move.
My child—I think—survived me. But what was funny
in the dream was, Rainer had written my requiem—
a long, beautiful poem, and calling me his friend.
I was *your* friend
but in the dream you didn't say a word.

In the dream his poem was like a letter
to someone who has no right
to be there but must be treated gently, like a guest
who comes on the wrong day. Clara, why don't I dream of you?
That photo of the two of us—I have it still,
you and I looking hard into each other
and my painting behind us. How we used to work
side by side! And how I've worked since then
trying to create according to our plan
that we'd bring, against all odds, our full power
to every subject. Hold back nothing
because we were women. Clara, our strength still lies
in the things we used to talk about:
how life and death take one another's hands,
the struggle for truth, our old pledge against guilt.
And now I feel dawn and the coming day.
I love waking in my studio, seeing my pictures
come alive in the light. Sometimes I feel
it is myself that kicks inside me,
myself I must give suck to, love . . .
I wish we could have done this for each other
all our lives, but we can't . . .
They say a pregnant woman
dreams of her own death. But life and death
take one another's hands. Clara, I feel so full
of work, the life I see ahead, and love
for you, who of all people
however badly I say this
will hear all I say and cannot say.

1975–1976

A Woman Dead in Her Forties

1.

Your breasts/   sliced-off   The scars
dimmed   as they would have to be
years later

All the women I grew up with are sitting
half-naked on rocks   in sun
we look at each other and
are not ashamed

and you too have taken off your blouse
but this was not what you wanted:

to show your scarred, deleted torso

I barely glance at you
as if my look could scald you
though I'm the one who loved you

I want to touch my fingers
to where your breasts had been
but we never did such things

You hadn't thought everyone
would look so perfect
unmutilated

you pull on
your blouse again: stern statement:

There are things I will not share
with everyone

2.

You send me back to share
my own scars   first of all
with myself

What did I hide from her
what have I denied her
what losses suffered

how in this ignorant body
did she hide

waiting for her release
till uncontrollable light began to pour

from every wound and suture
and all the sacred openings

3.

Wartime.   We sit on warm
weathered, softening grey boards

the ladder glimmers where you told me
the leeches swim

I smell the flame
of kerosene   the pine

boards where we sleep side by side
in narrow cots

the night–meadow exhaling
its darkness   calling

child into woman
child into woman
woman

4.

Most of our love from the age of nine
took the form of jokes and mute

loyalty: you fought a girl
who said she'd knock me down

we did each other's homework
wrote letters   kept in touch, untouching

lied about our lives: I wearing
the face of the proper marriage

you the face of the independent woman
We cleaved to each other across that space

fingering webs
of love and estrangement   till the day

the gynecologist touched your breast
and found a palpable hardness

5.

You played heroic, necessary
games with death

since in your neo-protestant tribe the void
was supposed not to exist

except as a fashionable concept
you had no traffic with

I wish you were here tonight   I want
to yell at you

Don't accept
Don't give in

But would I be meaning your brave
irreproachable life, you dean of women, or

your unfair, unfashionable, unforgivable
woman's death?

6.

You are every woman I ever loved
and disavowed

a bloody incandescent chord strung out
across years, tracts of space

How can I reconcile this passion
with our modesty

your calvinist heritage
my girlhood frozen into forms

how can I go on this mission
without you

you, who might have told me
everything you feel is true?

7.

Time after time in dreams you rise
reproachful

once from a wheelchair pushed by your father
across a lethal expressway

Of all my dead it's you
who come to me unfinished

You left me amber beads
strung with turquoise from an Egyptian grave

I wear them wondering
How am I true to you?

I'm half-afraid to write poetry
for you   who never read it much

and I'm left laboring
with the secrets and the silence

In plain language: I never told you how I loved you
we never talked at your deathbed of your death

8.

One autumn evening in a train
catching the diamond-flash of sunset

in puddles along the Hudson
I thought: *I understand*

life and death now, the choices
I didn't know your choice

or how by then you had no choice
how the body tells the truth in its rush of cells

Most of our love took the form
of mute loyalty

we never spoke at your deathbed of your death

but from here on
I want more crazy mourning, more howl, more keening

We stayed mute and disloyal
because we were afraid

I would have touched my fingers
to where your breasts had been
but we never did such things

1974–1977

Toward the Solstice

The thirtieth of November.
Snow is starting to fall.
A peculiar silence is spreading
over the fields, the maple grove.
It is the thirtieth of May,
rain pours on ancient bushes, runs
down the youngest blade of grass.
I am trying to hold in one steady glance
all the parts of my life.
A spring torrent races
on this old slanting roof,
the slanted field below
thickens with winter's first whiteness.
Thistles dried to sticks in last year's wind
stand nakedly in the green,
stand sullenly in the slowly whitening,
field.

      My brain glows
more violently, more avidly
the quieter, the thicker
the quilt of crystals settles,
the louder, more relentlessly
the torrent beats itself out
on the old boards and shingles.
It is the thirtieth of May,
the thirtieth of November,
a beginning or an end,
we are moving into the solstice
and there is so much here
I still do not understand.

If I could make sense of how
my life is still tangled
with dead weeds, thistles,
enormous burdocks, burdens
slowly shifting under
this first fall of snow,
beaten by this early, racking rain
calling all new life to declare itself strong
or die,
                if I could know
in what language to address
the spirits that claim a place
beneath these low and simple ceilings,
tenants that neither speak nor stir
yet dwell in mute insistence
till I can feel utterly ghosted in this house.

If history is a spider-thread
spun over and over though brushed away
it seems I might some twilight
or dawn in the hushed country light
discern its greyness stretching
from molding or doorframe, out
into the empty dooryard
and following it climb
the path into the pinewoods,
tracing from tree to tree
in the failing light, in the slowly
lucidifying day
its constant, purposive trail,
till I reach whatever cellar hole
filling with snowflakes or lichen,
whatever fallen shack
or unremembered clearing
I am meant to have found

and there, under the first or last
star, trusting to instinct
the words would come to mind
I have failed or forgotten to say
year after year, winter
after summer, the right rune
to ease the hold of the past
upon the rest of my life
and ease my hold on the past.

If some rite of separation
is still unaccomplished
between myself and the long-gone
tenants of this house,
between myself and my childhood,
and the childhood of my children,
it is I who have neglected
to perform the needed acts,
set water in corners, light and eucalyptus
in front of mirrors,
or merely pause and listen
to my own pulse vibrating
lightly as falling snow,
relentlessly as the rainstorm,
and hear what it has been saying.
It seems I am still waiting
for them to make some clear demand
some articulate sound or gesture,
for release to come from anywhere
but from inside myself.

A decade of cutting away
dead flesh, cauterizing
old scars ripped open over and over
and still it is not enough.

A decade of performing
the loving humdrum acts
of attention to this house
transplanting lilac suckers,
washing panes, scrubbing
wood-smoke from splitting paint,
sweeping stairs, brushing the thread
of the spider aside,
and so much yet undone,
a woman's work, the solstice nearing,
and my hand still suspended
as if above a letter
I long and dread to close.

1977

A Wild Patience Has
Taken Me This Far

Coast to Coast

There are days when housework seems the only
outlet   old funnel I've poured caldrons through
old servitude   In grief and fury bending
to the accustomed tasks   the vacuum cleaner plowing
realms of dust   the mirror scoured   grey webs
behind framed photographs   brushed away
the grey-seamed sky enormous in the west
snow gathering in corners   of the north

Seeing through the prism
you who gave it me
                    You, bearing ceaselessly
yourself   the witness
Rainbow dissolves the Hudson   This chary, stinting
skin of late winter   ice   forming and breaking up
The unprotected seeing it through
with their ordinary valor

Rainbow composed of ordinary light
February-flat
grey-white of a cheap enamelled pan
breaking into veridian, azure, violet
You write: *Three and a half weeks lost from writing.* . . .
I think of the word *protection*
who it is we try to protect   and why

Seeing through the prism   Your face, fog-hollowed   burning
cold of eucalyptus hung with butterflies
lavender of rockbloom
O and your anger uttered in silence word and stammer
shattering the fog   lances of sun

piercing the grey Pacific   unanswerable tide
carving itself in clefts and fissures of the rock
Beauty of your breasts   your hands
turning a stone a shell a weed a prism   in coastal light
traveller and witness
the passion of the speechless
driving your speech
protectless

If you can read and understand this poem
send something back: a burning strand of hair
a still-warm, still-liquid drop of blood
a shell
thickened from being battered year on year
send something back.

1978

Integrity

the quality or state of being complete: unbroken condition: entirely
—Webster

A wild patience has taken me this far

as if I had to bring to shore
a boat with a spasmodic outboard motor
old sweaters, nets, spray-mottled books
tossed in the prow
some kind of sun burning my shoulder-blades.
Splashing the oarlocks. Burning through.
Your fore-arms can get scalded, licked with pain
in a sun blotted like unspoken anger
behind a casual mist.

The length of daylight
this far north, in this
forty-ninth year of my life
is critical.

The light is critical: of me, of this
long-dreamed, involuntary landing
on the arm of an inland sea.
The glitter of the shoal
depleting into shadow
I recognize: the stand of pines
violet-black really, green in the old postcard
but really I have nothing but myself
to go by; nothing

stands in the realm of pure necessity
except what my hands can hold.

Nothing but myself? . . . My selves.
After so long, this answer.
As if I had always known
I steer the boat in, simply.
The motor dying on the pebbles
cicadas taking up the hum
dropped in the silence.

Anger and tenderness: my selves.
And now I can believe they breathe in me
as angels, not polarities.
Anger and tenderness: the spider's genius
to spin and weave in the same action
from her own body, anywhere—
even from a broken web.

The cabin in the stand of pines
is still for sale. I know this. Know the print
of the last foot, the hand that slammed and locked that door,
then stopped to wreathe the rain-smashed clematis
back on the trellis
for no one's sake except its own.
I know the chart nailed to the wallboards
the icy kettle squatting on the burner.
The hands that hammered in those nails
emptied that kettle one last time
are these two hands
and they have caught the baby leaping
from between trembling legs
and they have worked the vacuum aspirator
and stroked the sweated temples
and steered the boat here through this hot

misblotted sunlight, critical light
imperceptibly scalding
the skin these hands will also salve.

1978

Transit

When I meet the skier she is always
walking, skis and poles shouldered, toward the mountain
free-swinging in worn boots
over the path new-sifted with fresh snow
her greying dark hair almost hidden by
a cap of many colors
her fifty-year-old, strong, impatient body
dressed for cold and speed
her eyes level with mine

And when we pass each other I look into her face
wondering what we have in common
where our minds converge
for we do not pass each other, she passes me
as I halt beside the fence tangled in snow,
she passes me as I shall never pass her
in this life

Yet I remember us together
climbing Chocorua, summer nineteen-forty-five
details of vegetation beyond the timberline
lichens, wildflowers, birds,
amazement when the trail broke out onto the granite ledge
sloped over blue lakes, green pines, giddy air
like dreams of flying

When sisters separate they haunt each other
as she, who I might once have been, haunts me
or is it I who do the haunting
halting and watching on the path
how she appears again through lightly-blowing

crystals, how her strong knees carry her,
how unaware she is, how simple
this is for her, how without let or hindrance
she travels in her body
until the point of passing, where the skier
and the cripple must decide
to recognize each other?

1979

For Memory

Old words: *trust*   *fidelity*
Nothing new yet to take their place.

I rake leaves, clear the lawn, October grass
painfully green beneath the gold
and in this silent labor thoughts of you
start up
I hear your voice: *disloyalty*   *betrayal*
stinging the wires

I stuff the old leaves into sacks
and still they fall and still
I see my work undone

One shivering rainswept afternoon
and the whole job to be done over

I can't know what you know
unless you tell me
there are gashes in our understandings
of this world
We came together in a common
fury of direction
barely mentioning difference
(what drew our finest hairs
to fire
the deep, difficult troughs
unvoiced)
I fell through a basement railing
the first day of school and cut my forehead open—
did I ever tell you? More than forty years

and I still remember smelling my own blood
like the smell of a new schoolbook

And did you ever tell me
how your mother called you in from play
and from whom? To what? These atoms filmed by ordinary dust
that common life we each and all bent out of orbit from
to which we must return simply to say
this is where I came from
this is what I knew

The past is not a husk   yet change goes on

Freedom. It isn't once, to walk out
under the Milky Way, feeling the rivers
of light, the fields of dark—
freedom is daily, prose-bound, routine
remembering. Putting together, inch by inch
the starry worlds. From all the lost collections.

1979

What Is Possible

A clear night   if the mind were clear

If the mind were simple, if the mind were bare
of all but the most classic necessities:
wooden spoon   knife   mirror
cup   lamp   chisel
a comb passing through hair beside a window
a sheet
           thrown back by the sleeper

A clear night in which two planets
seem to clasp each other   in which the earthly grasses
shift like silk in starlight
                           If the mind were clear
and if the mind were simple   you could take this mind
this particular state   and say
This is how I would live if I could choose:
this is what is possible

A clear night.   But the mind
of the woman imagining all this   the mind
that allows all this to be possible
is not clear as the night
is never simple   cannot clasp
its truths as the transiting planets clasp each other
does not so easily
                   work free from remorse
does not so easily
                   manage the miracle
for which mind is famous

                or used to be famous
does not at will become abstract and pure

this woman's mind

does not even will that miracle
having a different mission
                        in the universe

If the mind were simple   if the mind were bare
it might resemble a room   a swept interior
but how could this now be possible

given the voices of the ghost-towns
their tiny and vast configurations
needing to be deciphered
                     the oracular night
with its densely working sounds

If it could ever come down to anything like
a comb passing through hair beside a window

no more than that
                a sheet
                thrown back by the sleeper
but the mind
of the woman thinking this   is wrapped in battle
is on another mission
a stalk of grass   dried feathery weed   rooted in snow
in frozen air stirring   a fierce wand graphing

Her finger also tracing
pages of a book
knowing better than the poem she reads

knowing through the poem
                    through ice-feathered panes
the winter
        flexing its talons
the hawk-wind
          poised to kill

1980

For Ethel Rosenberg

*convicted, with her husband, of "conspiracy to commit espionage": killed in the
electric chair June 19, 1953*

1.

Europe 1953:
throughout my random sleepwalk
the words

scratched on walls, on pavements
painted over railway arches
Liberez les Rosenberg!

Escaping from home I found
home everywhere:
the Jewish question, Communism

marriage itself
a question of loyalty
or punishment

my Jewish father writing me
letters of seventeen pages
finely inscribed harangues

questions of loyalty
and punishment
One week before my wedding

that couple gets the chair
the volts grapple her, don't
kill her fast enough

Liberez les Rosenberg!
I hadn't realized
our family arguments were so important

my narrow understanding
of crime   of punishment
no language for this torment

mystery of that marriage
always both faces
on every front page in the world

Something so shocking   so
unfathomable
it must be pushed aside

2.

She sank however into my soul   A weight of sadness
I hardly can register how deep
her memory has sunk   that wife and mother

like so many
who seemed to get nothing out of any of it
except her children

that daughter   of a family
like so many
needing its female monster

she, actually wishing to be   *an artist*
wanting out of poverty
possibly also really wanting

revolution

that woman   strapped in the chair
no fear and no regrets
charged by posterity

not with selling secrets to the Communists
but with wanting   *to distinguish*
herself   being a bad daughter   a bad mother

And I   walking to my wedding
by the same token a bad daughter   a bad sister
my forces focussed

on that hardly revolutionary effort
Her life and death   the possible
ranges of disloyalty

so painful   so unfathomable
they must be pushed aside
ignored for years

3.

Her mother testifies against her
Her brother testifies against her
After her death

she becomes a natural prey for pornographers
her death itself a scene
her body *sizzling   half-strapped   whipped like a sail*

She becomes the extremest victim
described nonetheless as *rigid of will*
what are her politics by then   no one knows

Her figure sinks into my soul
a drowned statue
sealed in lead

For years it has lain there   unabsorbed
first as part of that dead couple
on the front pages of the world   the week

I gave myself in marriage
then slowly severing   drifting apart
a separate death   a life unto itself

no longer *the Rosenbergs*
no longer the chosen scapegoat
the family monster

till I hear how she sang
a prostitute to sleep
in the Women's House of Detention

Ethel Greenglass Rosenberg   would you
have marched to take back the night
collected signatures

for battered women who kill
What would you have to tell us
would you have burst the net

4.

Why do I even want to call her up
to console my pain   (she feels no pain at all)
why do I wish to put such questions

to ease myself   (she feels no pain at all
she   finally burned to death   like so many)
why all this exercise of hindsight?

since   if I imagine her at all
I have to imagine first
the pain inflicted on her   by women

her mother testifies against her
her sister-in-law testifies against her
and how she sees it

not the impersonal forces
not the historical reasons
why they might have hated her strength

If I have held her at arm's length till now
if I have still believed it was
my loyalty, my punishment at stake

if I dare imagine her surviving
I must be fair to what she must have lived through
I must allow her to be at last

political in her ways   not in mine
her urgencies perhaps   impervious to mine
defining revolution as she defines it

or, bored to the marrow of her bones
with "politics"
bored with the vast boredom of long pain

small; tiny in fact; in her late sixties
liking her room   her private life
living alone perhaps

no one you could interview
maybe filling a notebook herself
with secrets she has never sold

1980

Heroines

Exceptional
        even deviant
                    you draw your long skirts
across the nineteenth century
                        Your mind
burns long after death
                    not like the harbor beacon
but like a pyre of driftwood
                        on the beach
                                You are spared
illiteracy
        death by pneumonia
                            teeth which leave the gums
the seamstress' clouded eyes
                        the mill-girl's shortening breath
by a collection
            of circumstances
                        soon to be known as
class privilege
            The law says you can possess nothing
                                in a world
where property is everything
                        You belong first to your father
then to him who
            chooses you
                        if you fail to marry
you are without recourse
                    unable to earn
                            a workingman's salary
forbidden to vote
                forbidden to speak
                            in public

if married you are legally dead
                              the law says
you may not bequeath property
                              save to your children
or male kin
              that your husband
                              has the right
of the slaveholder
              to hunt down and re-possess you
                              should you escape
You may inherit slaves
                              but have no power to free them
your skin is fair
              you have been taught that light
came
    to the Dark Continent
                              with white power
that the Indians
              live in filth
                              and occult animal rites
Your mother wore corsets
                              to choke her spirit
                              which if you refuse
you are jeered for refusing
                              you have heard many sermons
and have carried
              your own interpretations
                              locked in your heart
You are a woman
              strong in health
                              through a collection
of circumstances
              soon to be known
                              as class privilege

which if you break
                    the social compact
                                        you lose outright
When you open your mouth in public
                                        human excrement
                                                            is flung at you
you are exceptional
    .   in personal circumstance
                                                    in indignation
you give up believing
                        in protection
                                        in Scripture
in man-made laws
                    respectable as you look
                                            you are an outlaw
Your mind burns
                    not like the harbor beacon
                                                but like a fire
of fiercer origin
                    you begin speaking out
and a great gust of freedom
                                rushes in with your words
yet still you speak
                    in the shattered language
                                                of a partial vision
You draw your long skirts
                            deviant
                                    across the nineteenth century
registering injustice
                        failing to make it whole
How can I fail to love
                        your clarity and fury
how can I give you
                    all your due
                                take courage from your courage

honor your exact
                legacy as it is
recognizing
                as well
                        that it is not enough?

1980

Grandmothers

1. Mary Gravely Jones

We had no petnames, no diminutives for you,
always the formal guest under my father's roof:
you were "Grandmother Jones" and you visited rarely.
I see you walking up and down the garden,
restless, southern-accented, reserved, you did not seem
my mother's mother or anyone's grandmother.
You were Mary, widow of William, and no matriarch,
yet smoldering to the end with frustrate life,
ideas nobody listened to, least of all my father.
One summer night you sat with my sister and me
in the wooden glider long after twilight,
holding us there with streams of pent-up words.
You could quote every poet I had ever heard of,
had read *The Opium Eater,* Amiel and Bernard Shaw,
your green eyes looked clenched against opposition.
You married straight out of the convent school,
your background was country, you left an unperformed
typescript of a play about Burr and Hamilton,
you were impotent and brilliant, no one cared
about your mind, you might have ended
elsewhere than in that glider
reciting your unwritten novels to the children.

2. Hattie Rice Rich

Your sweetness of soul was a mystery to me,
you who slip-covered chairs, glued broken china,
lived out of a wardrobe trunk in our guestroom
summer and fall, then took the Pullman train

in your darkblue dress and straw hat, to Alabama,
shuttling half-yearly between your son and daughter.
Your sweetness of soul was a convenience for everyone,
how you rose with the birds and children, boiled your own egg,
fished for hours on a pier, your umbrella spread,
took the street-car downtown shopping
endlessly for your son's whims, the whims of genius,
kept your accounts in ledgers, wrote letters daily.
All through World War Two the forbidden word
Jewish was barely uttered in your son's house;
your anger flared over inscrutable things.
Once I saw you crouched on the guestroom bed,
knuckles blue-white around the bedpost, sobbing
your one brief memorable scene of rebellion:
you didn't want to go back South that year.
You were never "Grandmother Rich" but "Anana";
you had money of your own but you were homeless,
Hattie, widow of Samuel, and no matriarch,
dispersed among the children and grandchildren.

3. Granddaughter
Easier to encapsulate your lives
in a slide-show of impressions given and taken,
to play the child or victim, the projectionist,
easier to invent a script for each of you,
myself still at the center,
than to write words in which you might have found
yourselves, looked up at me and said
"Yes, I was like that; but I was something more. . . ."
Danville, Virginia; Vicksburg, Mississippi;
the "war between the states" a living memory
its aftermath the plague-town closing
its gates, trying to cure itself with poisons.
I can almost touch that little town. . . .
a little white town rimmed with Negroes,

making a deep shadow on the whiteness.
Born a white woman, Jewish or of curious mind
—twice an outsider, still believing in inclusion—
in those defended hamlets of half-truth
broken in two by one strange idea,
"blood" the all-powerful, awful theme—
what were the lessons to be learned? If I believe
the daughter of one of you—Amnesia was the answer.

1980

The Spirit of Place

For Michelle Cliff

I.

Over the hills in Shutesbury, Leverett
driving with you in spring   road
like a streambed unwinding downhill
fiddlehead ferns uncurling
spring peepers ringing sweet and cold

while we talk yet again
of dark and light, of blackness, whiteness, numbness
rammed through the heart like a stake
trying to pull apart the threads
from the dried blood of the old murderous uncaring

halting on bridges in bloodlight
where the freshets call out freedom
to frog-thrilling swamp, skunk-cabbage
trying to sense the conscience of these hills

knowing how the single-minded, pure
solutions bleached and dessicated
within their perfect flasks

for it was not enough to be New England
as every event since has testified:
New England's a shadow-country, always was

it was not enough to be for abolition
while the spirit of the masters
flickered in the abolitionist's heart

it was not enough to name ourselves anew
while the spirit of the masters
calls the freedwoman to forget the slave

With whom do you believe your lot is cast?
If there's a conscience in these hills
it hurls that question

unquenched, relentless, to our ears
wild and witchlike
ringing every swamp

II.

The mountain laurel in bloom
constructed like needlework
tiny half-pulled stitches piercing
flushed and stippled petals

here in these woods it grows wild
midsummer moonrise turns it opal
the night breathes with its clusters
protected species

meaning endangered
Here in these hills
this valley   we have felt
a kind of freedom

planting the soil   have known
hours of a calm, intense and mutual solitude
reading and writing
trying to clarify   connect

past and present   near and far
the Alabama quilt
the Botswana basket
history   the dark crumble

of last year's compost
filtering softly through your living hand
but here as well we face
instantaneous violence   ambush   male

dominion on a back road
to escape in a locked car   windows shut
skimming the ditch   your split-second
survival reflex taking on the world

as it is   not as we wish it
as it is   not as we work for it
to be

III.

Strangers are an endangered species

In Emily Dickinson's house in Amherst
cocktails are served   the scholars
gather in celebration
their pious or clinical legends
festoon the walls like imitations
of period patterns

   (. . . and, as I feared, my "life" was made a "victim")

The remnants pawed   the relics
the cult assembled in the bedroom

and you   whose teeth were set on edge by churches
resist your shrine
                    escape
                              are found
nowhere
            unless in words   (your own)

All we are strangers—dear—The world is not
acquainted with us, because we are not acquainted
with her. And Pilgrims!—Do you hesitate? and
Soldiers oft—some of us victors, but those I do
not see tonight owing to the smoke.—We are hungry,
and thirsty, sometimes—We are barefoot—and cold—

This place is large enough for both of us
the river-fog will do for privacy
this is my third and last address to you

with the hands of a daughter I would cover you
from all intrusion   even my own
saying   rest to your ghost

with the hands of a sister I would leave your hands
open or closed as they prefer to lie
and ask no more of who or why or wherefore

with the hands of a mother I would close the door
on the rooms you've left behind
and silently pick up my fallen work

IV.

The river-fog will do for privacy
on the low road a breath
here, there, a cloudiness floating on the blacktop

sunflower heads turned black and bowed
the seas of corn a stubble
the old routes flowing north, if not to freedom

no human figure now in sight
(with whom do you believe your lot is cast?)
only the functional figure of the scarecrow

the cut corn, ground to shreds, heaped in a shape
like an Indian burial mound
a haunted-looking, ordinary thing

The work of winter starts fermenting in my head
how with the hands of a lover or a midwife
to hold back till the time is right

force nothing, be unforced
accept no giant miracles of growth
by counterfeit light

trust roots, allow the days to shrink
give credence to these slender means
wait without sadness and with grave impatience

here in the north where winter has a meaning
where the heaped colors suddenly go ashen
where nothing is promised

learn what an underground journey
has been, might have to be; speak in a winter code
let fog, sleet, translate; wind, carry them.

V.

Orion plunges like a drunken hunter
over the Mohawk Trail   a parallelogram
slashed with two cuts of steel

A night so clear that every constellation
stands out from an undifferentiated cloud
of stars, a kind of aura

All the figures up there look violent to me
as a pogrom on Christmas Eve in some old country
I want our own earth   not the satellites, our

world as it is   if not as it might be
then as it is: male dominion, gangrape, lynching, pogrom
the Mohawk wraiths in their tracts of leafless birch

watching: will we do better?
The tests I need to pass are prescribed by the spirits
of place   who understand travel but not amnesia

The world as it is: not as her users boast
damaged beyond reclamation by their using
Ourselves as we are   in these painful motions

of staying cognizant: some part of us always
out beyond ourselves
knowing   knowing   knowing

Are we all in training for something we don't name?
to exact reparation for things
done long ago to us and to those who did not

survive what was done to them   whom we ought to honor
with grief   with fury   with action
On a pure night   on a night when pollution

seems absurdity when the undamaged planet seems to turn
like a bowl of crystal in black ether
they are the piece of us that lies out there
knowing   knowing   knowing

1980

Frame

Winter twilight. She comes out of the lab-
oratory, last class of the day
a pile of notebooks slung in her knapsack, coat
zipped high against the already swirling
evening sleet. The wind is wicked and the
busses slower than usual. On her mind
is organic chemistry and the issue
of next month's rent and will it be possible to
bypass the professor with the coldest eyes
to get a reference for graduate school,
and whether any of them, even those who smile
can see, looking at her, a biochemist
or a marine biologist, which of the faces
can she trust to see her at all, either today
or in any future. The busses are worm-slow in the
quickly gathering dark. *I don't know her. I am*
standing though somewhere just outside the frame
of all this, trying to see. At her back
the newly finished building suddenly looks
like shelter, it has glass doors, lighted halls
presumably heat. The wind is wicked. She throws a
glance down the street, sees no bus coming and runs
up the newly constructed steps into the newly
constructed hallway. *I am standing all this time*
just beyond the frame, trying to see. She runs
her hand through the crystals of sleet about to melt
on her hair. She shifts the weight of the books
on her back. It isn't warm here exactly but it's
out of that wind. Through the glass
door panels she can watch for the bus through the thickening
weather. Watching so, she is not

watching for the white man who watches the building
who has been watching her. This is Boston 1979.
I am standing somewhere at the edge of the frame
watching the man, we are both white, who watches the building
telling her to move on, get out of the hallway.
I can hear nothing because I am not supposed to be
present but I can see her gesturing
out toward the street at the wind-raked curb
I see her drawing her small body up
against the implied charges. The man
goes away. Her body is different now.
It is holding together with more than a hint of fury
and more than a hint of fear. She is smaller, thinner
more fragile-looking than I am. *But I am not supposed to be*
there. I am just outside the frame
of this action when the anonymous white man
returns with a white police officer. Then she starts
to leave into the wind-raked night but already
the policeman is going to work, the handcuffs are on her
wrists he is throwing her down his knee has gone into
her breast he is dragging her down the stairs *I am unable*
to hear a sound of all this all that I know is what
I can see from this position there is no soundtrack
to go with this and I understand at once
it is meant to be in silence that this happens
in silence that he pushes her into the car
banging her head in silence that she cries out
in silence that she tries to explain she was only
waiting for a bus
in silence that he twists the flesh of her thigh
with his nails in silence that her tears begin to flow
that she pleads with the other policeman as if
he could be trusted to see her at all
in silence that in the precinct she refuses to give her name
in silence that they throw her into the cell

in silence that she stares him
straight in the face in silence that he sprays her
in her eyes with Mace in silence that she sinks her teeth
into his hand in silence that she is charged
with trespass assault and battery in
silence that at the sleet-swept corner her bus
passes without stopping and goes on
in silence. *What I am telling you*
is told by a white woman who they will say
was never there. I say I am there.

1980

A Vision

(thinking of Simone Weil)

You. There, with your gazing eyes
Your blazing eyes

A hand or something passes across the sun. Your eyeballs slacken,
you are free for a moment. Then it comes back: this
test of the capacity to keep in focus
this
      unfair struggle with the forces of perception
this enforced
               (but at that word your attention changes)
this enforced   loss of self
in a greater thing of course, who has ever
lost herself in something smaller?

You with your cornea and iris and their power
you with your stubborn lids that have stayed open
at the moment of pouring liquid steel
you with your fear of blinding

Here it is. I am writing this almost
involuntarily on a bad, a junky typewriter that skips
and slides the text
Still these are mechanical problems, writing to you
is another kind of problem
and even so the words create themselves

What is your own will that it
can so transfix you
why are you forced to take this test

over and over and call it God
why not call it you and get it over

you with your hatred of enforcement
and your fear of blinding?

1981

Your Native Land, Your Life

Sources

For Helen Smelser
since 1949

I

Sixteen years.   The narrow, rough-gullied backroads
almost the same.   The farms: almost the same,
a new barn here, a new roof there, a rusting car,
collapsed sugar-house, trailer, new young wife
trying to make a lawn instead of a dooryard,
new names, old kinds of names: Rocquette, Desmarais,
Clark, Pierce, Stone.   Gossier.   No names of mine.

The vixen I met at twilight on Route 5
south of Willoughby: long dead.   She was an omen
to me, surviving, herding her cubs
in the silvery bend of the road
in nineteen sixty-five.

Shapes of things: so much the same
they feel like eternal forms: the house and barn
on the rise above May Pond; the brow of Pisgah;
the face of milkweed blooming,
brookwater pleating over slanted granite,
boletus under pine, the half-composted needles
it broke through patterned on its skin.
Shape of queen anne's lace, with the drop of blood.
Bladder-campion veined with purple.
Multifoliate heal-all.

II

I refuse to become a seeker for cures.
Everything that has ever
helped me has come through what already
lay stored in me.   Old things, diffuse, unnamed, lie strong
across my heart.
                    This is from where
my strength comes, even when I miss my strength
even when it turns on me
like a violent master.

III

From where?   the voice asks coldly.

This is the voice in cold morning air
that pierces dreams.   *From where does your strength come?*

Old things . . .
                    From where does your strength come, you Southern Jew?
split at the root, raised in a castle of air?

Yes.   I expected this.   I have known for years
the question was coming.   *From where*

(not from these, surely,
Protestant separatists, Jew-baiters, nightriders

who fired in Irasburg in nineteen-sixty-eight
on a black family newly settled in these hills)
                                        From where

the dew grows thick late August on the fierce green grass
and on the wooden sill and on the stone

the mountains stand in an extraordinary
point of no return   though still are green

collapsed shed-boards gleam like pewter in the dew
the realms of touch-me-not   fiery with tiny tongues

cover the wild ground of the woods

IV

With whom do you believe your lot is cast?
From where does your strength come?

I think somehow, somewhere
every poem of mine must repeat those questions

which are not the same.   There is a *whom, a where*
that is not chosen   that is given   and sometimes falsely given

in the beginning we grasp whatever we can
to survive

V

All during World War II
I told myself I had some special destiny:
there had to be a reason
I was not living in a bombed-out house
or cellar   hiding out with rats

there had to be a reason
I was growing up safe, American
with sugar rationed in a Mason jar

split at the root   white-skinned social christian
neither gentile nor Jew

through the immense silence
of the Holocaust

I had no idea of what I had been spared

still less of the women and men   my kin
the Jews of Vicksburg or Birmingham
whose lives must have been strategies no less
than the vixen's on Route 5

VI

If they had played the flute, or chess
I was told   I was not told what they told
their children when the Klan rode
how they might have seen themselves

                                        a chosen people

of shopkeepers
clinging by strategy to a way of life
that had its own uses for them

proud of their length of sojourn in America
deploring the late-comers   the peasants from Russia

I saw my father building
his rootless ideology

his private castle in air

in that most dangerous place, the family home
we were the chosen people

In the beginning we grasp whatever we can

VII

    For years I struggled with you: your categories, your theories, your will, the cruelty which came inextricable from your love.   For years all arguments I carried on in my head were with you.   I saw myself, the eldest daughter raised as a son, taught to study but not to pray, taught to hold reading and writing sacred: the eldest daughter in a house with no son, she who must overthrow the father, take what he taught her and use it against him.   All this in a castle of air, the floating world of the assimilated who know and deny they will always be aliens.

    After your death I met you again as the face of patriarchy, could name at last precisely the principle you embodied, there was an ideology at last which let me dispose of you, identify the suffering you caused, hate you righteously as part of a system, the kingdom of the fathers.   I saw the power and arrogance of the male as your true watermark; I did not see beneath it the suffering of the Jew, the alien stamp you bore, because you had deliberately arranged that it should be invisible to me.   It is only now, under a powerful, womanly lens, that I can decipher your suffering and deny no part of my own.

VIII

Back there in Maryland the stars
showed liquescent, diffuse

in the breathless summer nights
the constellations melted

I thought I was leaving a place of enervation
heading north where the Drinking Gourd

stood cold and steady at last
pointing the way

I thought I was following a track of freedom
and for awhile it was

IX

Why has my imagination stayed
northeast with the ones who stayed

Are there spirits in me, diaspora-driven
that wanted to lodge somewhere

hooked into the "New" Englanders who hung on
here in this stringent space

believing their Biblical language
their harping on righteousness?

And, myself apart, what was this like for them,
this unlikely growing season

after each winter so mean, so mean
the tying-down of the spirit

and the endless rocks in the soil, the endless
purifications of self

there being no distance, no space around
to experiment with life?

X

These upland farms are the farms
of invaders, these villages

white with rectitude and death
are built on stolen ground

The persecuted, pale with anger
know how to persecute

those who feel destined, under god's eye
need never ponder difference

and if they kill others for being who they are
or where they are

is this a law of history
or simply, *what must change?*

XI

If I try to conjure their lives
—who are not my people by any definition—

Yankee Puritans, Québec Catholics
mingled within sight of the Northern Lights

I am forced to conjure a passion
like the tropism in certain plants

bred of a natural region's
repetitive events

beyond the numb of poverty
christian hypocrisy, isolation

—a passion so unexpected
there is no name for it

so quick, fierce, unconditional
short growing season is no explanation.

XII

And has any of this to do with how
Mohawk or Wampanoag knew it?.

is the passion I connect with in this air
trace of the original

existences that knew this place
is the region still trying to speak with them

is this light a language
the shudder of this aspen-grove a way

of sending messages
the white mind barely intercepts

are signals also coming back
from the vast diaspora

of the people who kept their promises
as a way of life?

XIII

Coming back after sixteen years
I stare anew at things

that steeple pure and righteous
that clapboard farmhouse

seeing what I hadn't seen before
through barnboards, crumbling plaster

decades of old wallpaper roses
clinging to certain studs

—into that dangerous place
the family home:

There are verbal brutalities
borne thereafter like any burn or scar

there are words pulled down from the walls
like dogwhips

the child backed silent against the wall
trying to keep her eyes dry;   haughty;   in panic

I will never let you know
I will never
let you know

XIV

And if my look becomes the bomb that rips
the family home apart

is this betrayal, that the walls
slice off, the staircase shows

torn-away above the street
that the closets where the clothes hung

hang naked, the room the old
grandmother had to sleep in

the toilet on the landing
the room with the books

where the father walks up and down
telling the child to *work, work*

harder than anyone has worked before?
—But I can't stop seeing like this

more and more I see like this everywhere.

XV

It's an oldfashioned, an outrageous thing
to believe one has a "destiny"

—a thought often peculiar to those
who possess privilege—

but there is something else: the faith
of those despised and endangered

that they are not merely the sum
of damages done to them:

have kept beyond violence the knowledge
arranged in patterns like kente-cloth

unexpected as in batik
recurrent as bitter herbs and unleavened bread

of being a connective link
in a long, continuous way

of ordering hunger, weather, death, desire
and the nearness of chaos.

XVI

The Jews I've felt rooted among
are those who were turned to smoke

Reading of the chimneys against the blear air
I think I have seen them myself

the fog of northern Europe licking its way
along the railroad tracks

to the place where all tracks end
You told me not to look there

to become
a citizen of the world

bound by no tribe or clan
yet dying you followed the Six Day War

with desperate attention
and this summer I lie awake at dawn

sweating the Middle East through my brain
wearing the star of David

on a thin chain at my breastbone

XVII

But there was also the other Jew. The one you most feared,
the one from the *shtetl*, from Brooklyn, from the wrong part of
history, the wrong accent, the wrong class. The one I left you
for.   The one both like and unlike you, who explained you to
me for years, who could not explain himself.   The one who said,
as if he had memorized the formula, *There's nothing left now but
the food and the humor.*   The one who, like you, ended isolate,
who had tried to move in the floating world of the assimilated
who know and deny they will always be aliens.   Who drove
to Vermont in a rented car at dawn and shot himself.   For

so many years I had thought you and he were in opposition. I needed your unlikeness then; now it's your likeness that stares me in the face.   There is something more than food, humor, a turn of phrase, a gesture of the hands: there is something more.

XVIII

There is something more than self-hatred. That still outlives
these photos of the old Ashkenazi life:
we are gifted children at camp in the country
or orphaned children in kindergarten
we are hurrying along the rare book dealers' street
with the sunlight striking one side
we are walking the wards of the Jewish hospital
along diagonal squares   young serious nurses
we are part of a family group
formally taken in 1936
with tables, armchairs, ferns
(behind us, in our lives, the muddy street
and the ragged shames
the street-musician, the weavers lined for strike)
we are part of a family wearing white head-bandages
we were beaten in a pogrom

The place where all tracks end
is the place where history was meant to stop
but does not stop   where thinking
was meant to stop but does not stop
where the pattern was meant to give way at last

                                                          but only
becomes a different pattern
                                   terrible, threadbare
strained   familiar   on-going

XIX

They say such things are stored
in the genetic code—

half-chances, unresolved
possibilities, the life

passed on because unlived—
a mystic biology?—

I think of the women who sailed to Palestine
years before I was born—

halutzot, pioneers
believing in a new life

socialists, anarchists, jeered
as excitable, sharp of tongue

too filled with life
wanting equality in the promised land

carrying the broken promises
of Zionism in their hearts

along with the broken promises
of communism, anarchism—

makers of miracle who expected miracles
as stubbornly as any housewife does

that the life she gives her life to
shall not be cheap

that the life she gives her life to
shall not turn on her

that the life she gives her life to
shall want an end to suffering

Zion by itself is not enough.

XX

The faithful drudging child
the child at the oak desk whose penmanship,
hard work, style will win her prizes
becomes the woman with a mission, not to win prizes
but to change the laws of history.
How she gets this mission
is not clear, how the boundaries of perfection
explode, leaving her cheekbone grey with smoke
a piece of her hair singed off, her shirt
spattered with earth . . . Say that she grew up in a house
with talk of books, ideal societies—
she is gripped by a blue, a foreign air,
a desert absolute: dragged by the roots of her own will
into another scene of choices.

XXI

YERUSHALAYIM: a vault of golden heat
hard-pulsing from bare stones

the desert's hard-won, delicate green
the diaspora of the stars

thrilling like thousand-year-old locusts
audible yet unheard

a city on a hill
waking with first light to voices

piercing, original, intimate
as if my dreams mixed with the cries

of the oldest, earliest birds
and of all whose wrongs and rights

cry out for explication
as the night pales and one more day

breaks on this *Zion* of hope and fear
and broken promises
                              this promised land

XXII

I have resisted this for years, writing to you as if you could hear
me.   It's been different with my father: he and I always had
a kind of rhetoric going with each other, a battle between us, it
didn't matter if one of us was alive or dead.   But, you, I've had a
sense of protecting your existence, not using it merely as a theme
for poetry or tragic musings; letting you dwell in the minds of
those who have reason to miss you, in your way, or their way, not
mine. The living, writers especially, are terrible projectionists.   I
hate the way they use the dead.

Yet I can't finish this without speaking to you, not simply
of you.   You knew there was more left than food and
humor.   Even as you said that in 1953 I knew it was a formula
you had found, to stand between you and pain.   The deep
crevices of black pumpernickel under the knife, the sweet butter
and red onions we ate on those slices; the lox and cream cheese
on fresh onion rolls; bowls of sour cream mixed with cut radishes,
cucumber, scallions; green tomatoes and kosher dill pickles in

half-translucent paper; these, you said, were the remnants of the culture, along with the fresh *challah* which turned stale so fast but looked so beautiful.

That's why I want to speak to you now.   To say: no person, trying to take responsibility for her or his identity, should have to be so alone.   There must be those among whom we can sit down and weep, and still be counted as warriors.   (I make up this strange, angry packet for you, threaded with love.)   I think you thought there was no such place for you, and perhaps there was none then, and perhaps there is none now; but we will have to make it, we who want an end to suffering, who want to change the laws of history, if we are not to *give ourselves away.*

XXIII

Sixteen years ago I sat in this northeast kingdom
reading Gilbert White's *Natural History
of Selborne*   thinking
I can never know this land I walk upon
as that English priest knew his
—a comparable piece of earth—
rockledge   soil   insect   bird   weed   tree

I will never know it so well because . . .

*Because you have chosen
something else: to know other things
even the cities which
create of this a myth*

*Because you grew up in a castle of air
disjunctured*

Because without a faith
                    you are faithful

I have wished I could rest among the beautiful and common
weeds I cán name, both here and in other tracts of the
globe.   But there is no finite knowing, no such rest.   Innocent
birds, deserts, morning-glories, point to choices. leading away
from the familiar. When I speak of an end to suffering I don't
mean anesthesia. I mean knowing the world, and my place in
it, not in order to stare with bitterness or detachment, but as a
powerful and womanly series of choices: and here I write the
words, in their fullness:
powerful;   womanly.

August 1981–
August 1982

For the Record

The clouds and the stars didn't wage this war
the brooks gave no information
if the mountain spewed stones of fire into the river
it was not taking sides
the raindrop faintly swaying under the leaf
had no political opinions

and if here or there a house
filled with backed-up raw sewage
or poisoned those who lived there
with slow fumes, over years
the houses were not at war
nor did the tinned-up buildings

intend to refuse shelter
to homeless old women and roaming children
they had no policy to keep them roaming
or dying, no, the cities were not the problem
the bridges were non-partisan
the freeways burned, but not with hatred

Even the miles of barbed-wire
stretched around crouching temporary huts
designed to keep the unwanted
at a safe distance, out of sight
even the boards that had to absorb
year upon year, so many human sounds

so many depths of vomit, tears
slow-soaking blood
had not offered themselves for this

The trees didn't volunteer to be cut into boards
nor the thorns for tearing flesh
Look around at all of it

and ask whose signature
is stamped on the orders, traced
in the corner of the building plans
Ask where the illiterate, big-bellied
women were, the drunks and crazies,
the ones you fear most of all: ask where you were.

1983

North American Time

I

When my dreams showed signs
of becoming
politically correct
no unruly images
escaping beyond borders
when walking in the street I found my
themes cut out for me
knew what I would not report
for fear of enemies' usage
then I began to wonder

II

Everything we write
will be used against us
or against those we love.
These are the terms,
take them or leave them.
Poetry never stood a chance
of standing outside history.
One line typed twenty years ago
can be blazed on a wall in spraypaint
to glorify art as detachment
or torture of those we
did not love but also
did not want to kill

We move   but our words stand
become responsible
for more than we intended

and this is verbal privilege

III

Try sitting at a typewriter
one calm summer evening
at a table by a window
in the country, try pretending
your time does not exist
that you are simply you
that the imagination simply strays
like a great moth, unintentional
try telling yourself
you are not accountable
to the life of your tribe
the breath of your planet

IV

It doesn't matter what you think.
Words are found responsible
all you can do is choose them
or choose
to remain silent.   Or, you never had a choice,
which is why the words that do stand
are responsible

and this is verbal privilege

V

Suppose you want to write
of a woman braiding
another woman's hair—
straight down, or with beads and shells
in three-strand plaits or corn-rows—
you had better know the thickness
the length   the pattern
why she decides to braid her hair
how it is done to her
what country it happens in
what else happens in that country

You have to know these things

VI

Poet, sister: words—
whether we like it or not—
stand in a time of their own.
No use protesting   *I wrote that*
before Kollontai was exiled
Rosa Luxemburg, Malcolm,
Anna Mae Aquash, murdered,
before Treblinka, Birkenau,
Hiroshima, before Sharpeville,
Biafra, Bangladesh, Boston,
Atlanta, Soweto, Beirut, Assam
—those faces, names of places
sheared from the almanac
of North American time

VII

I am thinking this in a country
where words are stolen out of mouths
as bread is stolen out of mouths
where poets don't go to jail
for being poets, but for being
dark-skinned, female, poor.
I am writing this in a time
when anything we write
can be used against those we love
where the context is never given
though we try to explain, over and over
For the sake of poetry at least
I need to know these things

VIII

Sometimes, gliding at night
in a plane over New York City
I have felt like some messenger
called to enter, called to engage
this field of light and darkness.
A grandiose idea, born of flying.
But underneath the grandiose idea
is the thought that what I must engage
after the plane has raged onto the tarmac
after climbing my old stairs, sitting down
at my old window
is meant to break my heart and reduce me to silence.

IX

In North America time stumbles on
without moving, only releasing
a certain North American pain.
Julia de Burgos wrote:
That my grandfather was a slave
is my grief;   had he been a master
that would have been my shame.
A poet's words, hung over a door
in North America, in the year
nineteen-eighty-three.
The almost-full moon rises
timelessly speaking of change
out of the Bronx, the Harlem River
the drowned towns of the Quabbin
the pilfered burial mounds
the toxic swamps, the testing-grounds

and I start to speak again

1983

Virginia 1906

A white woman dreaming of innocence,
of a country childhood, apple-blossom driftings,
is held in a DC-10 above the purity
of a thick cloud ceiling in a vault of purest blue.
She feels safe.   Here, no one can reach her.
Neither men nor women have her in their power.

Because I have sometimes been her, because I am of her,
I watch her with eyes that blink away like a flash
cruelly, when she does what I don't want to see.
I am tired of innocence and its uselessness,
sometimes the dream of innocence beguiles me.
Nothing has told me how to think of her power.

Blurredly, apple-blossom drifts
across rough earth, small trees contort and twist
making their own shapes, wild.   Why should we love purity?
Can the woman in the DC-10 see this
and would she call this innocence?   If no one can reach her
she is drawing on unnamed, unaccountable power.

This woman I have been and recognize
must know that beneath the quilt of whiteness lies
a hated nation, hers,
earth whose wet places call to mind
still-open wounds: her country.
Do we love purity?   Where do we turn for power?

Knowing us as I do I cringe when she says
But I was not culpable,
I was the victim, the girl, the youngest,

the susceptible one, I was sick,
the one who simply had to get out, and did
: I am still trying how to think of her power.

And if she was forced, this woman, by the same
white Dixie boy who took for granted as prey
her ignored dark sisters?   What if at five years old
she was old to his fingers splaying her vulva open
what if forever after, in every record
she wants her name inscribed as *innocent*

and will not speak, refuses to know, can say
I have been numb for years
does not want to hear of any violation
like or unlike her own, as if the victim
can be innocent only in isolation
as if the victim dare not be intelligent

(I have been numb for years):   and if this woman
longs for an intact world, an intact soul,
longs for what we all long for, yet denies us all?
What has she smelled of power without once
tasting it in the mouth? For what protections
has she traded her wildness and the lives of others?

There is a porch in Salem, Virginia
that I have never seen, that may no longer stand,
honeysuckle vines twisting above the talk,
a driveway full of wheeltracks, paths going down
to the orchards, apple and peach,
divisions so deep a wild child lost her way.

A child climbing an apple-tree in Virginia
refuses to come down, at last comes down
for a neighbor's lying bribe.   Now, if that child, grown old

feels safe in a DC-10 above thick white clouds
and no one can reach her
and if that woman's child, another woman

chooses another way, yet finds the old vines
twisting across her path, the old wheeltracks
how does she stop dreaming the dream
of protection, how does she follow her own wildness
shedding the innocence, the childish power?
How does she keep from dreaming the old dreams?

1983

Dreams Before Waking

Despair is the question.
        —Elie Wiesel

Hasta tu país cambió. Lo has cambiado tú mismo.
        —Nancy Morejón

Despair falls:
the shadow of a building
they are raising in the direct path
of your slender ray of sunlight
Slowly the steel girders grow
the skeletal framework rises
yet the western light still filters
through it all
still glances off the plastic sheeting
they wrap around it
for dead of winter

At the end of winter something changes
a faint subtraction
from consolations you expected
an innocent brilliance that does not come
though the flower shops set out
once again on the pavement
their pots of tight-budded sprays
the bunches of jonquils stiff with cold
and at such a price
though someone must buy them
you study those hues as if with hunger

Despair falls
like the day you come home
from work, a summer evening
transparent with rose-blue light
and see they are filling in
the framework
the girders are rising
beyond your window
that seriously you live
in a different place
though you have never moved

and will not move, not yet
but will give away
your potted plants to a friend
on the other side of town
along with the cut crystal flashing
in the window-frame
will forget the evenings
of watching the street, the sky
the planes in the feathered afterglow:
will learn to feel grateful simply for this foothold

where still you can manage
to go on paying rent
where still you can believe
it's the old neighborhood:
even the woman who sleeps at night
in the barred doorway—wasn't she always there?
and the man glancing, darting
for food in the supermarket trash—
when did his hunger come to this?
what made the difference?
what will make it for you?

What will make it for you?
You don't want to know the stages
and those who go through them don't want to tell
You have your four locks on the door
your savings, your respectable past
your strangely querulous body, suffering
sicknesses of the city no one can name
You have your pride, your bitterness
your memories of sunset
you think you can make it straight through
if you don't speak of despair.

What would it mean to live
in a city whose people were changing
each other's despair into hope?—
You yourself must change it.—
what would it feel like to know
your country was changing?—
You yourself must change it.—
Though your life felt arduous
new and unmapped and strange
what would it mean to stand on the first
page of the end of despair?

1983

One Kind of Terror: A Love Poem

1.

From 1964: a color snapshot: you
riding a camel past the Great Pyramid

its rough earthy diagonal shouldering
the blue triangle of sky

I know your white shirt   dark skirt   your age
thirty-five   as mine was then

your ignorance like mine
in those years   and your curious mind

throw of your head   bend of your gilt knees
the laugh exchanged with whoever took the picture

I don't know how you were talking to yourself
I know I was thinking

with a schoolgirl's ardent rectitude
this will be the deciding year

I am sick of drift
Weren't we always trying to do better?

Then the voices began to say: *Your plans*
are not in the book of plans

written, printed and bound while you
were absent
          no, not here nor in Egypt
will you ever catch up

2.

So, then   as if by plan
I turn   and you are lost

How have I lived   knowing
that day of your laugh   so alive/so nothing

even the clothes you wore then
rotted away   How can I live believing

any year can be the deciding year
when I know the book of plans

how it disallows us
time for change   for growing older

truthfully   in our own way

3.

I used to think you ought to be
a woman   in charge   in a desperate time

of whole populations
such seemed the power of your restlessness

I saw you a rescuer
amid huge events   diasporas

scatterings and returnings
I needed this for us

I would have gone to help you
flinging myself into the fray

both of us treading free
of the roads we started on

4.

In the book of plans it is written
that our lifelines shall be episodic

faithless   frayed   lived out
under impure violent rains

and rare but violent sun
It is written there that we may reach

like wan vines across a window
trying to grasp each other

but shall lack care and tending
that water and air shall betray us

that the daughter born a poet
will die of dysentery

while the daughter born to organize
will die of cancer

5.

In the book of plans it says no one
will speak of the book of plans

the appearance will continue
that all this is natural

It says my grief for you is natural
but my anger for us is not

that the image of a white curtain trembling
across a stormy pane

is acceptable   but not
the image I make of you

arm raised hurling   signalling
the squatters   the refugees

storming the food supply
The book of plans says only that you must die

that we all, very soon, must die

6.

Well, I am studying a different book
taking notes wherever I go

the movement of the wrist does not change
but the pen plows deeper

my handwriting flows into words
I have not yet spoken

I'm the sole author of nothing
the book moves from field to field

of testimony   recording
how the wounded teach each other   the old

refuse to be organized
by fools   how the women say

in more than one language   *You have struck a rock—*
prepare to meet the unplanned

the ignored   the unforeseen   that which breaks
despair   which has always travelled

underground   or in the spaces
between the fixed stars

gazing full-faced   wild
and calm   on the Revolution

7.

Love: I am studying a different book
and yes, a book is a finite thing

In it your death will never be reversed
the deaths I have witnessed since   never undone

The light drained from the living eyes
can never flash again from those same eyes

I make you no promises
but something's breaking open here

there were certain extremes we had to know
before we could continue

Call it a book, or not
call it a map of constant travel

Call it a book, or not
call it a song   a ray

of images thrown on a screen
in open lots   in cellars

and among those images
one woman's meaning to another woman

long after death
in a different world

1983

What Was, Is;
What Might Have Been, Might Be

What's kept.   What's lost.   A snap decision.
Burn the archives.   Let them rot.
Begin by going ten years back.

A woman walks downstairs in a brownstone
in Brooklyn.   Late that night, some other night
snow crystals swarm in her hair
at the place we say, So long.

I've lost something.   I'm not sure what it is.
I'm going through my files.

Jewel-weed flashing
blue fire against an iron fence
Her head bent to a mailbox
long fingers ringed in gold   in red-eyed
golden serpents

the autumn sun
burns like a beak off the cars
parked along Riverside   we so deep in talk
in burnt September grass

I'm trying for exactitude
in the files I handle worn and faded labels
And how she drove, and danced, and fought, and worked
and loved, and sang, and hated
dashed into the record store   then out
with the Stevie Wonder   back in the car
flew on

Worn and faded labels . . . This was
our glamor for each other
underlined in bravado

Could it have been another way:
could we have been respectful comrades
parallel warriors   none of that
fast–falling

could we have kept a clean
and decent slate

1984

Poetry: I

Someone at a table under a brown metal lamp
is studying the history of poetry.
Someone in the library at closing-time
has learned to say *modernism,*
trope, vatic, text.
She is listening for shreds of music.
He is searching for his name
back in the old country.
They cannot learn without teachers.
They are like us   what we were
if you remember.

In a corner of night a voice
is crying in a kind of whisper:
More!

Can you remember?   when we thought
the poets taught   how to live?
That is not the voice of a critic
nor a common reader
it is someone young   in anger
hardly knowing what to ask
who finds our lines   our glosses
wanting   in this world.

1985

Poetry: II, Chicago

Whatever a poet is
at the point of conception   is
conceived in these projects
of beige and grey bricks   Yes, poets are born
in wasted tracts like these   whatever color, sex
comes to term in this winter's driving nights
And the child pushes like a spear
a cry   through cracked cement   through zero air
a spear, a cry of green   Yes, poets endure
these schools of fear   balked yet unbroken
where so much gets broken: trust
windows   pride   the mothertongue

Wherever a poet is born   enduring
depends on the frailest of chances:
Who listened to your murmuring
over your little rubbish   who let you be
who gave you the books
who let you know you were not
alone   showed you the twist
of old strands   raffia, hemp or silk
the beaded threads   the fiery lines
saying: *This belongs to you   you have the right*
you belong to the song
of your mothers and fathers   You have a people

1984

Poetry: III

Even if we knew the children were all asleep
and healthy   the ledgers balanced   the water running
clear in the pipes
                        and all the prisoners free

Even if every word we wrote by then
were honest   the sheer heft
of our living behind it
                                    not these sometimes
lax, indolent lines
                        these litanies

Even if we were told   not just by friends
that this was honest work

Even if each of us didn't wear
a brass locket with a picture
of a strangled woman   a girlchild sewn through the crotch

Even if someone had told us, young: *This is not a key*
nor a peacock feather
                                not a kite nor a telephone
This is the kitchen sink   the grinding-stone

would we give ourselves
more calmly over   feel less criminal joy
when the thing comes   as it does come
clarifying grammar
and the fixed and mutable stars—?

1984

Baltimore: a fragment from the Thirties

Medical textbooks propped in a dusty window.
Outside, it's summer.   Heat
swamping stretched awnings, battering dark-green shades.
The Depression, Monument Street,
ice-wagons trailing melt, the Hospital
with its segregated morgues . . .
I'm five years old and trying to be perfect
walking hand-in-hand with my father.
A Black man halts beside us
croaks in a terrible voice, *I'm hungry* . . .
I'm a lucky child but I've read about beggars—
how the good give, the evil turn away.
But I want to turn away.   My father gives.
We walk in silence.   Why did he sound like that?
Is it evil to be frightened?   I want to ask.
He has no roof in his mouth,
                              my father says at last.

1985

Homage to Winter

You: a woman too old
for passive contemplation
caught staring out a window
at bird-of-paradise spikes
jewelled with rain, across an alley
It's winter in this land
of roses, roses   sometimes
the fog lies thicker around you than your past
sometimes the Pacific radiance
scours the air to lapis
In this new world you feel
backward along the hem of your whole life
questioning every breadth
Nights you can watch the moon shed skin after skin
over and over, always a shape
of imbalance except
at birth and in the full
You, still trying to learn
how to live, what must be done
though in death you will be complete
whatever you do
But death is not the answer.

On these flat green leaves
light skates like a golden blade
high in the dull-green pine
sit two mushroom-colored doves
afterglow overflows
across the bungalow roof
between the signs for the three-way stop
over everything that is:

the cotton pants stirring on the line, the
empty Coke can by the fence
onto the still unflowering
mysterious acacia
and a sudden chill takes the air

Backward you dream to a porch
you stood on a year ago
snow flying quick as thought
sticking to your shoulder   gone
Blue shadows, ridged and fading
on a snow-swept road
the shortest day of the year
Backward you dream to glare ice
and ice-wet pussywillows
to Riverside Drive, the wind
cut loose from Hudson's Bay
driving tatters into your face
And back you come at last to that room
without a view, where webs of frost
blinded the panes at noon
where already you had begun
to make the visible world your conscience
asking things: *What can you tell me?*
what am I doing?   what must I do?

1985

Blue Rock

For Myriam Díaz-Diocaretz

Your chunk of lapis-lazuli shoots its stain
blue into the wineglass on the table

the full moon moving up the sky is plain
as the dead rose and the live buds on one stem

No, this isn't Persian poetry I'm quoting:
all this is here in North America

where I sit trying to kindle fire
from what's already on fire:

the light of a blue rock from Chile swimming
in the apricot liquid called "eye of the swan".

This is a chunk of your world, a piece of its heart:
split from the rest, does it suffer?

You needn't tell me.   Sometimes I hear it singing
by the waters of Babylon, in a strange land

sometimes it just lies heavy in my hand
with the heaviness of silent seismic knowledge

a blue rock in a foreign land, an exile
excised but never separated

from the gashed heart, its mountains,
winter rains, language, native sorrow.

At the end of the twentieth century
cardiac graphs of torture reply to poetry

line by line: in North America
the strokes of the stylus continue

the figures of terror are reinvented
all night, after I turn the lamp off, blotting

wineglass, rock and roses, leaving pages
like this scrawled with mistakes and love,

falling asleep; but the stylus does not sleep,
cruelly the drum revolves, cruelty writes its name.

Once when I wrote poems they did not change
left overnight on the page

they stayed as they were and daylight broke
on the lines, as on the clotheslines in the yard

heavy with clothes forgotten or left out
for a better sun next day

But now I know what happens while I sleep
and when I wake the poem has changed:

the facts have dilated it, or cancelled it;
and in every morning's light, your rock is there.

1985

Yom Kippur 1984

I drew solitude over me, on the lone shore.
    —*Robinson Jeffers, "Prelude"*

For whoever does not afflict his soul throughout this day, shall be cut off from his people.

                                                                    —*Leviticus 23:29*

What is a Jew in solitude?
What would it mean not to feel lonely or afraid
far from your own or those you have called your own?
What is a woman in solitude: a queer woman or man?
In the empty street, on the empty beach, in the desert
what in this world as it is can solitude mean?

The glassy, concrete octagon suspended from the cliffs
with its electric gate, its perfected privacy
is not what I mean
the pick-up with a gun parked at a turn-out in Utah or the Golan
                Heights
is not what I mean
the poet's tower facing the western ocean, acres of forest planted to
                the east, the woman reading in the cabin, her
                attack dog suddenly risen
is not what I mean

Three thousand miles from what I once called home
I open a book searching for some lines I remember
about flowers, something to bind me to this coast as lilacs in the
                dooryard once
bound me back there—yes, lupines on a burnt mountainside,
something that bloomed and faded and was written down
in the poet's book, forever:

Opening the poet's book
I find the hatred in the poet's heart: . . . *the hateful-eyed*
and human-bodied are all about me: you that love multitude may have
                    them

Robinson Jeffers, multitude
is the blur flung by distinct forms against these landward valleys
and the farms that run down to the sea; the lupines
are multitude, and the torched poppies, the grey Pacific unrolling
                    its scrolls of surf,
and the separate persons, stooped
over sewing machines in denim dust, bent under the shattering
                    skies of harvest
who sleep by shifts in never-empty beds have their various dreams
Hands that pick, pack, steam, stitch, strip, stuff, shell, scrape,
                    scour, belong to a brain like no other
Must I argue the love of multitude in the blur or defend
a solitude of barbed-wire and searchlights, the survivalist's final
                    solution, have I a choice?

To wander far from your own or those you have called your own
to hear strangeness calling you from far away
and walk in that direction, long and far, not calculating risk
to go to meet the Stranger without fear or weapon, protection
                    nowhere on your mind
(the Jew on the icy, rutted road on Christmas Eve prays for another
                    Jew
the woman in the ungainly twisting shadows of the street: *Make*
                    those be a woman's footsteps; as if she could believe in a
                    woman's god)

Find someone like yourself.   Find others.
Agree you will never desert each other.
Understand that any rift among you
means power to those who want to do you in.

Close to the center, safety; toward the edges, danger.
But I have a nightmare to tell: I am trying to say
that to be with my people is my dearest wish
but that I also love strangers
that I crave separateness
I hear myself stuttering these words
to my worst friends and my best enemies
who watch for my mistakes in grammar
my mistakes in love.
This is the day of atonement; but do my people forgive me?
If a cloud knew loneliness and fear, I would be that cloud.

To love the Stranger, to love solitude—am I writing merely about
          privilege
about drifting from the center, drawn to edges,
a privilege we can't afford in the world that is,
who are hated as being of our kind: faggot kicked into the icy
          river, woman dragged from her stalled car
into the mist-struck mountains, used and hacked to death
young scholar shot at the university gates on a summer evening
          walk, his prizes and studies nothing, nothing
          availing his Blackness
Jew deluded that she's escaped the tribe, the laws of her exclusion,
          the men too holy to touch her hand;   Jew who has
          turned her back
on *midrash* and *mitzvah* (yet wears the *chai* on a thong between her
          breasts) hiking alone
found with a swastika carved in her back at the foot of the cliffs
          (did she die as queer or as Jew?)

Solitude, O taboo, endangered species
on the mist-struck spur of the mountain, I want a gun to defend
          you
In the desert, on the deserted street, I want what I can't have:
your elder sister, Justice, her great peasant's hand outspread

161

her eye, half-hooded, sharp and true
And I ask myself, have I thrown courage away?

have I traded off something I don't name?
To what extreme will I go to meet the extremist?
What will I do to defend my want or anyone's want to search for
         her spirit-vision
far from the protection of those she has called her own?
Will I find O solitude
your plumes, your breasts, your hair
against my face, as in childhood, your voice like the mockingbird's
singing *Yes, you are loved, why else this song?*
in the old places, anywhere?

What is a Jew in solitude?
What is a woman in solitude, a queer woman or man?
When the winter flood-tides wrench the tower from the rock,
         crumble the prophet's headland, and the farms slide
         into the sea
when leviathan is endangered and Jonah becomes revenger
when center and edges are crushed together, the extremities
         crushed together on which the world was founded
when our souls crash together, Arab and Jew, howling our
         loneliness within the tribes
when the refugee child and the exile's child re-open the blasted and
         forbidden city
when we who refuse to be women and men as women and men are
         chartered, tell our stories of solitude spent in
         multitude
in that world as it may be, newborn and haunted, what will
         solitude mean?

1984–1985

Edges

In the sleepless sleep of dawn, in the dreamless dream
the kingfisher cuts through   flashing
spirit-fire from his wings   bluer than violet's edge
the slice of those wings

5 a.m., first light, hoboes of the past
are leaning through the window, what freightcars
did they hop here   I thought I'd left behind?
Their hands are stretched out but not for bread
they are past charity, they want me to hear   their names

Outside in the world where so much is possible
sunrise rekindles and the kingfisher—
the living kingfisher, not that flash of vision—
darts where the creek drags her wetness over stump and stone
where poison oak reddens   acacia pods collect
curled and secretive against the bulkhead

and the firstlight ghosts go transparent
while the homeless line for bread

1985

Contradictions: Tracking Poems

1.

Look: this is January   the worst onslaught
is ahead of us   Don't be lured
by these soft grey afternoons   these sunsets cut
from pink and violet tissue-paper   by the thought
the days are lengthening
Don't let the solstice fool you:
our lives will always be
a stew of contradictions
the worst moment of winter can come in April
when the peepers are stubbornly still   and our bodies
plod on without conviction
and our thoughts cramp down before the sheer
arsenal of everything that tries us:
this battering, blunt-edged life

2.

Heart of cold.   Bones of cold.   Scalp of cold.
the grey   the black   the blond   the red
hairs on a skull of cold.   Within that skull
the thought of war   the sovereign thought
the coldest of all thought.   Dreaming shut down
everything kneeling down to cold   intelligence
smirking with cold   memory
squashed and frozen cold   breath
half held-in for cold.   The freezing people
of a freezing nation   eating
luxury food or garbage
frozen tongues licking the luxury meat
or the pizza-crust   the frozen eyes

welded to other eyes   also frozen
the cold hands trying to stroke   the coldest sex.
Heart of cold   Sex of cold   Intelligence of cold
My country   wedged fast in history
stuck in the ice

3.

My mouth hovers across your breasts
in the short grey winter afternoon
in this bed   we are delicate
and tough   so hot with joy we amaze ourselves
tough   and delicate   we play rings
around each other   our daytime candle burns
with its peculiar light   and if the snow
begins to fall outside   filling the branches
and if the night falls   without announcement
these are the pleasures of winter
sudden, wild and delicate   your fingers
exact   my tongue exact at the same moment
stopping to laugh at a joke
my love   hot on your scent   on the cusp of winter

4.

He slammed his hand across my face   and I
let him do that until   I stopped letting him do it
so I'm in for life.

. . . . he kept saying I was crazy, he'd lock me up
until I went to Women's Lib and they
told me he'd been abusing me as much
as if he'd hit me: emotional abuse.
They told me how to answer back.   That I could
answer back.   But my brother-in-law's a shrink

with the State.   I have to watch my step.
If I stay just within bounds they can't come and get me.
Women's Lib taught me the words to say
to remind myself and him I'm a person with rights
like anyone.   But answering back's no answer.

5.

She is carrying my madness   and I dread her
avoid her when I can
She walks along I.S. 93   howling
in her bare feet
She is number 6375411
in a cellblock in Arkansas
and I dread what she is paying for   that is mine
She has fallen asleep at last in the battered
women's safe-house   and I dread
her dreams   that I also dream
If never I become exposed or confined like this
what am I hiding
O sister of nausea   of broken ribs   of isolation
what is this freedom I protect   how is it mine

6.

Dear Adrienne:
                    I'm calling you up tonight
as I might call up a friend   as I might call up a ghost
to ask what you intend to do
with the rest of your life.   Sometimes you act
as if you have all the time there is.
I worry about you when I see this.
The prime of life, old age
aren't what they used to be;
making a good death isn't either,

now you can walk around the corner of a wall
and see a light
that already has blown your past away.
Somewhere in Boston   beautiful literature
is being read around the clock
by writers   to signify
their dislike of this.
I hope you've got something in mind.
I hope you have some idea
about the rest of your life.

In sisterhood,

Adrienne

7.

Dear Adrienne,
I feel signified by pain

from my breastbone through my left shoulder down
through my elbow into my wrist is a thread of pain
I am typing this instead of writing by hand
because my wrist on the right side
blooms and rushes with pain
like a neon bulb
You ask me how I'm going to live
the rest of my life
Well, nothing is predictable with pain
Did the old poets write of this?
—in its odd spaces, free,
many have sung and battled—
But I'm already living the rest of my life
not under conditions of my choosing
wired   into pain

rider on the slow train

Yours, Adrienne

8.

I'm afraid of prison.   Have been all these years.
Afraid they'll take my aspirin away
and of other things as well:
beatings   damp and cold   I have my fears.
Unable one day to get up and walk
to do what must be done
Prison as idea   it fills me
with fear   this exposure to my own weakness
at someone else's whim
I watched that woman go over the barbed-wire fence
at the peace encampment
                        the wheelchair rider
I didn't want to do what she did
I thought, They'll get her for this
I thought, We are not such victims.

9.

Tearing but not yet torn: this page
The long late-winter rage
wild rain on the windshield
clenched stems   unyielding sticks
of maple, birch   bleached grass   the range
of things resisting change
And this is how I am
and this is how you are
when we resist the charmer's open sesame
the thief's light-fingered touch
staying closed because we will
not give ourselves away
until the agent   the manipulator   the false toucher
has left   and it is May

10.

Night   over the great and the little worlds
of Brooklyn   the shredded communities
in Chicago   Argentina   Poland
in Holyoke Massachusetts   Amsterdam   Manchester England
Night falls   the day of atonement begins
in how many divided hearts   how many defiant lives
Toronto   Managua   St. Johnsbury
and the great and little worlds of the women
Something ancient passes across the earth
lifting the dust of the blasted ghettos
You ask if I will eat and I say, Yes,
I have never fasted
but something crosses my life
not a shadow   the reflection of a fire

11.

I came out of the hospital like a woman
who'd watched a massacre
not knowing how to tell
my adhesions   the lingering infections
from the pain on the streets
In my room on Yom Kippur they took me off morphine
I saw shadows on the wall   the dying and the dead
They said Christian Phalangists did it
then Kol Nidre on the radio   and my own
unhoused spirit   trying to find a home
Was it then or another day
in what order did it happen
I thought   *They call this elective surgery*
but we all have died of this.

12.

Violence as purification: the one idea.
One massacre great enough to undo another
one last-ditch operation to solve the problem
of the old operation that was bungled
Look: I have lain on their tables under their tools
under their drugs   from the center of my body
a voice bursts   against these methods
(wherever you made a mistake
batter with radiation   defoliate   cut away)
and yes, there are merciful debridements
but burns turn into rotting flesh
for reasons of vengeance and neglect.
I have been too close to septic too many times
to play with either violence or non-violence.

13.

Trapped in one idea, you can't have your feelings,
feelings are always about more than one thing.
You drag yourself back home and it is autumn
you can't concentrate, you can't lie on the couch
so you drive yourself for hours on the quiet roads
crying at the wheel   watching the colors
deepening, fading   and winter is coming
and you long for one idea
one simple, huge idea to take this weight
and you know you will never find it, never
because you don't want to find it
You will drive and cry and come home and eat
and listen to the news
and slowly even at winter's edge
the feelings come back in their shapes
and colors   conflicting   they come back
   they are changed

14.

Lately in my dreams I hear long sentences
meaningless in ordinary American
like, *Your mother, too, was a missionary of poets*
and in another dream one of my old teachers
shows me a letter of reference
he has written for me, in a language
I know to be English but cannot understand,
telling me it's in "transformational grammar"
and that the student who typed the letter
does not understand this grammar either.
Lately I dreamed about my father,
how I found him, alive, seated on an old chair.
I think what he said to me was,
You don't know how lonely I am.

15.

You who think I find words for everything,
and you for whom I write this,
how can I show you what I'm barely
coming into possession of, invisible luggage
of more than fifty years, looking at first
glance like everyone else's, turning up
at the airport carousel
and the waiting for it, knowing what nobody
would steal must eventually come round—
feeling obsessed, peculiar, longing?

16.

It's true, these last few years I've lived
watching myself in the act of loss—the art of losing,
Elizabeth Bishop called it, but for me no art

only badly-done exercises
acts of the heart forced to question
its presumptions in this world   its mere excitements
acts of the body forced to measure
all instincts against pain
acts of parting   trying to let go
without giving up   yes   Elizabeth   a city here
a village there   a sister, comrade, cat
and more   no art to this but anger

17.

I have backroads I take   to places
like the hospital where night pain
is never tended enough but I can drive
under the overlacing boughs
of wineglass elm, oak, maple
from Mosquitoville to Wells River
along the double track with the greened hump
the slope with the great sugar-grove
New Age talk calls it "visualizing"   but I know
under torture I would travel
from the West Barnet burying-ground
to Joe's Brook   by heart   I know
all of those roads by heart
by heart I know what, and all, I have left behind

18.

The problem, unstated till now, is how
to live in a damaged body
in a world where pain is meant to be gagged
uncured   un-grieved-over   The problem is
to connect, without hysteria, the pain
of any one's body with the pain of the body's world

For it is the body's world
they are trying to destroy forever
The best world is the body's world
filled with creatures   filled with dread
misshapen so   yet the best we have
our raft among the abstract worlds
and how I longed to live on this earth
walking her boundaries   never counting the cost

19.

If to feel is to be unreliable
don't listen to us
if to be in pain is to be predictable
embittered   bullying
then don't listen to us
If we're in danger of mistaking
our personal trouble for the pain on the streets
don't listen to us
if my fury at being grounded frightens you
take off on your racing skis
in your beautiful tinted masks
Trapped in one idea, you can't have feelings
Without feelings perhaps you can feel like a god

20.

The tobacco fields lie fallow   the migrant pickers
no longer visible
where undocumented intelligences travailed
on earth they had no stake in
though the dark leaves growing beneath white veils
were beautiful   and the barns opened out like fans
All this of course could have been done differently
This valley itself: one more contradiction

the paradise fields   the brute skyscrapers
the pesticidal wells

I have been wanting for years
to write a poem   equal to these
material forces
and I have always failed
I wasn't looking for a muse
only a reader by whom   I could not be mistaken

21.

The cat-tails blaze in the corner   sunflowers
shed their pale fiery dust   on the dark stove-lid
others stand guard   heads bowed   over the garden
the fierce and flaring garden you have made
out of your woes and expectations
tilled into the earth   I circle close to your mind
crash into it sometimes   as you crash into mine
Given this strip of earth   given mere love
should we not be happy?
but happiness comes and goes as it comes and goes
the safe-house is temporary   the garden
lies open to vandals
this whole valley is one more contradiction
and more will be asked of us   we will ask more

22.

In a bald skull sits our friend   in a helmet
of third-degree burns
her quizzical melancholy grace
her irreplaceable self   in utter peril
In the radioactive desert walks a woman
in a black dress   white-haired   steady

as the luminous hand of a clock
in circles she walks   knitting
and unknitting her scabbed fingers
Her face is expressionless   shall we pray to her
shall we speak of the loose pine-needles   how they shook
like the pith of country summers
from the sacks of pitchblende ore in the tin-roofed shack
where it all began
Shall we accuse her of denial
first of the self   then of the mixed virtue
of the purest science   shall we be wise for her
in hindsight   shall we scream *It has come to this*
Shall we praise her   shall we let her wander
the atomic desert   in peace?

23.

You know the Government must have pushed them to settle,
the chemical industries   and pay
that hush-money to the men
who landed out there at twenty   not for belief
but because of who they were   and were called psychos
when they said their bodies contained dioxin
like memories they didn't want to keep
whose kids came out deformed
You know nothing has changed   no respect or grief
for the losers of a lost war everyone hated
nobody sent them to school like heroes
if they started sueing for everything that was done
there would be no end   there would be a beginning
My country   wedged fast in history
stuck in the ice

24.

Someone said to me: *It's just that we don't*
know how to cope with the loss of memory.
When your own grandfather doesn't know you
when your mother thinks you're somebody else
it's a terrible thing.
Now just like that is this idea
that the universe will forget us, everything we've done
will go nowhere
no one will know who we were.
No one will know who we were!

Not the young who will never   Nor even the old folk
who knew us when we were young   insatiable
for recognition from them
trying so fiercely not to be them
counting on them to know us   anywhere

25.

Did anyone ever know who we were
if *we* means more than a handful?
flower of a generation   young white men
cut off in the named, commemorated wars
I stare   Jewish   into that loss
for which all names become unspeakable
not ever just the best and brightest
but the most wretched and bedevilled
the obscure   the strange   the driven
the twins   the dwarfs   the geniuses   the gay
But ours was not the only loss
(to whom does annihilation speak
as if for the first time?)

26.

You: air-driven   reft   from the tuber-bitten soil
that was your portion   from the torched-out village
the Marxist study-group   the Zionist cell
café or *cheder*   Zaddik or Freudian   straight or gay
woman or man   O you
stripped   bared   appalled
stretched to mere spirit   yet still physical
your irreplaceable knowledge   lost
at the mud-slick bottom of the world
how you held fast   with your bone-meal fingers
to yourselves   each other   and strangers
how you touched   held-up from falling
what was already half-cadaver
how your life-cry taunted extinction
with its wild, crude   *so what?*
Grief for you has rebellion at its heart
it cannot simply mourn
You: air-driven: reft: are yet our teachers
trying to speak to us in sleep
trying to help us wake

27.

The Tolstoyans   the Afro-American slaves
knew this: you could be killed
for teaching people to read and write
I used to think the worst affliction
was to be forbidden pencil and paper
well, Ding Ling recited poems to prison walls
for years of the Cultural Revolution
and truly, the magic of written characters
looms and dwindles   shrinks small   grows swollen
depending on where you stand

and what is in your hand
and who can read and why
I think now the worst affliction
is not to know who you are or have been
I have learned this in part
from writers   Reading and writing
aren't sacred   yet people have been killed
as if they were

28.

This high summer we love will pour its light
the fields grown rich and ragged in one strong moment
then before we're ready will crash into autumn
with a violence we can't accept
a bounty we can't forgive
Night frost will strike when the noons are warm
the pumpkins wildly glowing   the green tomatoes
straining huge on the vines
queen anne and blackeyed susan will straggle rusty
as the milkweed stakes her claim
she who will stand at last   dark sticks barely rising
up through the snow   her testament of continuation
We'll dream of a longer summer
but this is the one we have:
I lay my sunburnt hand
on your table: this is the time we have

29.

You who think I find words for everything
this is enough for now
cut it short   cut loose from my words

You for whom I write this
in the night hours when the wrecked cartilage
sifts round the mystical jointure of the bones
when the insect of detritus crawls
from shoulder to elbow to wristbone
remember: the body's pain and the pain on the streets
are not the same   but you can learn
from the edges that blur   O you who love clear edges
more than anything   watch the edges that blur

1983–1985

Time's Power

Solfeggietto

1.

Your windfall at fifteen   your Steinway grand
paid for by fire insurance
came to me as birthright   a black cave
with teeth of ebony and ivory
twanging and thundering over the head
of the crawling child   until
that child was set on the big book on the chair
to face the keyboard world of black and white
—already knowing the world was black and white
The child's hands   smaller than a sand-dollar
set on the keys   wired to their mysteries
the child's wits facing the ruled and ruling staves

2.

For years we battled over music lessons
mine, taught by you   Nor did I wonder
what that keyboard meant to you
the hours of solitude   the practising
your life of prize-recitals   lifted hopes
Piatti's nephew praising you at sixteen
scholarships to the North
Or what it was to teach
boarding-school girls what won't be used
shelving ambition   beating time
to "On the Ice at Sweet Briar" or
"The Sunken Cathedral" for a child
counting the minutes and the scales to freedom

3.

Freedom: what could that mean, for you or me?
—Summers of '36, '37, Europe untuned
what I remember isn't lessons
not Bach or Brahms or Mozart
but the rented upright in the summer rental
One Hundred Best-Loved Songs on the piano rack
And so you played, evenings   and so we sang
"Steal Away" and "Swanee River,"
"Swing Low," and most of all
"Mine Eyes Have Seen the Glory of the Coming of the Lord"
How we sang out the chorus   how I loved
the watchfires of the hundred circling camps
and *truth is marching on* and *let us die to make men free*

4.

Piano lessons   The mother and the daughter
Their doomed exhaustion   their common mystery
worked out in finger-exercises   Czerny, Hanon
The yellow Schirmer albums   quarter-rests   double-holds
glyphs of an astronomy   the mother cannot teach
the daughter because this is not the story
of a mother teaching magic to her daughter
Side by side I see us locked
My wrists   your voice   are tightened
Passion lives in old songs   in the kitchen
where another woman cooks   teaches   and sings
He shall feed his flock like a shepherd
and in the booklined room
where the Jewish father reads and smokes and teaches
Ecclesiastes, Proverbs, the Song of Songs
The daughter struggles with the strange notations
—dark chart of music's ocean   flowers and flags

but would rather learn by ear and heart   The mother
says she must learn to read by sight   not ear and heart

5.

Daughter who fought her mother's lessons—
even today a scrip of music balks me—
I feel illiterate in this
your mother-tongue   Had it been Greek or Slovak
no more could your native alphabet have baffled
your daughter   whom you taught for years
held by a tether   over the ivory
and ebony teeth of the Steinway

                                        It is
the three hundredth anniversary of Johann
Sebastian Bach   My earliest life
woke to his English Suites   under your fingers
I understand a language I can't read
Music you played streams on the car radio
in the freeway night
You kept your passions deep   You have them still
I ask you, both of us
—Did you think mine was a virtuoso's hand?
Did I see power in yours?
What was worth fighting for?   What did you want?
What did I want from you?

1985–1988

This

Face flashing free   child-arms
lifting the collie pup
torn paper on the path
Central Park   April '72
behind you   minimal
those benches and that shade
that brilliant light in which
you laughed longhaired
and I'm the keeper of
this little piece of paper
this little piece of truth

I wanted this from you—
laughter   a child turning
into a boy   at ease
in the spring light   with friends
I wanted this for you

I could mutter   *Give back*
that day   give me again
that child   with the chance
of making it all right
I could yell   *Give back that light*
on the dog's teeth   the child's hair
but no rough drafts are granted
—Do you think I don't remember?
did you think I was all-powerful
unimpaired   unappalled?
yes   you needed that from me
I wanted this from you

1985

Negotiations

Someday if someday comes we will agree
that trust is not about safety
that keeping faith is not about deciding
to clip our fingernails exactly
to the same length or wearing
a uniform that boasts our unanimity

Someday if someday comes we'll know
the difference between liberal laissez-faire
pluralism and the way you cut your hair
and the way I clench my hand
against my cheekbone
both being possible gestures of defiance

Someday if there's a someday we will
bring food, you'll say I can't eat what you've brought
I'll say Have some in the name of our
trying to be friends, you'll say What about you?
We'll taste strange meat and we'll admit
we've tasted stranger

Someday if someday ever comes we'll go
back and reread those poems and manifestos
that so enraged us in each other's hand
I'll say, But damn, you wrote it so I
couldn't write it off   You'll say
I read you always, even when I hated you

1986

In a Classroom

Talking of poetry, hauling the books
arm–full to the table where the heads
bend or gaze upward, listening, reading aloud,
talking of consonants, elision,
caught in the how, oblivious of why:
I look in your face, Jude,
neither frowning nor nodding,
opaque in the slant of dust–motes over the table:
a presence like a stone, if a stone were thinking
What I cannot say, is me. For that I came.

1986

The Novel

All winter you went to bed early, drugging yourself on *War and*
                              Peace
Prince Andrei's cold eyes taking in the sky from the battlefield
were your eyes, you went walking wrapped in his wound
like a padded coat against the winds from the two rivers
You went walking in the streets as if you were ordinary
as if you hadn't been pulling with your raw mittened hand
on the slight strand that held your tattered mind
blown like an old stocking from a wire
on the wind between two rivers.
                              All winter you asked nothing
of that book though it lay heavy on your knees
you asked only for a shed skin, many skins in which to walk
you were old woman, child, commander
you watched Natasha grow into a neutered thing
you felt your heart go still while your eyes swept the pages
you felt the pages thickening to the left and on the right-
hand growing few, you knew the end was coming
you knew beyond the ending lay
your own, unwritten life

1986

In Memoriam: D.K.

A man walking on the street
feels unwell   has felt unwell
all week, a little   Yet the flowers crammed
in pots on the corner: furled anemones:
he knows they open
burgundy, violet, pink, amarillo
all the way to their velvet cores
The flowers hanging over the fence: fuchsias:
each tongued, staring,   all of a fire:
the flowers   He who has
been happy oftener than sad
carelessly happy   well oftener than sick
one of the lucky   is thinking about death
and its music   about poetry
its translations of his life

And what good will it do you
to go home and put on the Mozart Requiem?
Read Keats?   How will culture cure you?
                                        Poor, unhappy
unwell culture   what can it sing or say
six weeks from now, to you?

Give me your living hand   If I could take the hour
death moved into you   undeclared, unnamed
—even if sweet, if I could take that hour

between my forceps   tear at it like a monster
wrench it out of your flesh   dissolve its shape in quicklime
and make you well again

                              no, not again

but still. . . .

1986

Children Playing Checkers
at the Edge of the Forest

Two green–webbed chairs
                                    a three-legged stool between
Your tripod
                Spears of grass
                              longer than your bare legs
cast shadows on your legs
                      drawn up
                                from the red–and–black
cardboard squares
                      the board of play
                              the board of rules
But you're not playing, you're talking
                            It's midsummer
and greater rules are breaking
                    It's the last
innocent summer you will know
                    and I
will go on awhile pretending that's not true

When I have done pretending
                    I can see this:
the depth of the background
                shadows
                      not of one moment only
erased and charcoaled in again
                  year after year
how the tree looms back behind you
the first tree of the forest
                the last tree

from which the deer step out
                    from protection
                                        the first tree
into dreadfulness
              The last and the first tree

1987

Sleepwalking Next to Death

Sleep   *horns of a snail*
                              protruding, retracting
What we choose to know
                    or not know
                                        all these years
sleepwalking
                next to death

I

This snail could have been eaten
This snail could have been crushed
This snail could have dreamed it was a painter or a poet
This snail could have driven fast at night
putting up graffiti with a spray-gun:

This snail could have ridden
in the back of the pick-up, handing guns

II

Knows, chooses not to know
                        It has always
been about death and chances
                        The Dutch artist wrote and painted
one or more strange and usable things
For I mean to meet you
in any land   in any language
This is my promise:
I will be there
if you are there

III

In between this and that there are different places
of waiting, airports mostly where the air
is hungover, visibility low   boarding passes not guaranteed
If you wrote me, *I sat next to Naomi*
I would read that, *someone who felt like Ruth*
I would begin reading you like a dream
That's how extreme it feels

                           that's what I have to do

IV

Every stone around your neck you know the reason for
at this time in your life   Relentlessly
you tell me their names and furiously I
forget their names   Forgetting the names of the stones
you love, you lover of stones
what is it I do?

V

What is it I do? I refuse to take your place
in the world   I refuse to make myself
your courier   I refuse so much
I might ask, what is it I do?
I will not be the dreamer for whom
you are the only dream
I will not be your channel
I will wrestle you to the end
for our difference (as you have wrestled me)
I will change your name and confuse
the Angel

VI

I am stupid with you and practical with you
I remind you to take a poultice   forget a quarrel
I am a snail in the back of the pick-up handing you
vitamins you hate to take

VII

Calmly you look over my shoulder   at this page   and say
It's all about you   None of this
tells my story

VIII

Yesterday noon I stood by a river
and many waited to cross over
from the Juarez barrio
                              to El Paso del Norte
First day of spring   a stand of trees
in Mexico were in palegreen leaf
a man casting a net
                              into the Rio Grande
and women, in pairs, strolling
                                        across the border
as if taking a simple walk
                              Many thousands go

I stood by the river and thought of you
young   in Mexico   in a time of hope

IX

The practical nurse is the only nurse
with her plastic valise of poultices and salves

her hands of glove leather and ebony
her ledgers of pain
The practical nurse goes down to the river
in her runover shoes and her dollar necklace
eating a burrito in hand

                              it will be a long day
a long labor
                    the midwife will be glad to see her
it will be a long night   someone bleeding
from a botched abortion   a beating   Will you let her touch you
                    now?
Will you tell her you're fine?

X

I'm afraid of the border patrol
                              Not those men
of La Migra who could have run us
into the irrigation canal with their van
                              I'm afraid
of the patrollers
the sleepwalker in me
                    the loner in you

XI

I want five hours with you
in a train running south
                         maybe ten hours
in a Greyhound bound for the border
the two seats side-by-side that become a home
an island of light in the continental dark
the time that takes the place of a lifetime
I promise I won't fall asleep when the lights go down
I will not be lulled

Promise you won't jump the train
vanish into the bus depot at three a.m.
that you won't defect
                        that we'll travel
like two snails
                  our four horns erect

1987

Delta

If you have taken this rubble for my past
raking through it for fragments you could sell
know that I long ago moved on
deeper into the heart of the matter

If you think you can grasp me, think again:
my story flows in more than one direction
a delta springing from the riverbed
with its five fingers spread

1987

6/21

It's June and summer's height
the longest bridge of light
leaps from all the rivets
of the sky
Yet it's of earth
and nowhere else I have to speak
Only on earth has this light taken on
these swivelled meanings, only on this earth
where we are dying befouled, gritting our teeth
losing our guiding stars
                                    has this light
found an alphabet   a mouth

1987

Dreamwood

In the old, scratched, cheap wood of the typing stand
there is a landscape, veined, which only a child can see
or the child's older self,
a woman dreaming when she should be typing
the last report of the day.   If this were a map,
she thinks, a map laid down to memorize
because she might be walking it, it shows
ridge upon ridge fading into hazed desert,
here and there a sign of aquifers
and one possible watering-hole.   If this were a map
it would be the map of the last age of her life,
not a map of choices but a map of variations
on the one great choice. It would be the map by which
she could see the end of touristic choices,
of distances blued and purpled by romance,
by which she would recognize that poetry
isn't revolution but a way of knowing
why it must come.   If this cheap, massproduced
wooden stand from the Brooklyn Union Gas Co.,
massproduced yet durable, being here now,
is what it is yet a dream-map
so obdurate, so plain,
she thinks, the material and the dream can join
and that is the poem and that is the late report.

1987

Harpers Ferry

Where do I get this landscape? Two river-roads
glittering at each other's throats, the Virginia mountains fading
across the gorge, the October-shortened sun, the wooden town,
rebellion sprouting encampments in the hills
and a white girl running away from home
who will have to see it all. But where do I get this, how
do I know how the light quails from the trembling
waters, autumn goes to ash from ridge to ridge
how behind the gunmetal pines the guns
are piled, the sun drops, and the watchfires burn?

I know the men's faces tremble like smoky
crevices in a cave where candle-stumps have been stuck
on ledges by fugitives. The men are dark and sometimes pale
like her, their eyes pouched or blank or squinting, all by now
are queer, outside, and out of bounds and have no membership
in any brotherhood but this: where power is handed from
the ones who can get it to the ones
who have been refused. It's a simple act,
to steal guns and hand them to the slaves. Who would have thought
                    it.

Running away from home is slower than her quick feet thought
and this is not the vague and lowering North, ghostland of deeper
                    snows
than she has ever pictured
but this is one exact and definite place,
a wooden village at the junction of two rivers
two trestle bridges hinged and splayed,
low houses crawling up the mountains.

Suppose she slashes her leg on a slashed pine's tooth, ties the leg
                    in a kerchief
knocks on the door of a house, the first on the edge of town
has to beg water, won't tell her family name, afraid someone will
                    know her family face
lies with her throbbing leg on the vined verandah where the woman
                    of the house
wanted her out of there, that was clear
yet with a stern and courteous patience leaned above her
with cold tea, water from the sweetest spring, mint from the same
                    source
later with rags wrung from a boiling kettle
and studying, staring eyes. Eyes ringed with watching. A peachtree
                    shedding yellowy leaves
and a houseful of men who keep off. So great a family of men, and
                    then this woman
who wanted her gone yet stayed by her, watched over her.
But this girl is expert in overhearing
and one word leaps off the windowpanes like the crack of dawn,
the translation of the babble of two rivers. What does this girl
with her little family quarrel, know about arsenals?
Everything she knows is wrapped up in her leg
without which she won't get past Virginia, though she's running
                    north.

Whatever gave the girl the idea you could run away
from a family quarrel? Displace yourself, when nothing else
would change? It wasn't books:

it was half-overheard, a wisp of talk:
escape   flight   free soil
softing past her shoulder

She has never dreamed of arsenals, though
she's a good rifle-shot, taken at ten
by her brothers, hunting

and though they've climbed her over and over
leaving their wet clots in her sheets
on her new-started maidenhair

she has never reached for a gun to hold them off
for guns are the language of the strong to the weak
—How many squirrels have crashed between her sights

what vertebrae cracked at her finger's signal
what wings staggered through the boughs
whose eyes, ringed and treed, has she eyed as prey?

There is a strategy of mass flight
a strategy of arming
questions of how, of when, of where:

the arguments soak through the walls
of the houseful of men where running from home
the white girl lies in her trouble.

There are things overheard and things unworded, never sung
or pictured, things that happen silently
as the peachtree's galactic blossoms open in mist, the frost-star
hangs in the stubble, the decanter of moonlight pours its mournless
                    liquid down
steadily on the solstice fields
the cotton swells in its boll and you feel yourself engorged,
                    unnameable
you yourself feel encased and picked-open, you feel yourself
                    unenvisaged

There is no quarrel possible in this silence
You stop yourself listening for a word that will not be spoken:
                    listening instead to the overheard
fragments, phrases melting on air: *No more   Many thousand go*

And you know they are leaving as fast as they can, you whose child's
                eye followed each face wondering
not how could they leave but when: you knew they would leave
and so could you but not with them, you were not their child, they
                had their own children
you could leave the house where you were daughter, sister, prey
picked open and left to silence, you could leave alone

This would be my scenario of course: that the white girl understands
what I understand and more, that the leg torn in flight
had not betrayed her, had brought her to another point of struggle
that when she takes her place she is clear in mind and her anger
true with the training of her hand and eye, her leg cured on the
                porch of history
ready for more than solitary defiance. That when the General passes
                through
in her blazing headrag, this girl knows her for Moses, pleads to
                stand with the others in the shortened light
accepts the scrutiny, the steel-black gaze; but Moses passes and is
                gone to her business elsewhere
leaving the men to theirs, the girl to her own.
But who would she take as leader?
would she fade into the woods
will she die in an *indefensible position, a miscarried raid*
does she lose the family face at last
pressed into a gully above two rivers, does Shenandoah or Potomac
                carry her
north or south, will she wake in the mining camps to stoke the
                stoves
and sleep at night with her rifle blue and loyal under her hand
does she ever forget how they left, how they taught her leaving?

1988

Living Memory

Open the book of tales you knew by heart,
begin driving the old roads again,
repeating the old sentences, which have changed
minutely from the wordings you remembered.
A full moon on the first of May
drags silver film on the Winooski River.
The villages are shut
for the night, the woods are open
and soon you arrive at a crossroads
where late, late in time you recognize
part of yourself is buried.   Call it Danville,
village of water-witches.

From here on instinct is uncompromised and clear:
the tales come crowding like the Kalevala
longing to burst from the tongue.   Under the trees
of the backroad you rumor the dark
with houses, sheds, the long barn
moored like a barge on the hillside.
Chapter and verse.   A mailbox.   A dooryard.
A drink of springwater from the kitchen tap.
An old bed, old wallpaper.   Falling asleep like a child
in the heart of the story.

Reopen the book.   A light mist soaks the page,
blunt naked buds tip the wild lilac scribbled
at the margin of the road, no one knows when.
Broken stones of drywall mark the onset
of familiar paragraphs slanting up and away
each with its own version, nothing ever
has looked the same from anywhere.

We came like others to a country of farmers—
Puritans, Catholics, Scotch Irish, Québecois:
bought a failed Yankee's empty house and barn
from a prospering Yankee,
Jews following Yankee footprints,
prey to many myths but most of all
that Nature makes us free.   That the land can save us.
Pioneer, indigenous; we were neither.

You whose stories these farms secrete,
you whose absence these fields publish,
all you whose lifelong travail
took as given this place and weather
who did what you could with the means you had—
it was pick and shovel work
done with a pair of horses, a stone boat
a strong back, and an iron bar: clearing pasture—
Your memories crouched, foreshortened in our text.
Pages torn.   New words crowding the old.

I knew a woman whose clavicle was smashed
inside a white clapboard house with an apple tree
and a row of tulips by the door.   I had a friend
with six children and a tumor like a seventh
who drove me to my driver's test and in exchange
wanted to see Goddard College, in Plainfield.   She'd heard
women without diplomas could study there.
I knew a woman who walked
straight across cut stubble in her bare feet away,
women who said, *He's a good man, never*
laid a hand to me as living proof.
A man they said fought death
to keep fire for his wife for one more winter, leave
a woodpile to outlast him.

I was left the legacy of a pile of stovewood
split by a man in the mute chains of rage.
The land he loved as landscape
could not unchain him.   There are many,
Gentile and Jew, it has not saved.   Many hearts have burst
over these rocks, in the shacks
on the failure sides of these hills.   Many guns
turned on brains already splitting
in silence.   Where are those versions?
Written-across like nineteenth-century letters
or secrets penned in vinegar, invisible
till the page is held over flame.

I was left the legacy of three sons
—as if in an old legend of three brothers
where one changes into a rufous hawk
one into a snowy owl
one into a whistling swan
and each flies to the mother's side
as she travels, bringing something she has lost,
and she sees their eyes are the eyes of her children
and speaks their names and they become her sons.
But there is no one legend and one legend only.

This month the land still leafless, out from snow
opens in all directions, the transparent woods
with sugar-house, pond, cellar-hole unscreened.
Winter and summer cover the closed roads
but for a few weeks they lie exposed,
the old nervous-system of the land.   It's the time
when history speaks in a row of crazy fence-poles
a blackened chimney, houseless, a spring
soon to be choked in second growth
a stack of rusting buckets, a rotting sledge.

It's the time when your own living
laid open between seasons
ponders clues like the *One Way* sign defaced
to *Bone Way*, the stones
of a graveyard in Vermont, a Jewish cemetery
in Birmingham, Alabama.
How you have needed these places,
as a tall gaunt woman used to need to sit
at the knees of bronze-hooded *Grief*
by Clover Adams' grave.
But you will end somewhere else, a sift of ashes
awkwardly flung by hands you have held and loved
or, nothing so individual, bones reduced
with, among, other bones, anonymous,
or wherever the Jewish dead
have to be sought in the wild grass overwhelming
the cracked stones.   Hebrew spelled in wilderness.

All we can read is life.   Death is invisible.
A yahrzeit candle belongs
to life.   The sugar skulls
eaten on graves for the Day of the Dead
belong to life.   To the living.   The Kaddish is to the living,
the Day of the Dead, for the living.   Only the living
invent these plumes, tombs, mounds, funeral ships,
living hands turn the mirrors to the walls,
tear the boughs of yew to lay on the casket,
rip the clothes of mourning.   Only the living
decide death's color: is it white or black?
The granite bulkhead
incised with names, the quilt of names, were made
by the living, for the living.
                                        I have watched
films from a Pathé camera, a picnic
in sepia, I have seen my mother

tossing an acorn into the air;
my grandfather, alone in the heart of his family;
my father, young, dark, theatrical;
myself, a six-month child.
Watching the dead we see them living
their moments, they were at play, nobody thought
they would be watched so.
                          When Selma threw
her husband's ashes into the Hudson
and they blew back on her and on us, her friends,
it was life.   Our blood raced in that gritty wind.

Such details get bunched, packed, stored
in these cellar-holes of memory
so little is needed
to call on the power, though you can't name its name:
It has its ways of coming back:
a truck going into gear on the crown of the road
the white-throat sparrow's notes
the moon in her fullness standing
right over the concrete steps the way
she stood the night they landed there.
                              From here
nothing has changed, and everything.

The scratched and treasured photograph Richard showed me
taken in '29, the year I was born:
it's the same road I saw
strewn with the Perseids one August night,
looking older, steeper than now
and rougher, yet I knew it.   Time's
power, the only just power—would you
give it away?

1988

An Atlas of the
Difficult World

An Atlas of the Difficult World

I

A dark woman, head bent, listening for something
—a woman's voice, a man's voice or
voice of the freeway, night after night, metal streaming downcoast
past eucalyptus, cypress, agribusiness empires
THE SALAD BOWL OF THE WORLD, gurr of small planes
dusting the strawberries, each berry picked by a hand
in close communion, strawberry blood on the wrist,
Malathion in the throat, communion,
the hospital at the edge of the fields,
prematures slipping from unsafe wombs,
the labor and delivery nurse on her break watching
planes dusting rows of pickers.
Elsewhere declarations are made: at the sink
rinsing strawberries flocked and gleaming, fresh from market
one says: "On the pond this evening is a light
finer than my mother's handkerchief
received from her mother, hemmed and initialled
by the nuns in Belgium."
One says: "I can lie for hours
reading and listening to music. But sleep comes hard.
I'd rather lie awake and read."   One writes:
"Mosquitoes pour through the cracks
in this cabin's walls, the road
in winter is often impassable,
I live here so I don't have to go out and act,
I'm trying to hold onto my life, it feels like nothing."
One says: "I never knew from one day to the next
where it was coming from: I had to make my life happen
from day to day.   Every day an emergency.
Now I have a house, a job from year to year.
What does that make me?"

In the writing workshop a young man's tears
wet the frugal beard he's grown to go with his poems
hoping they have redemption stored
in their lines, maybe will get him home free.   In the classroom
eight-year-old faces are grey.   The teacher knows which children
have not broken fast that day,
remembers the Black Panthers spooning cereal.

.   .   .

I don't want to hear how he beat her after the earthquake,
tore up her writing, threw the kerosene
lantern into her face waiting
like an unbearable mirror of his own.   I don't
want to hear how she finally ran from the trailer
how he tore the keys from her hands, jumped into the truck
and backed it into her.   I don't want to think
how her guesses betrayed her—that he meant well, that she
was really the stronger and ought not to leave him
to his own apparent devastation.   I don't want to know
wreckage, dreck and waste, but these are the materials
and so are the slow lift of the moon's belly
over wreckage, dreck, and waste, wild treefrogs calling in
another season, light and music still pouring over
our fissured, cracked terrain.

.   .   .

Within two miles of the Pacific rounding
this long bay, sheening the light for miles
inland, floating its fog through redwood rifts and over
strawberry and artichoke fields, its bottomless mind
returning always to the same rocks, the same cliffs, with
ever-changing words, always the same language
—this is where I live now.   If you had known me

once, you'd still know me now though in a different
light and life.   This is no place you ever knew me.

But it would not surprise you
to find me here, walking in fog, the sweep of the great ocean
eluding me, even the curve of the bay, because as always
I fix on the land.   I am stuck to earth.   What I love here
is old ranches, leaning seaward, lowroofed spreads between rocks
small canyons running through pitched hillsides
liveoaks twisted on steepness, the eucalyptus avenue leading
to the wrecked homestead, the fogwreathed heavy-chested cattle
on their blond hills.   I drive inland over roads
closed in wet weather, past shacks hunched in the canyons
roads that crawl down into darkness and wind into light
where trucks have crashed and riders of horses tangled
to death with lowstruck boughs.   These are not the roads
you knew me by.   But the woman driving, walking, watching
for life and death, is the same.

II

Here is a map of our country:
here is the Sea of Indifference, glazed with salt
This is the haunted river flowing from brow to groin
we dare not taste its water
This is the desert where missiles are planted like corms
This is the breadbasket of foreclosed farms
This is the birthplace of the rockabilly boy
This is the cemetery of the poor
who died for democracy   This is a battlefield
from a nineteenth-century war   the shrine is famous
This is the sea-town of myth and story   when the fishing fleets
went bankrupt   here is where the jobs were   on the pier
processing frozen fishsticks   hourly wages and no shares
These are other battlefields   Centralia   Detroit

here are the forests primeval   the copper   the silver lodes
These are the suburbs of acquiescence   silence rising fumelike
                  from the streets
This is the capital of money and dolor whose spires
flare up through air inversions whose bridges are crumbling
whose children are drifting blind alleys pent
between coiled rolls of razor wire
I promised to show you a map you say but this is a mural
then yes let it be   these are small distinctions
where do we see it from is the question

III

Two five-pointed star-shaped glass candleholders, bought at the
                  Ben Franklin, Barton, twenty-three years ago, one
                  chipped
—now they hold half-burnt darkred candles, and in between
a spider is working, the third point of her filamental passage
a wicker basket-handle.   All afternoon I've sat
at this table in Vermont, reading, writing, cutting an apple in
                  slivers
and eating them, but mostly gazing down through the windows
at the long scribble of lake due south
where the wind and weather come from.   There are bottles set in
                  the windows
that children dug up in summer woods or bought for nickels and
                  dimes
in dark shops that are no more, gold-brown, foam-green or
                  cobalt glass, blue that gave way to the cobalt
                  bomb.   The woods
are still on the hill behind the difficult unknowable
incommensurable barn.   The wind's been working itself up
in low gusts gnashing the leaves left chattering on branches
or drifting over still-green grass;   but it's been a warm wind.

An autumn without a killing frost so far, still warm
feels like a time of self-deception, a memory of pushing
limits in youth, that intricate losing game of innocence long
                    overdue.
Frost is expected tonight, gardens are gleaned, potplants taken in,
                    there is talk of withering, of wintering-over.

. . .

North of Willoughby the back road to Barton
turns a right-hand corner on a high plateau
bitten by wind now and rimed grey-white
—farms of rust and stripping paint, the shortest growing season
south of Quebec, a place of sheer unpretentious hardship, dark
                    pines stretching away
toward Canada.   There was a one-room schoolhouse
by a brook where we used to picnic, summers, a little world
of clear bubbling water, cowturds, moss, wild mint, wild mush-
                    rooms under the pines.
One hot afternoon I sat there reading Gaskell's *Life of Charlotte
                    Brontë*—the remote
upland village where snow lay long and late, the deep-rutted
                    roads, the dun and grey moorland
—trying to enfigure such a life, how genius
unfurled in the shortlit days, the meagre means of that house. I
                    never thought
of lives at that moment around me, what girl dreamed
and was extinguished in the remote back-country I had come to
                    love,
reader reading under a summer tree in the landscape
of the rural working poor.

Now the panes are black and from the south the wind still stag-
                    gers, creaking the house:

brown milkweeds toss in darkness below but I cannot see them
the room has lost the window and turned into itself: two corner
            shelves of things
both useful and unused, things arrived here by chance or choice,
            two teapots, one broken-spouted, red and blue
came to me with some books from my mother's mother, my
            grandmother Mary
who travelled little, loved the far and strange, bits of India, Asia
and this teapot of hers was Chinese or she thought it was
—the other given by a German Jew, a refugee who killed herself
Midlands flowered ware, and this too cannot be used because
            coated inside—why?—with flaking paint:

"You will always use it for flowers," she instructed when she
            gave it.
In a small frame, under glass, my father's bookplate, engraved in
            his ardent youth, the cleft tree-trunk and the win-
            tering ants:
Without labor, no sweetness—motto I breathed in from him and
            learned in grief and rebellion to take and use
—and later learned that not all labor ends in sweetness.
A little handwrought iron candlestick, given by another German
            woman
who hidden survived the Russian soldiers beating the walls in
            1945,
emigrated, married a poet.   I sat many times at their table.
            They are now long apart.
Some odd glasses for wine or brandy, from an ignorant, passion-
            ate time—we were in our twenties—
with the father of the children who dug for old medicine bottles
            in the woods
—afternoons listening to records, reading Karl Shapiro's *Poems
            of a Jew* and Auden's "In Sickness and in Health"
            aloud, using the poems to talk to each other

—now it's twenty years since last I heard that intake
of living breath, as if language were too much to bear,
that voice overcast like klezmer with echoes, uneven, edged,
            torn, Brooklyn street crowding Harvard Yard
—I'd have known any syllable anywhere.

Stepped out onto the night-porch.   That wind has changed,
            though still from the south
it's blowing up hard now, no longer close to earth but driving
            high
into the crowns of the maples, into my face
almost slamming the stormdoor into me.   But it's warm, warm,
pneumonia wind, death of innocence wind, unwinding wind,
time-hurtling wind.   And it has a voice in the house.   I hear
conversations that can't be happening, overhead in the bedrooms
and I'm not talking of ghosts.   The ghosts are here of course but
            they speak plainly
—haven't I offered food and wine, listened well for them all
            these years,
not only those known in life but those before our time
of self-deception, our intricate losing game of innocence long
            overdue?

. . .

The spider's decision is made, her path cast, candle-wick to
            wicker handle to candle,
in the air, under the lamp, she comes swimming toward me
(have I been sitting here so long?)   she will use everything,
            nothing comes without labor, she is working so
            hard and I know
nothing all winter can enter this house or this web, not all labor
            ends in sweetness.
But how do I know what she needs?   Maybe simply

to spin herself a house within a house, on her own terms
in cold, in silence.

IV

Late summers, early autumns, you can see something that binds
the map of this country together: the girasol, orange gold-
                petalled
with her black eye, laces the roadsides from Vermont to
                California
runs the edges of orchards, chain-link fences
milo fields and malls, schoolyards and reservations
truckstops and quarries, grazing ranges, graveyards
of veterans, graveyards of cars hulked and sunk, her tubers the
                jerusalem artichoke
that has fed the Indians, fed the hobos, could feed us all.
Is there anything in the soil, cross-country, that makes for
a plant so generous?   *Spendtbrift* we say, as if
accounting nature's waste.   Ours darkens
the states to their strict borders, flushes
down borderless streams, leaches from lakes to the curdled foam
down by the riverside.

Waste.   Waste.   The watcher's eye put out, hands of the
                builder severed, brain of the maker starved
those who could bind, join, reweave, cohere, replenish
now at risk in this segregate republic
locked away out of sight and hearing, out of mind, shunted aside
those needed to teach, advise, persuade, weigh arguments
those urgently needed for the work of perception
work of the poet, the astronomer, the historian, the architect of
                new streets
work of the speaker who also listens
meticulous delicate work of reaching the heart of the desperate
                woman, the desperate man

—never-to-be-finished, still unbegun work of repair—it cannot
        be done without them
and where are they now?

V

Catch if you can your country's moment, begin
where any calendar's ripped-off: Appomattox
Wounded Knee, Los Alamos, Selma, the last airlift from Saigon
the ex-Army nurse hitch-hiking from the debriefing center; medal
        of spit on the veteran's shoulder
—catch if you can this unbound land these states without a cause
earth of despoiled graves and grazing these embittered brooks
these pilgrim ants pouring out from the bronze eyes, ears,
        nostrils,
the mouth of Liberty
        over the chained bay waters
                San Quentin:
once we lost our way and drove in under the searchlights to the
        gates
end of visiting hours, women piling into cars
the bleak glare aching over all
            Where are we moored?   What
            are the bindings?   What be-
            hooves us?

Driving the San Francisco-Oakland Bay Bridge
no monument's in sight but fog
prowling Angel Island muffling Alcatraz
poems in Cantonese inscribed on fog
no icon lifts a lamp here
history's breath blotting the air
over Gold Mountain   a transfer
of patterns like the transfer of African appliqué
to rural Alabama   voices alive in legends, curses

tongue-lashings
                    poems on a weary wall

And when light swivels off Angel Island and Alcatraz
when the bays leap into life
                              views of the Palace of Fine Arts,
                              TransAmerica
when sunset bathes the three bridges
                                        still
old ghosts crouch hoarsely whispering
under Gold Mountain

. . .

North and east of the romantic headlands there are roads into tule
                    fog
places where life is cheap poor quick unmonumented
Rukeyser would have guessed it coming West for the opening
of the great red bridge   *There are roads to take* she wrote
when you think of your country   driving south
to West Virginia Gauley Bridge silicon mines the flakes of it
                    heaped like snow, death-angel white
—poet journalist pioneer mother
uncovering her country: *there are roads to take*

. . .

I don't want to know how he tracked them
along the Appalachian Trail, hid close
by their tent, pitched as they thought in seclusion
killing one woman, the other
dragging herself into town   his defense they had teased his
                    loathing
of what they were   I don't want to know

but this is not a bad dream of mine   these are the materials
and so are the smell of wild mint and coursing water remembered
and the sweet salt darkred tissue I lay my face
upon, my tongue within.

A crosshair against the pupil of an eye
could blow my life from hers
a cell dividing without maps, sliver of ice beneath a wheel
could do the job.   Faithfulness isn't the problem.

VI

A potato explodes in the oven.   Poetry and famine:
the poets who never starved, whose names we know
the famished nameless taking ship with their hoard of poetry
Annie Sullivan half-blind in the workhouse enthralling her child-
        mates
with lore her father had borne in his head from Limerick along
        with the dream of work
and *hatred of England smouldering like a turf-fire.* But a poetry older
        than hatred. Poetry
in the workhouse, laying of the rails, a potato splattering oven
        walls
poetry of cursing and silence, bitter and deep, shallow and
        drunken
poetry of priest-talk, of I.R.A.-talk, kitchen-talk, dream-talk,
        tongues despised
in cities where in a mere fifty years language has rotted to jargon,
        lingua franca of inclusion
from turns of speech ancient as the potato, muttered at the coals
        by women and men
rack-rented, harshened, numbed by labor ending
in root-harvest rotted in field. 1847. No relief. No succour.
America. Meat three times a day, they said.   Slaves—You would
        not be that.

VII (The Dream-Site)

Some rooftop, water-tank looming, street-racket strangely quelled
and others known and unknown there, long sweet summer eve-
                    ning on the tarred roof:
leaned back your head to the nightvault swarming with stars
the Pleiades broken loose, not seven but thousands
every known constellation flinging out fiery threads
and you could distinguish all
—cobwebs, tendrils, anatomies of stars
coherently hammocked, blueblack avenues between
—you knew your way among them, knew you were part of them
until, neck aching, you sat straight up and saw:

It was New York, the dream-site
the lost city the city of dreadful light
where once as the sacks of garbage rose
like barricades around us we
stood listening to riffs from Pharaoh Sanders' window
on the brownstone steps
went striding the avenues in our fiery hair
in our bodies young and ordinary riding the subways reading
or pressed against other bodies
feeling in them the maps of Brooklyn Queens Manhattan
The Bronx unscrolling in the long breakneck
express plunges
                    as darkly we felt our own blood
streaming   a living city overhead
coherently webbed and knotted   bristling
we and all the others
                    known and unknown
living its life

VIII

He thought there would be a limit and that it would stop him.
            He depended on that:
the cuts would be made by someone else, the direction
come from somewhere else, arrows flashing on the freeway.
That he'd end somewhere gazing
straight into It was what he imagined and nothing beyond.
That he'd end facing as limit a thing without limits and so he
            flung
and burned and hacked and bled himself toward that (if I
            understand
this story at all). What he found: FOR SALE: DO NOT
            DISTURB
OCCUPANT on some cliffs;   some ill-marked, ill-kept roads
ending in warnings about shellfish in Vietnamese, Spanish and
            English.
But the spray was any color he could have dreamed
—gold, ash, azure, smoke, moonstone—
and from time to time the ocean swirled up through the eye of a
            rock and taught him
limits.   Throwing itself backward, singing and sucking, no
            teacher, only its violent
self, the Pacific, dialectical waters rearing
their wild calm constructs, momentary, ancient.

. . .

If your voice could overwhelm those waters, what would it say?
What would it cry of the child swept under, the mother
on the beach then, in her black bathing suit, walking straight
            out
into the glazed lace as if she never noticed, what would it say of
            the father
facing inland in his shoes and socks at the edge of the tide,
what of the lost necklace glittering twisted in foam?

. . .

If your voice could crack in the wind hold its breath still as the
        rocks
what would it say to the daughter searching the tidelines for a
        bottled message
from the sunken slaveships?   what of the huge sun slowly de-
        faulting into the clouds
what of the picnic stored in the dunes at high tide, full of the
        moon, the basket
with sandwiches, eggs, paper napkins, can-opener, the meal
packed for a family feast, excavated now by scuttling
ants, sandcrabs, dune-rats, because no one understood
all picnics are eaten on the grave?

IX

On this earth, in this life, as I read your story, you're lonely.
Lonely in the bar, on the shore of the coastal river
with your best friend, his wife, and your wife, fishing
lonely in the prairie classroom with all the students who love
        you. You know some ghosts
come everywhere with you yet leave them unaddressed
for years.   You spend weeks in a house
with a drunk, you sober, whom you love, feeling lonely.
You grieve in loneliness, and if I understand you fuck in
        loneliness.

I wonder if this is a white man's madness.
I honor your truth and refuse to leave it at that.

What have I learned from stories of the hunt, of lonely men in
        gangs?
But there were other stories:
one man riding the Mohave Desert

another man walking the Grand Canyon.
I thought those solitary men were happy, as ever they had been.

Indio's long avenues
of Medjool date-palm and lemon sweep to the Salton Sea
in Yucca Flats the high desert reaches higher, bleached and spare
        of talk.
At Twentynine Palms I found the grave
of Maria Eleanor Whallon, eighteen years, dead at the watering-
        hole in 1903, under the now fire-branded palms
Her mother travelled on alone to cook in the mining camps.

X

Soledad. = f. Solitude, loneliness, homesickness; lonely retreat.
Winter sun in the rosetrees.
An old Mexican with a white moustache prunes them back
        spraying
the cut branches with dormant oil.   The old paper-bag-brown
        adobe walls
stretch apart from the rebuilt mission, in their own time.   It is
        lonely here
in the curve of the road winding through vast brown fields
        machine-engraved in furrows
of relentless precision.   In the small chapel
La Nuestra Señora de la Soledad dwells in her shallow arch
painted on either side with columns.   She is in black lace crisp as
        cinders
from head to foot.   Alone, solitary, homesick
in her lonely retreat.   Outside black olives fall and smash
littering and staining the beaten path.   The gravestones of the
        padres
are weights pressing down on the Indian artisans.   It is the sixth
        day of another war.

. . .

Across the freeway stands another structure
from the other side of the mirror   *it destroys*
the logical processes of the mind, a man's thoughts
become completely disorganized, madness streaming from every throat
frustrated sounds from the bars, metallic sounds from the walls
the steel trays, iron beds bolted to the wall, the smells, the human waste.
To determine how men will behave once they enter prison
it is of first importance to know that prison.   (From the freeway
gun-turrets planted like water-towers in another garden,
                    outbuildings spaced in winter sun
and the concrete mass beyond: who now writes letters deep
                    inside that cave?)

If my instructor tells me that the world and its affairs
are run as well as they possibly can be, that I am governed
by wise and judicious men, that I am free and should be happy,
and if when I leave the instructor's presence and encounter
the exact opposite, if I actually sense or see confusion, war,
recession, depression, death and decay, is it not reasonable
that I should become perplexed?

                              From eighteen to twenty-eight
                                    of his years
a young man schools himself, argues,
debates, trains, lectures to himself,
teaches himself Swahili, Spanish, learns
five new words of English every day,
chainsmokes, reads, writes letters.
In this college of force he wrestles bitterness,
self-hatred, sexual anger, cures his own nature.
Seven of these years in solitary.   Soledad.

But the significant feature of the desperate man reveals itself
when he meets other desperate men, directly or vicariously;
and he experiences his first kindness, someone to strain with him,
to strain to see him as he strains to see himself,

someone to understand, someone to accept the regard,
the love, that desperation forces into hiding.
Those feelings that find no expression in desperate times
store themselves up in great abundance, ripen, strengthen,
and strain the walls of their repository to the utmost;
where the kindred spirit touches this wall it crumbles—
no one responds to kindness, no one is more sensitive to it
than the desperate man.

XI

One night on Monterey Bay the death-freeze of the century:
a precise, detached calliper-grip holds the stars and the quarter-
                    moon
in arrest: the hardiest plants crouch shrunken, a "killing frost"
on bougainvillea, Pride of Madeira, roseate black-purple succu-
                    lents bowed
juices sucked awry in one orgy of freezing
slumped on their stems like old faces evicted from cheap hotels
—*into the streets of the universe, now!*

Earthquake and drought followed by freezing followed by war
Flags are blossoming now where little else is blossoming
and I am bent on fathoming what it means to love my country.
The history of this earth and the bones within it?
Soils and cities, promises made and mocked, plowed contours of
                    shame and of hope?
Loyalties, symbols, murmurs extinguished and echoing?
Grids of states stretching westward, underground waters?
Minerals, traces, rumors I am made from, morsel, minuscule
                    fibre, one woman
like and unlike so many, fooled as to her destiny, the scope of
                    her task?
One citizen like and unlike so many, touched and untouched in
                    passing

—each of us now a driven grain, a nucleus, a city in crisis
some busy constructing enclosures, bunkers, to escape the com-
        mon fate
some trying to revive dead statues to lead us, breathing their
        breath against marble lips
some who try to teach the moment, some who preach the
        moment
some who aggrandize, some who diminish themselves in the face
        of half-grasped events
—power and powerlessness run amuck, a tape reeling backward
        in jeering, screeching syllables—
some for whom war is new, others for whom it merely continues
        the old paroxysms of time
some marching for peace who for twenty years did not march for
        justice
some for whom peace is a white man's word and a white man's
        privilege
some who have learned to handle and contemplate the shapes of
        powerlessness and power
as the nurse learns hip and thigh and weight of the body he has
        to lift and sponge, day upon day
as she blows with her every skill on the spirit's embers still burn-
        ing by their own laws in the bed of death.
A patriot is not a weapon.   A patriot is one who wrestles for the
        soul of her country
as she wrestles for her own being, for the soul of his country
(gazing through the great circle at Window Rock into the sheen
        of the Viet Nam Wall)
as he wrestles for his own being.   A patriot is a citizen trying to
        wake
from the burnt-out dream of innocence, the nightmare
of the white general and the Black general posed in their
        camouflage,
to remember her true country, remember his suffering land:
        remember

that blessing and cursing are born as twins and separated at birth
           to meet again in mourning
that the internal emigrant is the most homesick of all women and
           of all men
that every flag that flies today is a cry of pain.
                    Where are we moored?
                    What are the bindings?
                    What behooves us?

XII

What homage will be paid to a beauty built to last
from inside out, executing the blueprints of resistance and mercy
drawn up in childhood, in that little girl, round-faced with
                    clenched fists, already acquainted with mourning
in the creased snapshot you gave me?   What homage will be
                    paid to beauty
that insists on speaking truth, knows the two are not always the
                    same,
beauty that won't deny, is itself an eye, will not rest under
                    contemplation?
Those low long clouds we were driving under a month ago in
                    New Mexico, clouds an arm's reach away
were beautiful and we spoke of it but I didn't speak then
of your beauty at the wheel beside me, dark head steady, eyes
                    drinking the spaces
of crimson, indigo, Indian distance, Indian presence,
your spirit's gaze informing your body, impatient to mark what's
                    possible, impatient to mark
what's lost, deliberately destroyed, can never any way be
                    returned,
your back arched against all icons, simulations, dead letters
your woman's hands turning the wheel or working with shears,
                    torque wrench, knives, with salt pork, onions, ink
                    and fire

your providing sensate hands, your hands of oak and silk, of
                    blackberry juice and drums
—I speak of them now.

(FOR M.)

XIII (Dedications)

I know you are reading this poem
late, before leaving your office
of the one intense yellow lamp-spot and the darkening window
in the lassitude of a building faded to quiet
long after rush-hour.   I know you are reading this poem
standing up in a bookstore far from the ocean
on a grey day of early spring, faint flakes driven
across the plains' enormous spaces around you.
I know you are reading this poem
in a room where too much has happened for you to bear
where the bedclothes lie in stagnant coils on the bed
and the open valise speaks of flight
but you cannot leave yet.   I know you are reading this poem
as the underground train loses momentum and before running
                    up the stairs
toward a new kind of love
your life has never allowed.
I know you are reading this poem by the light
of the television screen where soundless images jerk and slide
while you wait for the newscast from the *intifada*.
I know you are reading this poem in a waiting-room
of eyes met and unmeeting, of identity with strangers.
I know you are reading this poem by fluorescent light
in the boredom and fatigue of the young who are counted out,
count themselves out, at too early an age.   I know
you are reading this poem through your failing sight, the thick

lens enlarging these letters beyond all meaning yet you read on
because even the alphabet is precious.

I know you are reading this poem as you pace beside the stove
warming milk, a crying child on your shoulder, a book in your
                    hand
because life is short and you too are thirsty.
I know you are reading this poem which is not in your language
guessing at some words while others keep you reading
and I want to know which words they are.
I know you are reading this poem listening for something, torn
                    between bitterness and hope
turning back once again to the task you cannot refuse.
I know you are reading this poem because there is nothing else
                    left to read
there where you have landed, stripped as you are.

1990–1991

That Mouth

This is the girl's mouth, the taste
daughters, not sons, obtain:
These are the lips, powerful rudders
pushing through groves of kelp,
the girl's terrible, unsweetened taste
of the whole ocean, its fathoms: this is that taste.

This is not the father's kiss, the mother's:
a father can try to choke you,
a mother drown you to save you:
all the transactions have long been enacted.
This is neither a sister's tale nor a brother's:
strange trade-offs have long been made.

This is the swallow, the splash
of krill and plankton, that mouth
described as a girl's—
enough to give you a taste:
Are you a daughter, are you a son?
Strange trade-offs have long been made.

1988

Marghanita

at the oak table under the ceiling fan
Marghanita at the table counting up
a dead woman's debts.
Kicks off a sandal, sips
soda from a can, wedges the last bills
under the candelabrum.   She is here
because no one else was there when worn-to-skeleton
her enemy died.   Her love.   Her twin.
Marghanita dreamed the intravenous, the intensive
the stainless steel
before she ever saw them.   She's not practical,
you know, they used to say.
She's the artist, she got away.

In her own place Marghanita glues bronze
feathers into wings, smashes green and clear
bottles into bloodletting particles
crushed into templates of sand
scores mirrors till they fall apart and sticks them up
in driftwood boughs, drinks golden
liquid with a worm's name, forgets
her main enemy, her twin;
scores her wrist on a birthday
dreams the hospital dream.

When they were girl and boy together, boy and girl
she pinned his arm against his back
for a box containing false
lashes and fingernails, a set of veils, a string of pearls,
she let go and listened to his tales
she breathed their breath, he hers,
they each had names only the other knew.

Marghanita in the apartment everyone has left:
not a nephew, not a niece,
nobody from the parish
—gone into hiding, emigrated, lost?
where are the others?
Marghanita comes back because she does,
adding up what's left:
a rainsoaked checkbook, snapshots
razed from an album,
colors ground into powder, brushes, wands
for eyelids, lashes, brows,
beads of bath-oil, tubes of glycerin
—a dead woman's luxuries.

Marghanita will
take care of it all.   Pay if nothing else
the last month's rent.   The wings of the fan
stir corners of loose paper,
light ebbs from the window-lace,
she needs to go out and eat.   And so
hating and loving come down
to a few columns of figures,
an aching stomach, a care taken: something done.

1989

Tattered Kaddish

Taurean reaper of the wild apple field
messenger from earthmire gleaning
transcripts of fog
in the nineteenth year and the eleventh month
speak your tattered Kaddish for all suicides:

Praise to life though it crumbled in like a tunnel
on ones we knew and loved

    Praise to life though its windows blew shut
    on the breathing-room of ones we knew and loved

Praise to life though ones we knew and loved
loved it badly, too well, and not enough

    Praise to life though it tightened like a knot
    on the hearts of ones we thought we knew loved us

Praise to life giving room and reason
to ones we knew and loved who felt unpraisable

    Praise to them, how they loved it, when they could.

1989

Through Corralitos Under Rolls of Cloud

I

Through Corralitos under rolls of cloud
between winter-stiff, ranged apple-trees
each netted in transparent air,
thin sinking light, heartsick within and filmed
in heartsickness around you, gelatin cocoon
invisible yet impervious—to the hawk
steering against the cloudbank, to the clear
oranges burning at the rancher's gate
rosetree, agave, stiff beauties holding fast
with or without your passion,
the pruners freeing up the boughs
in the unsearched faith these strange stiff shapes will bear.

II

Showering after 'flu;   stripping the bed;
running the shrouds of sickness through the wash;
airing the rooms;   emptying the trash;
it's as if part of you had died in the house
sometime in that last low-lit afternoon
when your dreams ebbed salt-thick into the sheets
and now this other's left to wash the corpse,
burn eucalyptus, turn the mirrors over—
this other who herself barely came back,
whose breath was fog to your mist, whose stubborn shadow
covered you as you lay freezing, she survived
uncertain who she is or will be without you.

III

If you know who died in that bed, do you know
who has survived?   If you say, *she was weaker,*
held life less dear, expected others
to fight for her   if pride lets you name her
victim   and the one who got up and threw
the windows open, stripped the bed, *survivor*
—what have you said, what do you know
of the survivor when you know her
only in opposition to the lost?
What does it mean to say *I have survived*
until you take the mirrors and turn them outward
and read your own face in their outraged light?

IV

That light of outrage is the light of history
springing upon us when we're least prepared,
thinking maybe a little glade of time
leaf-thick and with clear water
is ours, is promised us, for all we've hacked
and tracked our way through: to this:
What will it be?   Your wish or mine?   your
prayers or my wish then: that those we love
be well, whatever that means, to be well.
Outrage: who dare claim protection for their own
amid such unprotection?   What kind of prayer
is that?   To what kind of god?   What kind of wish?

V

She who died on that bed sees it her way:
She who went under peers through the translucent shell
cupping her death and sees her other well,

through a long lens, in silvered outline, well
she sees her other and she cannot tell
why when the boom of surf struck at them both
she felt the undertow and heard the bell,
thought death would be their twinning, till the swell
smashed her against the reef, her other still
fighting the pull, struggling somewhere away
further and further, calling her all the while:
she who went under summons her other still.

1989–1990

Darklight

I

Early day.   Grey the air.
Grey the boards of the house, the bench,
red the dilated potflower's petals
blue the sky that will rend through
this fog.
                    Dark summer's outer reaches:
thrown husk of a moon
sharpening
in the last dark blue.
I think of your eye
                              (dark the light
that washes into a deeper dark).

An eye, coming in closer.
                              Under the lens
lashes and veins grow huge
and huge the tear that washes out the eye,
the tear that clears the eye.

II

When heat leaves the walls at last
and the breeze comes
or seems to come, off water
or off the half-finished moon
her silver roughened by a darkblue rag
this is the ancient hour
between light and dark, work and rest
earthly tracks and star-trails

the last willed act of the day
and the night's first dream

If you could have this hour
for the last hour of your life.

1988–1990

For a Friend in Travail

Waking from violence: the surgeon's probe left in the foot
paralyzing the body from the waist down.
Dark before dawn: wrapped in a shawl, to walk the house
the Drinking-Gourd slung in the northwest,
half-slice of moon to the south
through dark panes.   A time to speak to you.

What are you going through? she said, is the great question.
Philosopher of oppression, theorist
of the victories of force.

We write from the marrow of our bones.   What she did not
ask, or tell: how victims save their own lives.

That crawl along the ledge, then the ravelling span of fibre strung
from one side to the other, I've dreamed that too.
Waking, not sure we made it.   Relief, appallment, of waking.
Consciousness.   O, no.   To sleep again.
O to sleep without dreaming.

How day breaks, when it breaks, how clear and light the moon
melting into moon-colored air
moist and sweet, here on the western edge.
Love for the world, and we are part of it.
How the poppies break from their sealed envelopes
she did not tell.

What are you going through, there on the other edge?

1990

Final Notations

it will not be simple, it will not be long
it will take little time, it will take all your thought
it will take all your heart, it will take all your breath
it will be short, it will not be simple

it will touch through your ribs, it will take all your heart
it will not be long, it will occupy your thought
as a city is occupied, as a bed is occupied
it will take all your flesh, it will not be simple

You are coming into us who cannot withstand you
you are coming into us who never wanted to withstand you
you are taking parts of us into places never planned
you are going far away with pieces of our lives

it will be short, it will take all your breath
it will not be simple, it will become your will

1991

Dark Fields of the Republic

What Kind of Times Are These

What Kind of Times Are These

There's a place between two stands of trees where the grass grows
        uphill
and the old revolutionary road breaks off into shadows
near a meeting-house abandoned by the persecuted
who disappeared into those shadows.

I've walked there picking mushrooms at the edge of dread, but
        don't be fooled,
this isn't a Russian poem, this is not somewhere else but here,
our country moving closer to its own truth and dread,
its own ways of making people disappear.

I won't tell you where the place is, the dark mesh of the woods
meeting the unmarked strip of light—
ghost-ridden crossroads, leafmold paradise:
I know already who wants to buy it, sell it, make it disappear.

And I won't tell you where it is, so why do I tell you
anything? Because you still listen, because in times like these
to have you listen at all, it's necessary
to talk about trees.

1991

In Those Years

In those years, people will say, we lost track
of the meaning of *we*, of *you*
we found ourselves
reduced to *I*
and the whole thing became
silly, ironic, terrible:
we were trying to live a personal life
and, yes, that was the only life
we could bear witness to

But the great dark birds of history screamed and plunged
into our personal weather
They were headed somewhere else but their beaks and pinions drove
along the shore, through the rags of fog
where we stood, saying *I*

1991

To the Days

From you I want more than I've ever asked,
all of it—the newscasts' terrible stories
of life in my time, the knowing it's worse than that,
much worse—the knowing what it means to be lied to.

Fog in the mornings, hunger for clarity,
coffee and bread with sour plum jam.
Numbness of soul in placid neighborhoods.
Lives ticking on as if.

A typewriter's torrent, suddenly still.
Blue soaking through fog, two dragonflies wheeling.
Acceptable levels of cruelty, steadily rising.
Whatever you bring in your hands, I need to see it.

Suddenly I understand the verb without tenses.
To smell another woman's hair, to taste her skin.
To know the bodies drifting underwater.
To be human, said Rosa—I can't teach you that.

A cat drinks from a bowl of marigolds—his moment.
Surely the love of life is never-ending,
the failure of nerve, a charred fuse?
I want more from you than I ever knew to ask.

Wild pink lilies erupting, tasseled stalks of corn
in the Mexican gardens, corn and roses.
Shortening days, strawberry fields in ferment
with tossed-aside, bruised fruit.

1991

Miracle Ice Cream

MIRACLE's truck comes down the little avenue,
Scott Joplin ragtime strewn behind it like pearls,
and, yes, you can feel happy
with one piece of your heart.

Take what's still given: in a room's rich shadow
a woman's breasts swinging lightly as she bends.
Early now the pearl of dusk dissolves.
Late, you sit weighing the evening news,
fast-food miracles, ghostly revolutions,
the rest of your heart.

1992

Rachel

There's a girl born in abrupt August light
far north, a light soon to be peeled
like an onion, down to nothing. Around her ions are falling
in torrents, glacial eyes are staring, the monster's body
trapped in the bay goes through its spasms.
What she opens her gray eyes on
is drastic. Even the man and woman gazing
into her unfocused gaze, searching for focus,
are drastic.
                    It's the end of a century.
If she gets to grow old, if there's anything
: anyone to speak, will they say of her,
She grew up to see it, she was our mother, but
she was born one of them?

1992

Amends

Nights like this: on the cold apple-bough
a white star, then another
exploding out of the bark:
on the ground, moonlight picking at small stones

as it picks at greater stones, as it rises with the surf
laying its cheek for moments on the sand
as it licks the broken ledge, as it flows up the cliffs,
as it flicks across the tracks

as it unavailing pours into the gash
of the sand-and-gravel quarry
as it leans across the hangared fuselage
of the crop-dusting plane

as it soaks through cracks into the trailers
tremulous with sleep
as it dwells upon the eyelids of the sleepers
as if to make amends

1992

Calle Visión

1

Not what you thought: just a turn-off
leading downhill not up

narrow, doesn't waste itself
has a house at the far end

scrub oak and cactus in the yard
some cats   some snakes

in the house there is a room
in the room there is a bed

on the bed there is a blanket
that tells the coming of the railroad

under the blanket there are sheets
scrubbed transparent here and there

under the sheets there's a mattress
the old rough kind, with buttons and ticking

under the mattress is a frame
of rusting iron   still strong

the whole bed smells of soap and rust
the window smells of old tobacco-dust and rain

this is your room
in Calle Visión

if you took the turn-off
it was for you

2

Calle Visión   sand in your teeth
granules of cartilage in your wrists

Calle Visión   firestorm behind
shuttered eyelids   fire in your foot

Calle Visión   rocking the gates
of your locked bones

Calle Visión   dreamnet dropped
over your porous sleep

3

Lodged in the difficult hotel
all help withheld

a place not to live but to die in
not an inn but a hospital

a friend's love came to me
touched and took me away

in a car   love
of a curmudgeon, a short-fuse

and as he drove   eyes on the road
I felt his love

and that was simply the case   the way things were
unstated and apparent

and like the rest of it
clear as a dream

4

Calle Visión   your heart beats on unbroken
   how is this possible

Calle Visión   wounded knee
   wounded spine   wounded eye

      Have you ever worked around metal?
      Are there particles under your skin?

Calle Visión   but your heart is still whole
   how is this possible

since what can be   will be taken
   when not offered in trust and faith

by the collectors of collectibles
   the professors of what–has–been–suffered

      The world is falling down   hold my hand
      It's a lonely sound   hold my hand

Calle Visión   never forget
   the body's pain

never divide it

5

Ammonia
          carbon dioxide
                    carbon monoxide
                              methane
                    hydrogen sulfide
:   the gasses that rise from urine and feces

in the pig confinement units known as nurseries
can eat a metal doorknob off in half a year

pig-dander
          dust from dry manure
—lung-scar: breath-shortedness an early symptom

And the fire shall try
every man's work   :Calle Visión:
and every woman's

if you took the turn-off
this is your revelation   this the source

6

The repetitive motions of slaughtering
   —fire in wrists   in elbows—
the dead birds coming at you along the line
   —how you smell them in your sleep—
fire in your wrist   blood packed
   under your fingernails   heavy air
doors padlocked on the outside
   —you might steal a chicken—
fire in the chicken factory fire
   in the carpal tunnel   leaping the frying vats

yellow smoke from soybean oil
   and wasted parts and insulating wire
—some fleeing to the freezer some
   found "stuck in poses of escape"—

7

You can call on beauty still and it will leap
from all directions

you can write beauty into the cruel file
of things done   things left undone   but

once we were dissimilar
yet unseparate   that's beauty   that's what you catch

in the newborn's midnight gaze
the fog that melts the falling stars

the virus from the smashed lianas driven
searching now for us

8

In the room   in the house
in Calle Visión

all you want   is to lie down
alone on your back   let your hands

slide lightly over your hipbones
But she's there with her remnants her cross-sections

trying to distract you
with her childhood her recipes her

cargo of charred pages her
carved and freckled neck-stones

her crying-out-for-witness her
backward-forward timescapes

her suitcase in Berlin
and the one lost and found

in her island go-and-come
—is she terrified you will forget her?

9

In the black net
of her orange wing

the angry nightblown butterfly
hangs on a piece of lilac in the sun

carried overland like her
from a long way off

She has travelled hard and far
and her interrogation goes:

—*Hands dripping with wet earth*
head full of shocking dreams

O what have you buried all these years
what have you dug up?

. . .

This place is alive with the dead and with the living
I have never been alone here

I wear my triple eye as I walk along the road
past, present, future all are at my side

Storm-beaten, tough-winged passenger
there is nothing I have buried that can die

10

On the road there is a house
scrub oak and cactus in the yard

lilac carried overland
from a long way off

in the house there is a bed
on the bed there is a blanket

telling the coming of the railroad
under the mattress there's a frame

of rusting iron   still strong
the window smells of old tobacco-dust and rain

the window smells of old
tobacco-dust and rain

1992–1993

Reversion

This woman/   the heart of the matter.
This woman flung into solitary by the prayers of her tribe.
This woman waking/   reaching for scissors/   starting to cut
     her hair
Hair long shaven/   growing out.
To snip to snip to snip/   creak of sharpness meeting itself against
     the roughness of her hair.

This woman whose voices drive her into exile.
(Exile, exile.)
Drive her toward the other side.
By train and foot and ship, to the other side.
Other side.   Of a narrow sea.

This woman/   the heart of the matter.
Heart of the law/   heart of the prophets.
Their voices buzzing like raspsaws in her brain.
Taking ship without a passport.
How does she do it.   Even the ships have eyes.
Are painted like birds.
This woman has no address book.
This woman perhaps has a toothbrush.
Somewhere dealing for red/blue dyes to crest her
     rough-clipped hair.

On the other side: stranger to women and to children.
Setting her bare footsole in the print of the stranger's bare foot in
     the sand.
Feeding the stranger's dog from the sack of her exhaustion.
Hearing the male prayers of the stranger's tribe/   rustle of the
     stranger's river.
Lying down asleep and dreamless in one of their doorways.

She has long shed the coverings.
On the other side she walks bare-armed, bare-legged, clothed
     in voices.
Here or there picks up a scarf/   a remnant.
Day breaks cold on her legs and in her sexual hair.
Her punk hair/   her religious hair.

Passing the blue rectangles of the stranger's doors.
Not one opens to her.
Threading herself into declining alleys/   black on white plaster/
     olive on violet.
To walk to walk to walk.
To lie on a warm stone listening to familiar insects.
(Exile, exile.)

This woman/   the heart of the matter.
Circling back to the city where her name crackles behind
     creviced stones.
This woman who left alone and returns alone.
Whose hair again is covered/   whose arms and neck are covered/
     according to the law.
Underneath her skin has darkened/   her footsoles roughened.
Sand from the stranger's doorway sifting from her plastic
          carry-all/   drifting into the sand
               whirling around in her old quarter.

1993

Then or Now

Is it necessary for me to write obliquely
about the situation? Is that what
you would have me do?

Food Packages: 1947

Powdered milk, chocolate bars, canned fruit, tea,
salamis, aspirin:
Four packages a month to her old professor in Heidelberg
and his Jewish wife:
Europe is trying to revive an intellectual life
and the widow of the great sociologist needs flour.

Europe is trying/to revive/
with the Jews somewhere else.

The young ex-philosopher tries to feed her teachers
all the way from New York, with orders for butter from
    Denmark,
sending dispatches into the fog
of the European spirit:
I am no longer German. I am a Jew and the German language
was once my home.

1993

Innocence: 1945

"The beauty of it was the guilt.
It entered us, quick *schnapps*,
forked tongue of ice.   The guilt
made us feel innocent again.
We had done nothing while some
extreme measures were taken.   We drifted.   In the
Snow Queen's huge ballroom had dreamed
of the whole world and a new pair of skates.
But we had suffered too.
The miracle was: felt
nothing.   Felt we had done
nothing.   Nothing to do.   Felt free.
And we had suffered, too.
It was that freedom we craved,
cold needle in the bloodstream.
Guilt after all was a feeling."

1993

Sunset, December, 1993

Dangerous of course to draw
parallels   Yet more dangerous to write

as if there were a steady course, we and our poems
protected: the individual life, protected

poems, ideas, gliding
in mid-air, innocent

I walked out on the deck and every board
was luminous with cold dew   It could freeze tonight

Each board is different of course but each does gleam
wet, under a complicated sky: mounds of swollen ink

heavy gray unloading up the coast
a rainbow suddenly and casually

unfolding its span
Dangerous not to think

how the earth still was   in places
while the chimneys shuddered with the first dischargements

1993

264

Deportations

It's happened already while we were still
searching for patterns   A turn of the head
toward a long horizontal window overlooking the city
to see people being taken
neighbors, vendors, paramedicals
hurried from their porches, their tomato stalls
their auto-mechanic arguments
and children from schoolyards
There are far more of the takers-away than the taken
at this point anyway

Then: dream-cut: our house:
four men walk through the unlatched door
One in light summer wool and silken tie
One in work clothes browned with blood
One with open shirt, a thin
thong necklace hasped with silver around his neck
One in shorts naked up from the navel

And they have come for us, two of us and four of them
and I think, perhaps they are still human
and I ask them   *When do you think this all began?*

as if trying to distract them from their purpose
as if trying to appeal to a common bond
as if one of them might be you
as if I were practicing for something
yet to come

1994

And Now

And now as you read these poems
—you whose eyes and hands I love
—you whose mouth and eyes I love
—you whose words and minds I love—
don't think I was trying to state a case
or construct a scenery:
I tried to listen to
the public voice of our time
tried to survey our public space
as best I could
—tried to remember and stay
faithful to details, note
precisely how the air moved
and where the clock's hands stood
and who was in charge of definitions
and who stood by receiving them
when the name of compassion
was changed to the name of guilt
when to feel with a human stranger
was declared obsolete.

1994

Six Narratives

1

You drew up the story of your life   I was in that story
Nights on the coast I'd meet you flashlight in hand
curving my soles over musseled rocks   cracked and raw we'd lick
           inside the shells for danger
You'd drop into the bar   I'd sit upstairs at my desk writing
           the pages
you hoped would make us famous   then in the face of my
           turned back
you went to teach at the freedom school as if
you were teaching someone else to get free from me   this was
           your story
Like a fogsmeared planet over the coast
I'd walked into, served, your purposeful longings   I knew, I did
           not stop   till I turned my back

2

You drew up a story about me   I fled that story
Aching in mind I noticed names on the helms of busses:
          COP CITY   SHEEPSHEAD BAY
I thought I saw the city where the cops came home
to lay kitchen linoleum   barbecue on balconies
I saw the bloodied head of the great sheep dragged through
          the underpasses
trucked to the bay where the waters would not touch it
left on the beach in its shroud of flies
On the bus to La Guardia my arms ached with all my findings
anchored under my breasts with all my will
I cried *sick day, O sick day, this is my day and I, for this I will*
          not pay
as the green rushed bleeding out through the snarled cracks of
          the expressway

3

You were telling a story about women to young men   It was
            not my story
it was not a story about women it was a story about men
Your hunger a spear gripped in hand a tale unspun in your
            rented campground
clothed in captured whale-songs tracked with synthesized
            Andes flutes
it was all about you   beaded and bearded   misfeathered and
            miscloaked
where the TV cameras found you in your sadness

4

You were telling a story about love   it was your story
I came and stood outside
listening :   : death was in the doorway
death was in the air but the story
had its own life   no pretenses
about women in that lovesong for a man
Listening I went inside the bow scraping the bass-string
inside the horn's heartbroken cry
I was the breath's intake the bow's rough mutter:
Vigil for boy of responding kisses, (never again on earth responding,)
Vigil for comrade swiftly slain . . .

5

I was telling you a story about love
how even in war it goes on speaking its own language

Yes you said but the larynx is bloodied
the knife was well-aimed into the throat

Well I said love is hated   it has no price

No you said   you are talking about feelings
Have you ever felt nothing?   that is what war is now

Then a shadow skimmed your face
Go on talking in a normal voice   you murmured
Nothing is listening

6

You were telling a story about war   it is our story
an old story   and still it must be told
the story of the new that fled the old
how the big dream strained and shifted
the ship of hope shuddered on the iceberg's breast
the private affections swayed and staggered
So we are thrown together   so we are racked apart
in a republic shivering on   its glassy lips
parted   as if the fundamental rift
had not been calculated from the first into the mighty scaffold.

1994

Inscriptions

One: comrade

Little as I knew you I know you: little as you knew me you
        know me
—that's the light we stand under when we meet.
I've looked into flecked jaws
walked injured beaches footslick in oil
watching licked birds stumble in flight
while you drawn through the pupil of your eye
across your own oceans in visionary pain and in relief
headlong and by choice took on the work of charting
your city's wounds ancient and fertile
listening for voices within and against.
My testimony: yours: Trying to keep faith
not with each other exactly yet it's the one known and unknown
who stands for, imagines the other   with whom faith could
        be kept.

In city your mind burns wanes waxes with hope
(no stranger to bleakness you: worms have toothed at
        your truths
but you were honest regarding that).
You conspired to compile the illegal discography
of songs forbidden to sing or to be heard.
If there were ethical flowers one would surely be yours
and I'd hand it to you headlong across landmines
across city's whyless sleeplight I'd hand it
purposefully, with love, a hand trying to keep beauty afloat
on the bacterial waters.

When a voice learns to sing it can be heard as dangerous
when a voice learns to listen it can be heard as desperate.

The self unlocked to many selves.
A mirror handed to one who just released
from the locked ward from solitary from preventive detention
sees in her thicket of hair her lost eyebrows
whole populations.
One who discharged from war stares in the looking-glass of home
at what he finds there, sees in the undischarged tumult of his
       own eye
how thickskinned peace is, and those who claim to promote it.

Two: **movement**

Old backswitching road bent toward the ocean's light
Talking of angles of vision   movements   a black or a red tulip
          opening
Times of walking across a street   thinking
not *I have joined a movement* but   *I am stepping in this deep current*
Part of my life washing behind me   terror I couldn't swim with
part of my life waiting for me   a part I had no words for
I need to live each day through   have them and know them all
though I can see from here where I'll be standing at the end.

. . .

When does a life bend toward freedom?   grasp its direction?
How do you know you're not circling in pale dreams, nostalgia,
          stagnation
but entering that deep current   malachite, colorado
requiring all your strength wherever found
your patience and your labor
desire pitted against desire's inversion
all your mind's fortitude?
Maybe through a teacher: someone with facts with numbers
          with poetry
who wrote on the board: IN EVERY GENERATION ACTION FREES
          OUR DREAMS.
Maybe a student: one mind unfurling like a redblack peony
quenched into percentile, dropout, stubbed-out bud
—Your journals Patricia: Douglas your poems: but the repeti-
          tive blows
on spines whose hope you were, on yours:
to see that quenching and decide.

—And now she turns her face brightly on the new morning in
        the new classroom
new in her beauty her skin her lashes her lively body:
Race, class . . . all that . . . but isn't all that just history?
Aren't people bored with it all?

She could be
myself at nineteen   but free of reverence for past ideas
ignorant of hopes piled on her   She's a mermaid
momentarily precipitated from a solution
which could stop her heart   She could swim or sink
like a beautiful crystal.

Three: origins

Turning points.   We all like to hear about those.   Points
        on a graph.
Sudden conversions.   Historical swings.   Some kind of
        dramatic structure.
But a life doesn't unfold that way   it moves
in loops   by switchbacks loosely strung
around the swelling of one hillside toward another
one island toward another
A child's knowing   a child's forgetting   remain childish
till you meet them   mirrored and echoing   somewhere else
Don't ask me when I learned love
Don't ask me when I learned fear
Ask about the size of rooms   how many lived in them
    what else the rooms contained
    what whispers of the histories of skin

Should I simplify my life for you?
The Confederate Women of Maryland
on their dried-blood granite pedestal incised
        IN DIFFICULTY AND IN DANGER . . .
           "BRAVE AT HOME"
—words a child could spell out
standing in wetgreen grass stuck full of yellow leaves
monumental women bandaging wounded men
Joan of Arc in a book   a peasant in armor
Mussolini   Amelia Earhart   the President on the radio
    —what's taught, what's overheard

Four: history

Should I simplify my life for you?
Don't ask how I began to love men.
Don't ask how I began to love women.
Remember the forties songs, the slowdance numbers
the small sex-filled gas-rationed Chevrolet?
Remember walking in the snow and who was gay?
Cigarette smoke of the movies, silver-and-gray
profiles, dreaming the dreams of he-and-she
breathing the dissolution of the wisping silver plume?
Dreaming that dream we leaned applying lipstick
by the gravestone's mirror when we found ourselves
playing in the cemetery.   In Current Events she said
the war in Europe is over, the Allies
and she wore no lipstick have won the war
and we raced screaming out of Sixth Period.

Dreaming that dream
we had to maze our ways through a wood
where lips were knives breasts razors and I hid
in the cage of my mind scribbling
this map stops where it all begins
into a red-and-black notebook.
Remember after the war when peace came down
as plenty for some and they said we were saved
in an eternal present and we knew the world could end?
—remember after the war when peace rained down
on the winds from Hiroshima Nagasaki Utah Nevada?
and the socialist queer Christian teacher jumps from the
        hotel window?
and L.G. saying *I want to sleep with you but not for sex*

and the red-and-black enamelled coffee-pot dripped slow through
        the dark grounds
—appetite terror power tenderness
the long kiss in the stairwell the switch thrown
on two Jewish Communists married to each other
the definitive crunch of glass at the end of the wedding?
(When shall we learn, what should be clear as day,
We cannot choose what we are free to love?)

Five:　　**voices**

"That year I began to understand the words *burden of proof*
—how the free market of ideas depended
on certain lives laboring under that burden.
I started feeling in my body
how that burden was bound to our backs
keeping us cramped in old repetitive motions
crouched in the same mineshaft year on year
or like children in school striving to prove
proofs already proven over and over
to get into the next grade
but there is no next grade no movement onward only this

and the talk goes on, the laws, the jokes, the deaths, the way of
　　　　life goes on
as if you had proven nothing as if this burden were what
　　　　you are."

· · ·

(Knotted crowns of asparagus lowered by human hands
into long silver trenches fogblanched mornings
the human spine translated into fog's
almost unbearable rheumatic beauty flattering pain
into a daze a mystic text of white and white's
absolute faceless romance　:　:　the photographer's
darkroom thrill discerning two phantoms caught
trenchside deep in the delicate power
of fog　:　:　phantoms who nonetheless have to know
the length of the silvery trenches how many plants how long
this bending can go on and for what wage and what
that wage will buy in the Great Central Valley 1983.)

. . .

"Desire disconnected   meetings and marches
for justice and peace   the sex of the woman
the bleached green-and-gold   of the cotton print bedspread
in the distance the sound   of the week's demonstration
July sun louvered shutters   off Riverside Drive
shattered glass in the courtyard   the sex of the woman
her body entire aroused to the hair
the sex of the women our bodies entire
molten in purpose each body a tongue
each body a river and over and over

and after to walk   in the streets still unchanging
a stormy light, evening   tattered emblems, horse-droppings
DO NOT CROSS POLICE BARRIER   yellow boards kicked awry
the scattering crowds   at the mouth of the subway

A thumbprint on a glass of icy water
memory that scours and fogs

nights when I threw my face
on a sheet of lithic scatter
wrapped myself in a sack of tears"

. . .

"My thief   my counsellor
        tell me how it was then under the bridge
        in the long cashmere scarf
        the opera-lover left
silken length rough flesh violet light meandering
the splash that trickled down the wall
O tell me what you hissed to him and how he groaned to you
tell me the opera-lover's body limb by limb and touch by touch
how his long arms arched dazzling under the abutment

as he played himself to the hilt
     cloak flocked with light
My thief   my counsellor
tell me was it good or bad, was it good and bad, in the
     unbefriended archway of your first ardor?
was it an oilstain's thumbprint on moving water?
the final drench and fizzle on the wall?
was it freedom from names from rank from color?
Thieving the leather trenchcoat of the night, my counsellor?
Breathing the sex of night of water never having to guess its
     source, my thief?

O thief
I stand at your bedside   feed you segments of orange
O counsellor
you have too many vanishing children to attend
There were things I was meant to learn from you   they wail out
     like a train leaving the city
Desire the locomotive   death the tracks   under the bridge
the silken roughness drench of freedom the abruptly
     floodlit parapet
LOVE CONQUERS ALL spelled out in flickering graffiti
—my counsellor, my thief"

· · ·

"In the heart of the capital of Capital
against banked radiations of azalea
I found a faux-marble sarcophagus inscribed
          HERE LIES THE WILL OF THE PEOPLE
I had been wondering why for so long so little
had been heard from that quarter.
I found myself there by deepest accident
wandering among white monuments
looking for the Museum of Lost Causes.

A strangely focused many-lumened glare
was swallowing alive the noon.
I saw the reviewing stand the podium draped and swagged
the huge screen all-enhancing and all-heightening
I heard the martial bands the choirs the speeches
amplified in the vacant plaza
swearing to the satellites it had been a natural death."

Six: edgelit

Living under fire in the raincolored opal of your love
I could have forgotten other women I desired
so much I wanted to love them but
here are some reasons love would not let me:
One had a trick of dropping her lashes along her cheekbone
in an amazing screen so she saw nothing.
Another would stand in summer arms rounded and warm
catching wild apricots that fell
either side of a broken fence but she caught them on one
                    side only.
One, ambitious, flushed
to the collarbone, a shapely coward.
One keen as mica, glittering,
full at the lips, absent at the core.
One who flirted with danger
had her escape route planned when others had none
and disappeared.
One sleepwalking on the trestle
of privilege dreaming of innocence
tossing her cigarette into the dry gully
—an innocent gesture.

. . .

Medbh's postcard from Belfast:
                    one's poetry seems aimless
covered in the blood and lies
                    oozing corrupt & artificial
but of course one will continue . . .

This week I've dredged my pages
for anything usable
                    head, heart, perforated
by raw disgust and fear
If I dredge up anything it's suffused
by what it works in, "like the dyer's hand"
I name it unsteady, slick, unworthy
                                    and I go on

In my sixty-fifth year I know something about language:
it can eat or be eaten by experience
Medbh, poetry means refusing
the choice to kill or die

but this life of continuing is for the sane mad
and the bravest monsters

. . .

The bright planet that plies her crescent shape
in the western air   that through the screendoor gazes
with her curved eye now speaks: *The beauty of darkness*
is how it lets you see.   Through the screendoor
she told me this and half-awake I scrawled
her words on a piece of paper.
She is called Venus but I call her You
You   who sees me   You   who calls me to see
You   who has other errands far away in space and time
You   in your fiery skin   acetylene
scorching the claims of the false mystics
You   who like the moon arrives in crescent
changeable changer   speaking truth from darkness

. . .

Edgelit: firegreen yucca under fire-ribbed clouds
blue-green agave   grown huge in flower
cries of birds streaming over

The night of the eclipse the full
moon
swims clear between flying clouds until

the hour of the occlusion   It's not of aging
anymore and its desire
which is of course unending

it's of dying   young or old
in full desire

Remember me . . . . O, O, O,
O, remember me

these vivid stricken cells
precarious living marrow
this my labyrinthine filmic brain
this my dreaded blood
this my irreplaceable
footprint vanishing from the air

dying in full desire
thirsting for the coldest water
hungering for hottest food
gazing into the wildest light

edgelight from the high desert
where shadows drip from tiniest stones
sunklight of bloody afterglow

torque of the Joshua tree
flinging itself forth in winter
factoring freeze into its liquid consciousness

These are the extremes I stoke
into the updraft of this life
still roaring

                    into thinnest air

1993–1994

Midnight Salvage

The Art of Translation

1

To have seen you exactly, once:
red hair over cold cheeks fresh from the freeway
your lingo, your daunting and dauntless
eyes. But then to lift toward home, mile upon mile
back where they'd barely heard your name
—neither as terrorist nor as genius would they detain you—

to wing it back to my country bearing
your war-flecked protocols—

that was a mission, surely: my art's pouch
crammed with your bristling juices
sweet dark drops of your spirit
that streaked the pouch, the shirt I wore
and the bench on which I leaned.

2

It's only a branch like any other
green with the flare of life in it
and if I hold this end, you the other
that means it's broken

broken between us, broken despite us
broken and therefore dying
broken by force, broken by lying
green, with the flare of life in it

3

But say we're crouching on the ground like children
over a mess of marbles, soda caps, foil, old foreign coins
—the first truly precious objects. Rusty hooks, glass.

Say I saw the earring first but you wanted it.
Then you wanted the words I'd found. I'd give you
the earring, crushed lapis if it were,

I would look long at the beach glass and the sharded self
of the lightbulb. Long I'd look into your hand
at the obsolete copper profile, the cat's-eye, the lapis.

Like a thief I would deny the words, deny they ever
existed, were spoken, or could be spoken,
like a thief I'd bury them and remember where.

4

The trade names follow trade
the translators stopped at passport control:
Occupation: no such designation—
Journalist, maybe spy?

That the books are for personal use
only—could I swear it?
That not a word of them
is contraband—how could I prove it?

1995

Midnight Salvage

1

Up skyward through a glazed rectangle I
sought the light of a so-called heavenly body
: : a planet or our moon in some event and caught

nothing nothing but a late wind
pushing around some Monterey pines
themselves in trouble and rust-limbed

Nine o'clock : : July : the light
undrained : : that blotted blue
that lets has let will let

thought's blood ebb between life- and death-time
darkred behind darkblue
bad news pulsing back and forth of "us" and "them"

And all I wanted was to find an old
friend an old figure an old trigonometry
still true to our story in orbits flaming or cold

2

Under the conditions of my hiring
I could profess or declare anything at all
since in that place nothing would change
So many fountains, such guitars at sunset

Did not want any more to sit under such a window's
deep embrasure, wisteria bulging on spring air
in that borrowed chair
with its collegiate shield at a borrowed desk

under photographs of the spanish steps, Keats' death mask
and the english cemetery all so under control and so eternal
in burnished frames : : or occupy the office
of the marxist-on-sabbatical

with Gramsci's fast-fading eyes
thumbtacked on one wall opposite a fading print
of the same cemetery : : had memories
and death masks of my own : : could not any more

peruse young faces already straining for
the production of slender testaments
to swift reading and current thinking : : would not wait
for the stroke of noon to declare all passions obsolete

Could not play by the rules
in that palmy place : : nor stand at lectern professing
anything at all
                    in their hire

3

Had never expected hope would form itself
completely in my time : : was never so sanguine
as to believe old injuries could transmute easily
through any singular event or idea : : never
so feckless as to ignore the managed contagion
of ignorance the contrived discontinuities
the felling of leaders and future leaders
the pathetic erections of soothsayers

But thought I was conspiring, breathing-along
with history's systole-diastole
twenty thousand leagues under the sea a mammal heartbeat
sheltering another heartbeat

plunging from the Farallons all the way to Baja
sending up here or there a blowhole signal
and sometimes beached
making for warmer waters
where the new would be delivered : : though I would not see it

4

But neither was expecting in my time
to witness this : : wasn't deep
lucid or mindful you might say enough
to look through history's bloodshot eyes
into this commerce this dreadnought wreck cut loose
from all vows, oaths, patents, compacts, promises : :
                                                    To see

not O my Captain
fallen cold & dead by the assassin's hand

but cold alive & cringing : : drinking with the assassins
in suit of noir Hong Kong silk
pushing his daughter in her famine-
waisted flamingo gown
out on the dance floor with the traffickers
in nerve gas saying to them *Go for it*
and to the girl *Get with it*

5

When I ate and drank liberation once I walked
arm-in-arm with someone who said she had something to teach me
It was the avenue and the dwellers
free of home : roofless : : women
without pots to scour or beds to make
or combs to run through hair
or hot water for lifting grease or cans

to open or soap to slip in that way
under arms then beneath breasts then downward to thighs

Oil-drums were alight under the freeway
and bottles reached from pallets of cardboard corrugate
and piles of lost and found to be traded back and forth
and figures arranging themselves from the wind
Through all this she walked me : : And said
My name is Liberation and I come from here
Of what are you so afraid?

We've hung late in the bars like bats
kissed goodnight at the stoplights
—did you think I wore this city without pain?
did you think I had no family?

6

Past the curve where the old craftsman was run down
there's a yard called Midnight Salvage
He was walking in the road which was always safe
The young driver did not know that road
its curves or that people walked there
or that you could speed yet hold the curve
watching for those who walked there
such skills he did not have being in life unpracticed

but I have driven that road in madness and driving rain
thirty years in love and pleasure and grief-blind
on ice I have driven it and in the vague haze of summer
between clumps of daisies and sting of fresh cowflop odors
lucky I am I hit nobody old or young
killed nobody left no trace
practiced in life as I am

7

This horrible patience which is part of the work
This patience which waits for language for meaning for the
                least sign
This encumbered plodding state doggedly dragging
the IV up and down the corridor
with the plastic sack of bloodstained urine

Only so can you start living again
waking to take the temperature of the soul
when the black irises lean at dawn
from the mouth of the bedside pitcher
This condition in which you swear *I will*
submit to whatever poetry is
I accept no limits   Horrible patience

8

You cannot eat an egg   You don't know where it's been
The ordinary body of the hen
vouchsafes no safety   The countryside refuses to supply
Milk is powdered   meat's in both senses high

Old walls the pride of architects   collapsing
find us in crazed niches   sleeping like foxes
we wanters we unwanted we
wanted for the crime of being ourselves

Fame slides on its belly like any other animal after food
Ruins are disruptions of system leaking in
weeds and light   redrawing
the City of Expectations

You cannot eat an egg   Unstupefied not unhappy
we braise wild greens and garlic   feed the feral cats
and when the fog's irregular documents break open
scan its fissures for young stars
                    in the belt of Orion

1996

Char

1

There is bracken there is the dark mulberry
there is the village where no villager survived
there are the hitlerians there are the foresters
feeding the partisans from frugal larders

there is the moon ablaze in every quarter
there is the moon "of tin and sage" and unseen pilots dropping
explosive gifts into meadows of fog and crickets
there is the cuckoo and the tiny snake

there is the table set at every meal
for freedom whose chair stays vacant
the young men in their newfound passions
(Love along with them the ones they love)

Obscurity, code, the invisible existence
of a thrush in the reeds, the poet watching
as the blood washes off the revolver in the bucket
Redbreast, your song shakes loose a ruin of memories

A horrible day . . . Perhaps he knew, at that final instant?
The village had to be spared at any price . . .
How can you hear me? I speak from so far . . .
The flowering broom hid us in a blazing yellow mist . . .

2

This war will prolong itself beyond any platonic armistice. The implanting
of political concepts will go on amid upheavals and under cover of self-
confident hypocrisy. Don't smile. Thrust aside both skepticism and

resignation and prepare your soul to face an intramural confrontation with
demons as cold-blooded as microbes.

The poet in wartime, the Surréalistes' younger brother
turned realist (*the village had to be spared at any price*)
all eyes on him in the woods crammed with maquisards ex-
pecting him to signal to fire and save their comrade
shook his head and watched Bernard's execution
knowing that *the random shooting of a revolver*
may be the simplest surreal act but never
changes the balance of power and that real acts are not simple
The poet, prone to exaggerate, thinks clearly under torture

knowing the end of the war
would mean no end to the microbes frozen in each soul
the young freedom fighters
in love with the Resistance
fed by a thrill for violence
familiar as his own jaw under the razor

3

Insoluble riverrain conscience echo of the future
I keep vigil for you here by the reeds of Elkhorn Slough
and the brown mouth of the Salinas River going green
where the white egret fishes the fragile margins
Hermetic guide in resistance I've found you and lost you
several times in my life   You were never just
the poet appalled and transfixed by war you were the maker
of terrible delicate decisions and that did not smudge
your sense of limits   You saw squirrels crashing
from the tops of burning pines when the canister exploded
and worse and worse and you were in charge of every risk
the incendiary motives of others were in your charge
and the need for a courage wrapped in absolute tact

and you decided and lived like that and you
held poetry at your lips a piece of wild thyme ripped
from a burning meadow a mimosa twig
from still unravaged country   You kept your senses
about you like that and like this I keep vigil for you.

1996

Modotti

Your footprints of light on sensitive paper
that typewriter you made famous
my footsteps following you up stair-
wells of scarred oak and shredded newsprint
these windowpanes smeared with stifled breaths
corridors of tile and jaundiced plaster
if this is where I must look for you
then this is where I'll find you

From a streetlamp's wet lozenge bent
on a curb plastered with newsprint
the headlines aiming straight at your eyes
to a room's dark breath-smeared light
these footsteps I'm following you with
down tiles of a red corridor
if this is a way to find you
of course this is how I'll find you

Your negatives pegged to dry in a darkroom
rigged up over a bathtub's lozenge
your footprints of light on sensitive paper
stacked curling under blackened panes
the always upstairs of your hideout
the stern exposure of your brows
—these footsteps I'm following you with
aren't to arrest you

The bristling hairs of your eyeflash
that typewriter you made famous
your enormous will to arrest and frame
what was, what is, still liquid, flowing

your exposure of manifestos, your
lightbulb in a scarred ceiling
well if this is how I find you
Modotti so I find you

In the red wash of your darkroom
from your neighborhood of volcanoes
to the geranium nailed in a can
on the wall of your upstairs hideout
in the rush of breath a window
of revolution allowed you
on this jaundiced stair in this huge lashed eye

                                    these

footsteps I'm following you with

1996

Shattered Head

A life hauls itself uphill
    through hoar-mist steaming
the sun's tongue licking
    leaf upon leaf into stricken liquid
When? When? cry the soothseekers
    but time is a bloodshot eye
seeing its last of beauty its own
    foreclosure
        a bloodshot mind
finding itself unspeakable
    What is the last thought?
Now I will let you know?
    or, *Now I know?*
(porridge of skull-splinters, brain tissue
    mouth and throat membrane, cranial fluid)

Shattered head on the breast
    of a wooded hill
laid down there endlessly so
    tendrils soaked into matted compost
become a root
    torqued over the faint springhead
groin whence illegible
    matter leaches: worm-borings, spurts of silt
volumes of sporic changes
    hair long blown into far follicles
blasted into a chosen place

Revenge on the head (genitals, breast, untouched)
    revenge on the mouth
packed with its inarticulate confessions
    revenge on the eyes
green-gray and restless
    revenge on the big and searching lips
             the tender tongue
revenge on the sensual, on the nose the
    carrier of history
revenge on the life devoured
in another incineration

You can walk by such a place, the earth is made of them
where the stretched tissue of a field or woods is humid
      with belovéd matter
the soothseekers have withdrawn
you feel no ghost, only a sporic chorus
when that place utters its worn sigh
   let us have peace

And the shattered head answers back
   I believed I was loved, I believed I loved,
     who did this to us?

1996–1997

Letters to a Young Poet

1

Your photograph won't do you justice
those wetted anthill mounds won't let you focus
that lens on the wetlands

five swans chanting overhead
distract your thirst for closure
and quick escape

2

Let me turn you around in your frozen nightgown and say
one word to you: Ineluctable

—meaning, you won't get quit
of this: the worst of the new news

history running back and forth
panic in the labyrinth

—I will not touch you further:
your choice to freeze or not

to say, you and I are caught in
a laboratory without a science

3

Would it gladden you to think
poetry could purely

take its place beneath lightning sheets
or fogdrip   live its own life

screamed at, howled down
by a torn bowel of dripping names

—composers visit Terezin, film-makers Sarajevo
Cabrini-Green or Edenwald Houses

   ineluctable

if a woman as vivid as any artist
can fling any day herself from the 14th floor

would it relieve you to decide   *Poetry*
doesn't make this happen?

4

From the edges of your own distraction turn
the cloth-weave up, its undersea-fold venous

with sorrow's wash and suck, pull and release,
      annihilating rush

to and fro, fabric of caves, the onset of your fear
kicking away their lush and slippery flora nurseried
      in liquid glass

trying to stand fast in rootsuck, in distraction,
      trying to wade this
undertow of utter repetition

Look: with all my fear I'm here with you, trying what it
      means, to stand fast; what it means to move

5

Beneaped. Rowboat, pirogue, caught between the lowest
and highest tides of spring. Beneaped. Befallen,
becalmed, benighted, yes, begotten.
—*Be*—infernal prefix of the actionless.
—*Be*—as in Sit, Stand, Lie, Obey.
The dog's awful desire that takes his brain
and lays it at the boot-heel.

You can be like this forever—*Be*
as without movement.

6

But this is how
I come, anyway, pushing up from below
my head wrapped in a chequered scarf a lanterned helmet on this
                    head
pushing up out of the ore
this sheeted face this lanterned head facing the seep of death
my lips having swum through silt
        clearly pronouncing
Hello and farewell

Who, anyway, wants to know
this pale mouth, this stick
of crimson lipsalve Who my
dragqueen's vocal chords my bitter beat
my overshoulder backglance flung
at the great strophes and antistrophes
my chant my ululation my sacred parings
nails, hair my dysentery my hilarious throat

my penal colony's birdstarved ledge my face downtown
in films by Sappho and Artaud?

Everyone.   For a moment.

7

It's not the déjà vu that kills
it's the foreseeing
the head that speaks from the crater

I wanted to go somewhere
the brain had not yet gone
I wanted not to be
there so alone.

1997

Camino Real

Hot stink of skunk
crushed at the vineyards' edge

hawk–skied, carrion–clean
clouds ranging themselves
over enormous autumn

that scribble   edged and skunky
as the great road winds on
toward my son's house seven hours south

Walls of the underpass
smudged and blistered eyes gazing from armpits
THE WANTER WANTED   ARMED IN LOVE AND
              DANGEROUS
WANTED FOR WANTING

To become the scholar of : :
: : to list compare contrast events to footnote lesser evils
calmly to note "bedsprings"
describe how they were wired
to which parts of the body
to make clear-eyed assessments of the burnt-out eye: : investigate
the mouth–bit and the mouth
the half-swole slippery flesh the enforced throat
the whip they played you with the backroad games the beatings by
              the river

O to list collate commensurate to quantify:
I was the one, I suffered, I was there

never
to trust to memory only

to go back   notebook in hand
dressed as no one there was dressed

over and over to quantify
on a gridded notebook page

The difficulty of proving
such things were done for no reason
that every night
"in those years"
people invented reasons for torture

Asleep now,   head in hands
hands over ears   O you
Who do this work
every one of you
every night

Driving south: santabarbara's barbarous
landscaped mind: lest it be forgotten
in the long sweep downcoast

let it not be exonerated

but O the light
on the raw Pacific silks

Charles Olson: "Can you afford not to make
                    the magical study
                        which happiness is?"

I take him to mean
that happiness is in itself a magical study
a glimpse of the *unhandicapped life*
as it might be for anyone, somewhere

a kind of alchemy, a study of transformation
else it withers, wilts

—that happiness is not to be
mistrusted or wasted
though it ferment in grief

George Oppen to June Degnan: "I don't know how
to measure happiness"
—Why measure? in itself it's the measure—
at the end of a day
        of great happiness if there be such a day

drawn by love's unprovable pull

I write this, sign it
                    Adrienne

1997

Seven Skins

1

Walk along back of the library
in 1952
someone's there to catch your eye
Vic Greenberg in his wheelchair
paraplegic GI—
Bill of Rights Jew
graduate student going in
by the only elevator route
up into the great stacks where
all knowledge should and is
and shall be stored like sacred grain
while the loneliest of lonely
American decades goes aground
on the postwar rock
and some unlikely
shipmates found ourselves
stuck amid so many smiles

Dating Vic Greenberg you date
crutches and a chair
a cool wit an outrageous form:
"—just back from a paraplegics' conference,
guess what the biggest meeting was about—
Sex with a Paraplegic!—for the wives—"
In and out of cabs his chair
opening and closing round his
electrical monologue the air
furiously calm around him
as he transfers to the crutches

But first you go for cocktails
in his room at Harvard
he mixes the usual martinis, plays Billie Holiday
talks about Melville's vision of evil
and the question of the postwar moment:
Is there an American civilization?
In the bathroom huge
grips and suction-cupped
rubber mats long-handled sponges
the reaching tools a veteran's benefits
in plainest sight

And this is only memory, no more
so this is how you remember

Vic Greenberg takes you to the best restaurant
which happens to have no stairs
for talk about movies, professors, food
Vic orders wine and tastes it
you have lobster, he Beef Wellington
the famous dessert is baked alaska
ice cream singed in a flowerpot
from the oven, a live tulip inserted there

Chair to crutches, crutches to cab
chair in the cab and back to Cambridge
memory shooting its handheld frames
Shall I drop you, he says, or shall
we go back to the room for a drink?
It's the usual question
a man has to ask it
a woman has to answer
you don't even think

2

What a girl I was then what a body
ready for breaking open like a lobster
what a little provincial village
what a hermit crab seeking nobler shells
what a beach of rattling stones what an offshore raincloud
what a gone-and-come tidepool

what a look into eternity I took and did not return it
what a book I made myself
what a quicksilver study
bright little bloodstain
liquid pouches escaping

What a girl pelican-skimming over fear what a mica lump
            splitting
into tiny sharp-edged mirrors through which
the sun's eclipse could seem normal
what a sac of eggs what a drifting flask
eager to sink   to be found
to disembody   what a mass of swimmy legs

3

Vic into what shoulder could I have pushed your face
laying hands first on your head
onto whose thighs pulled down your head
which fear of mine would have wound itself
around which of yours   could we have taken it   nakedness
without sperm   in what insurrectionary
convulsion would we have done it   mouth to mouth
mouth-tongue to vulva-tongue to anus   earlobe to nipple
what seven skins each have to molt what seven shifts
what tears boil up through sweat to bathe
what humiliatoriums   what layers of imposture

What heroic tremor
released into pure moisture
might have soaked our shape   two-headed   avid
into your heretic
linen-service
sheets?

1997

Rusted Legacy

Imagine a city where nothing's
forgiven   your deed adheres
to you like a scar, a tattoo   but almost everything's
forgotten   deer flattened leaping a highway for food
the precise reason for the shaving of the confused girl's head
the small boys' punishing of the frogs
—a city memory-starved but intent on retributions
Imagine the architecture   the governance
the men and the women in power
—tell me if it is not true you still
          live in that city.

Imagine a city partitioned   divorced from its hills
where temples and telescopes used to probe the stormy codices
a city brailling through fog
thicket and twisted wire
into dark's velvet dialectic
sewers which are also rivers
art's unchartered aquifers   the springhead
sprung open in civic gardens left unlocked at night
I finger the glass beads I strung and wore
under the pines while the arrests were going on
(transfixed from neck to groin I wanted to save what I could)
They brought trays with little glasses of cold water
into the dark park   a final village gesture
before the villages were gutted.
They were trying to save what they could
—tell me if this is not the same city.

I have forced myself to come back like a daughter
required to put her mother's house in order
whose hands need terrible gloves to handle
the medicinals   the disease packed in those linens
Accomplished criminal I've been but
can I accomplish justice here? Tear the old wedding sheets
into cleaning rags? Faithless daughter
like stone   but with water pleating across
Let water be water let stone be stone
Tell me is this the same city.

This *I*—must she, must she lie scabbed with rust
crammed with memory in a place
of little anecdotes   no one left
to go around gathering the full dissident story?
Rusting her hands and shoulders stone her lips
yet leaching down from her eyesockets tears
—for one self only? each encysts a city.

1997

A Long Conversation

—warm bloom of blood in the child's arterial tree
could you forget?   do you
remember?   not to
know you were cold?   Altercations
from porches   color still high in your cheeks
the leap for the catch
the game getting wilder as the lights come on
catching your death it was said

                        your death of cold
something you couldn't see ahead, you couldn't see

                    (energy: Eternal Delight)

—•—

a long conversation

        between persistence and impatience
        between the bench of forced confessions
            hip from groin swiveled
            apart
            young tongues torn in the webbing
            the order of the cities
            founded on disorder

        and intimate resistance
        desire exposed and shameless
        as the flags go by

—•—

Sometime looking backward
into this future, straining
neck and eyes I'll meet your shadow
with its enormous eyes
 you who will want to know
 what this was all about

 Maybe this is the beginning of madness
 Maybe it's your conscience . . .

as you, straining neck and eyes
gaze forward into this past:
what did it mean to you?
 —to receive "full human rights"
 or the blue aperture of hope?

———•———

 Mrs. Bartender, will you tell us dear
 who came in when the nights were
 cold and drear and who sat where
 well helmeted and who
 was showing off his greasy hair
 Mrs. Bartender tell me quickly
 who spoke thickly or not at all
 how you decided what you'd abide
 what was proud and thus allowed
 how you knew what to do
 with all the city threw at you
 Mrs. Bartender tell me true
 we've been keeping an eye on you
 and this could be a long conversation
 we could have a long accommodation

———•———

On the oilcloth of a certain table, in the motel room of a certain time and country, a white plastic saucer of cheese and hard salami, winter radishes, cold cuts, a chunk of bread, a bottle of red wine, another of water proclaimed drinkable. Someone has brought pills for the infection that is ransacking this region. Someone else came to clean birds salvaged from the oil spill. Here we eat, drink from thick tumblers, try to pierce this thicket with mere words.

Like a little cell. Let's not aggrandize ourselves; we are not a little cell, but we are like a little cell.

Music arrives, searching for us. What hope or memory without it. Whatever we may think. After so many words.

————•————

A long conversation
                    pierced, jammed, scratched out:
                         bans, preventive detention, broken mouths
                         and on the scarred bench sequestered
                              a human creature with bloody wings
                                   its private parts
                                        reamed
                                        still trying to speak

A hundred and fifty years. In 1848 a pamphlet was published, one of many but the longest-read. One chapter in the long book of memories and expectations.   A chapter described to us as evil; if not evil out-of-date, naïve and mildewed.   Even the book they say is out of print, lacking popular demand.

So we have to find out what in fact that manifesto said. Evil, we can judge. Mildew doesn't worry us. We don't want to be more

naïve or out-of-date than necessary. Some old books are probably
more useful than others.

*The bourgeoisie cannot exist without constantly revolutionizing the
instruments of production, thereby the relations of production, and with them
the whole relations of society . . . it creates a world after its own image.*

*In proportion as the bourgeoisie, i.e., capital, is developed, in the same
proportion is the proletariat, the modern working class developed—a
class of laborers who live only so long as they find work, and who find
work only so long as their labor increases capital. These laborers, who
must sell themselves piecemeal, are a commodity, like every other article
of commerce, and are consequently exposed to all the vicissitudes of
competition, to all the fluctuations of the market.*

—Can we say if or how we find this true in our lives today?

She stands before us as if we are a class, in school, but we are long
out of school. Still, there's that way she has of holding the book in
her hands, as if she knew it contained the answer to her question.

Someone: —Technology's changing the most ordinary forms of
human contact—who can't see that, in their own life?

—But technology is nothing but a means.

—Someone, I say, makes a killing off war. You: —I've been
telling you, that's the engine driving the free market. Not
information, militarization. Arsenals spawning wealth.

Another woman: —But surely then patriarchal nationalism is the
key?

He comes in late, as usual he's been listening to sounds outside,
the tide scraping the stones, the voices in nearby cottages, the

way he used to listen at the beach, as a child. He doesn't speak like a teacher, more like a journalist come back from war to report to us. —It isn't nations anymore, look at the civil wars in all the cities. Is there a proletariat that can act effectively on this collusion, between the state and the armed and murderous splinter groups roaming at large? How could all these private arsenals exist without the export of increasingly sophisticated arms approved by the metropolitan bourgeoisie?

Now someone gets up and leaves, cloud-faced: —I can't stand that kind of language. I still care about poetry.

All kinds of language fly into poetry, like it or not, or even if you're only
       as we were   trying
           to keep an eye
                on the weapons on the street
                   and under the street

Just here, our friend L.: bony, nerve-driven, closeted, working as a nurse when he can't get teaching jobs. Jew from a dynasty of converts, philosopher trained as an engineer, he can't fit in where his brilliant and privileged childhood pointed him. He too is losing patience: *What is the use of studying philosophy if all that it does for you is enable you to talk with some plausibility about some abstruse questions of logic, etc . . . & if it does not improve your thinking about the important questions of everyday life, if it does not make you more conscientious than any journalist in the use of the dangerous phrases such people use for their own ends?*

You see, I know that it's difficult to think well about "certainty," "probability," perception, etc. But it is, if possible, still more difficult to think, or try to think, really honestly about your life and other people's lives. And thinking about these things is NOT THRILLING, but often downright nasty. And when it's nasty then it's MOST important.

His high-pitched voice with its darker, hoarser undertone.

At least he didn't walk out, he stayed, long fingers drumming.

———•———

So now your paledark face thrown up
into pre-rain silver light your white shirt takes
on the hurl and flutter of the gulls' wings
over your dark leggings their leathery legs
flash past your hurling arm one hand
snatching crusts from the bowl another hand holds close

You, barefoot on that narrow strand
with the iceplant edges and the long spindly pier
you just as the rain starts leaping into the bay
in your cloud of black, bronze and silvering hair

———•———

Later by the window on a fast-gathering winter evening
my eyes on the page then catch your face your breasts that light

> *. . . small tradespeople,*
> *shopkeepers, retired tradesmen, handicraftsmen and peasants—*
> *all these sink gradually into the proletariat*

> *partly because their*
> *diminutive capital does not suffice for the scale on which*
> *modern industry is carried on, and is swamped in the*
> *competition with the large capitalists*

> *partly because their specialized*
> *skill is rendered worthless by new methods of production.*

Thus, the proletariat is recruited
from all classes of the population. . . .

pelicans and cormorants stumbling up the bay
the last gash of light abruptly bandaged in darkness

———•———

1799, Coleridge to Wordsworth: *I wish*
you would write a poem
addressed to those who, in consequence
of the complete failure of the French Revolution
have thrown up all hopes
of the amelioration of mankind
and are sinking into an almost epicurean
selfishness, disguising the same
under the soft titles of domestic attachment
and contempt for visionary philosophes

A generation later, revolutions scorching Europe:
the visionaries having survived despite
rumors of complete failure

the words have barely begun   to match the desire

when the cold fog blows back in
organized and disordering
muffling words and faces

Your lashes, visionary! screening
in sudden rushes this
shocked, abraded crystal

———•———

325

I can imagine a sentence that might someday end with the
word, love. Like the one written by that asthmatic young man,
which begins, *At the risk of appearing ridiculous* . . . It would have
to contain losses, resiliencies, histories faced; it would have to
contain a face—his yours hers mine—by which I could do well,
embracing it like water in my hands, because by then we could
be sure that "doing well" by one, or some, was immiserating
nobody. A true sentence then, for greeting the newborn.
(—Someplace else. In our hopes.)

But where ordinary collective affections carry a price (swamped,
or accounted worthless) I'm one of those driven seabirds stamping
oil-distempered waters   maimed "by natural causes."

The music's pirated from somewhere else: Catalan songs reaching
us after fifty years. Old *nuevos canciones*, after twenty years? In
them, something about the sweetness of life, the memory of
tradition of mercy, struggles for justice. A long throat, casting
memory forward.

———•———

"it's the layers of history
we have to choose, along
with our own practice: what must be tried again
over and over and
what must not be repeated
and at what depth   which layer
will we meet others"

        the words barely begin
        to match the desire

and the mouth crammed with dollars doesn't testify

. . . the eye has become a human eye
when its object has become a human, social object

BRECHT BECOMES GERMAN ICON ANEW
FORGIVEN MARXIST IDEAS

. . . the Arts, you know—they're Jews, they're left-wing,
in other words, stay away . . .

———•———

So, Bo Kunstelaar, tell us true
how you still do what you do
your old theories forgiven
—the public understands
it was one thing then but now is now
and everyone says your lungs are bad
and your liver very sad
and the force of your imagination
has no present destination
though subversive has a certain charm
and art can really do no harm
but still they say you get up and go
every morning to the studio
Is it still a thrill?
or an act of will?
Mr. Kunstelaar?

———•———

—After so long, to be asked an opinion? Most of that time, the
opinions unwelcome. But opinion anyway was never art. Along
the way I was dropped by some; others could say I had dropped
them. I tried to make in my studio what I could not make outside
it. Even to have a studio, or a separate room to sleep in, was

a point in fact. In case you miss the point: I come from hod-carriers, lint-pickers, people who hauled cables through half-dug tunnels. Their bodies created the possibility of my existence. I come from the kind of family where loss means not just grief but utter ruin—adults and children dispersed into prostitution, orphanages, juvenile prisons, emigration—never to meet again. I wanted to show those lives—designated insignificant—as beauty, as terror. They were significant to me and what they had endured terrified me. I knew such a life could have been my own. I also knew they had saved me from it.

—I tried to show all this and as well to make an art as impersonal as it demanded.

—I have no theories. I don't know what I am being forgiven. I am my art: I make it from my body and the bodies that produced mine. I am still trying to find the pictorial language for this anger and fear rotating on an axle of love. If I still get up and go to the studio—it's there I find the company I need to go on working.

———•———

"This is for you
this little song
without much style
because your smile
fell like a red leaf
through my tears
in those fogbound years
when without ado
you gave me a bundle of fuel to burn
when my body was utterly cold
This is for you
who would not applaud
when with a kick to the breast or groin

they dragged us into the van
when flushed faces cheered
at our disgrace
or looked away   this is
for you who stayed
to see us through
delivered our bail and disappeared
This little song
without much style
may it find you
somewhere   well."

———•———

In the dark windowglass
a blurred face
—is it still mine?

Who out there hoped to change me—
what out there has tried?

What sways and presses against the pane
what can't I see beyond or through—

charred, crumpled, ever-changing human language
is that still *you?*

1997–1998

Fox

Victory

Something spreading underground won't speak to us
under skin won't declare itself
not all life-forms want dialogue with the
machine-gods in their drama   hogging down
the deep bush   clear-cutting refugees
from ancient or transient villages into
our opportunistic fervor   to search
                    crazily for a host   a lifeboat

Suddenly instead of art we're eyeing
organisms traced and stained on cathedral transparencies
cruel blues   embroidered purples   succinct yellows
a beautiful tumor

———•———

I guess you're not alone   I fear you're alone
There's, of course, poetry:
awful bridge rising over naked air: I first
took it as just a continuation of the road:
"a masterpiece of engineering
praised, etc."   then on the radio:
"incline too steep for ease of, etc."
Drove it nonetheless because I had to
this being how—   So this is how
I find you: alive and more

———•———

As if (how many conditionals must we suffer?)
I'm driving to your side
—an intimate collusion—

packed in the trunk my bag of foils for fencing with pain
glasses of varying spectrum for sun or fog or sun-struck
                        rain or bitterest night my sack of hidden
poetries, old glue shredding from their spines

my time exposure of the Leonids
                          over Joshua Tree

As if we're going to win this   O because

———•———

If you have a sister I am not she
nor your mother nor you my daughter
nor are we lovers or any kind of couple
      except in the intensive care
                  of poetry and
death's master plan   architecture-in-progress
draft elevations of a black-and-white mosaic dome
the master left on your doorstep
with a white card in black calligraphy:
        Make what you will of this
    As if leaving purple roses

———•———

If (how many conditionals must we suffer)
I tell you a letter from the master
is lying on my own doorstep
glued there with leaves and rain
and I haven't bent to it yet
              if I tell you I surmise
   he writes differently to me:

Do as you will, you have had your life
  many have not

signing it in his olden script:

  Meister aus Deutschland

———•———

In coldest Europe   end of that war
frozen domes   iron railings frozen   stoves lit in the
    streets
memory banks of cold

the Nike of Samothrace
on a staircase   wings in blazing
backdraft   said to me
: : to everyone she met
    Displaced, amputated   never discount me

Victory
    indented in disaster   striding
        at the head of stairs

for Tory Dent

1998

For This

If I've reached for your lines   (I have)
   like letters from the dead that stir the nerves
dowsed you for a springhead
   to water my thirst
dug into my compost skeletons and petals
   you surely meant to catch the light:

—at work in my wormeaten wormwood-raftered
   stateless underground
     have I a plea?

If I've touched your finger
   with a ravenous tongue
     licked from your palm a rift of salt
if I've dreamt or thought you
   a pack of blood   fresh-drawn
     hanging darkred from a hook
higher than my heart
   (you who understand transfusion)
     where else should I appeal?

A pilot light lies low
   while the gas jets sleep
     (a cat getting toed from stove
into nocturnal ice)
   language uncommon and agile as truth
     melts down the most intractable silence

A lighthouse keeper's ethics:
    you tend for all or none
        for this you might set your furniture on fire
A *this* we have blundered over
    as if the lamp could be shut off at will
        rescue denied for some

and still a lighthouse be

1999

Regardless

An idea declared itself between us
clear as a washed wineglass
that we'd love
regardless of manifestos I wrote or signed
my optimism of the will
regardless
your wincing at manifestos
your practice of despair you named
anarchism
: : an idea we could meet
somewhere else   a road
straggling unmarked through ice-plant
toward an ocean   heartless as eternity

Still hungry for freedom   I walked off
from glazed documents   becalmed
passions   time of splintering and sawdust
pieces lying still   I was not myself but
I found a road like that   it straggled
The ocean still
looked like eternity
I drew it on a
napkin mailed it to you

On your hands you wear work gloves stiffened
in liquids your own body has expressed
: : what stiffens hardest?   tears? blood? urine? sweat? the first
    drops from the penis?
Your glove then meets my hand   this is our meeting
Which of us has gone furthest?

To meet you like this I've had to rise
from love in a room
of green leaves larger than my clitoris or my brain
in a climate where winter never precisely
does or does not engrave its name on the windowpane
while the Pacific lays down its right of way
to the other side of the world

: : to a table where singed manifestos
curl back crying to be reread

but can I even provoke you
joking or
in tears
you   in long-stiffened gloves   still
protector of despair?

for H.C.

1998–1999

Architect

Nothing he had done before
   or would try for later
      will explain or atone
this facile suggestion of crossbeams
languid elevations traced on water
his stake in white colonnades cramping his talent
               showing up in
facsimile mansions overbearing the neighborhood
his leaving the steel rods out of the plinths
   (bronze raptors gazing from the boxwood)

You could say he spread himself too thin   a plasterer's term
      you could say he was then
skating thin ice   his stake in white colonnades against the
   thinness of
ice itself   a slickened ground
      Could say he did not then love
his art enough to love anything more

Could say he wanted the commission so
badly betrayed those who hired him   an artist
      who in dreams followed
         the crowds who followed him

Imagine commandeering those oversize those prized
    hardwood columns to be hoisted and hung
by hands expert and steady on powerful machines
    his knowledge using theirs as the one kind does the
    other (as it did in Egypt)

        —while devising the little fountain to run all night
        outside the master bedroom

1998–1999

Fox

I needed fox   Badly I needed
a vixen for the long time none had come near me
I needed recognition from a
triangulated face   burnt-yellow eyes
fronting the long body the fierce and sacrificial tail
I needed history of fox   briars of legend it was said she had run
    through
I was in want of fox

And the truth of briars she had to have run through
I craved to feel on her pelt   if my hands could even slide
past or her body slide between them   sharp truth distressing
    surfaces of fur
lacerated skin calling legend to account
a vixen's courage in vixen terms

For a human animal to call for help
on another animal
is the most riven the most revolted cry on earth
come a long way down
Go back far enough it means tearing and torn   endless and
    sudden
back far enough it blurts
into the birth-yell of the yet-to-be human child
pushed out of a female   the yet-to-be woman

1998

Messages

I love the infinity of these silent spaces
Darkblue shot with deathrays but only a short distance
Keep of course water and batteries, antibiotics
Always look at California for the last time

We weren't birds, were we, to flutter past each other
But what were we meant to do, standing or lying down
Together on the bare slope where we were driven
The most personal feelings become historical

Keep your hands knotted deep inside your sweater
While the instruments of force are more credible than beauty
Inside a glass paperweight dust swirls and settles (Manzanar)
Where was the beauty anyway when we shouldered past each
    other

Where is it now in the hollow lounge
Of the grounded airline where the cameras
For the desouling project are being handed out
Each of us instructed to shoot the others naked

If you want to feel the true time of our universe
Put your hands over mine on the stainless pelvic rudder
No, here   (sometimes the most impassive ones will shudder)
The infinity of these spaces comforts me
Simple textures falling open like a sweater

1999

Fire

      in the old city   incendiaries abound
who hate this place stuck to their foot soles
Michael Burnhard is being held and I
can tell you about him   pushed-out and living
across the river   low-ground given to flooding
in a shotgun house
his mother working for a hospital
or restaurant   dumpsters   she said a restaurant
hospital cafeteria who cares
what story
you bring home with the food

I can tell you Michael knows beauty
from the frog-iris in mud
the squelch of ankles
stalking the waterlily
the blues beat flung across water from the old city

Michael Burnhard in Black History Month
not his month only he was born there
not black and almost without birthday one
February 29 Michael Burnhard
on the other side of the river
glancing any night at his mother's wrists
crosshatched raw
beside the black-opal stream

Michael Burnhard still beside himself
when fire took the old city
lying like a black spider on its back
under the satellites and a few true stars

1999

Grating

I

Not having worn
   the pearly choker
      of innocence around my throat
willed by a woman
   whose leavings I can't afford
      Not having curled up like that girl
   in maternal gauze
                Not
     having in great joy gazing
on another woman's thick fur
   believed I was unsexed for that

Now let me not
   you   not I   but who ought to be
hang like a leaf twisting
      endlessly toward the past
   nor reach for a woman's skinned-off mask
   to hide behind
        You
            not I but who ought to be
get me out of this, human
            through some
   air vent, grating

II

There's a place where beauty names itself:
"I am beauty," and becomes irreproachable
to the girl transfixed beside the mother
the artist and her mother

There must be a color for the mother's
Otherness   must be some gate of chalk some slit or stain
through which the daughter sees outside that otherness
Long ago must have been burnt a bunch of rags
still smelling of umbrage
that can be crushed into a color
there must be such a color
if, lying full length
on the studio floor
the artist were to paint herself
in monochrome
from a mirror in the ceiling
an elongated figure suspended across the room
first horizontal

then straight up and naked
free of beauty
ordinary in fact

III

The task is to row a strong-boned, legally blind
hundred-and-one-year-old woman
across the Yangtze River

An emergency or not, depending
Others will have settled her in the boat with pillows but the arms
wielding the oars will be yours
crepitus of the shoulders yours
the conversation still hers

*Three days' labor
with you . . . **that** was torture*

—to pilot through current and countercurrent
requiring silence and concentration

There is a dreadfulness that charm o'erlies
—as might have been said
in an older diction

Try to row deadweight someone without
death skills

Shouldering the river a pilot figures
how

The great rock shoulders overlook
in their immensity all decisions

1999–2000

Noctilucent Clouds

Late night on the underside   a spectral glare
abnormal   Everything below
must and will betray itself
as a floodlit truckstop out here
on the North American continent stands revealed
and we're glad because it's late evening and no town
but this, diesel, regular, soda, coffee, chips, beer and video
no government no laws but LIGHT in the continental dark
and then   and then   what smallness the soul endures
rolling out on the ramp from such an isle
onto the harborless Usonian plateau

Dear Stranger   can I raise a poem
to justice   you not here
with your sheet-lightning apprehension
of nocturne
your surveyor's eye for distance
as if any forest's fallen tree were for you
a possible hypotenuse

Can I wake as I once woke with no thought of you
into the bad light of a futureless motel

This thing I am calling justice:
I could slide my hands into your leather gloves
but my feet would not fit into your boots

Every art leans on some other: yours
on mine in spasm retching
last shreds of vanity
We swayed together like cripples when the wind
suddenly turned a corner   or was it we who turned

Once more I invite you into this
in retrospect it will be clear

1999

If Your Name Is on the List

If your name is on the list of judges
you're one of them
though you fought their hardening
assumptions   went and stood
alone by the window while they
concurred
It wasn't enough to hold your singular
minority opinion
You had to face the three bridges
down the river
your old ambitions
flamboyant in bloodstained mist

You had to carry off under arm
and write up in perfect loneliness
your soul-splitting dissent

Yes, I know a soul can be partitioned like a country
In all the new inhere old judgments
loyalties crumbling send up sparks and smoke
We want to be part of the future   dragging in
what pure futurity can't use

Suddenly a narrow street a little beach a little century
screams   *Don't let me go*

Don't let me die   Do you forget
what we were to each other

1999

Terza Rima

1

Hail-spurting sky   sun
splashing off persimmons left
in the quit garden

of the quit house   The realtor's swaying name
against this cloudheap this
surrendered acre

I would   so help me   tell you if I could
how some great teacher
came to my side and said:

Let's go down   into the underworld
—the earth already crazed
Let me take your hand

—but who would that be?
already trembling on the broken crust
who would I trust?

I become the default derailed memory-raided
limping
teacher I never had   I lead and   I follow

2

Call it the earthquake trail:
I lead through live-oak meadows
to the hillside   where the plates shuddered

rewind the seismic story
point to the sundered
fence of 1906   the unmatching rocks

trace the loop under dark bay branches
blurred with moss
behaving like a guide

Like a novice I lag
behind with the little snake
dead on the beaten path

This will never happen again

3

At the end of the beaten path we're sold free
tickets for the celebration
of the death of history

The last page of the calendar
will go up   a sheet of flame
(no one will be permitted on the bridge)

We'll assemble by letters
alphabetical
each ticket a letter

to view ourselves as giants
on screen–surround
in the parking lot

figures of men and women firmly pushing
babies in thickly padded prams
through disintegrating malls

into the new era

4

I have lost our way   the fault is mine
ours   the fault belongs
to us   I become   the guide

who should have defaulted
who should have remained the novice
I   as guide   failed

I as novice   trembled
I should have been stronger   held us
together

5

I thought I was
stronger   my will the ice-sail
speeding my runners

along frozen rivers
bloodied by sunset
thought I could be forever

will-ful   my sail filled
with perfect ozone   my blades
flashing clean into the ice

6

Was that youth?   that clear
sapphire on snow
a distinct hour

in Central Park   that smell
on sidewalk and windowsill
fresh and unmixt

the blizzard's peace and drama
over the city
a public privacy

                    waiting
in the small steamed-up copy shop
slush tracked in across a wooden floor

then shivering   elated
in twilight
at the bus stop   with others   a public happiness

7

Not simple is it to do
a guide's work   the novices
irrupting hourly with their own bad vigor

knowing not who they are
every phase of moon an excuse
for fibrillating

besides the need   in today's world
to consider
outreach   the new thinking

—Or: love will strongly move you
or commerce will
You want a priest?   go to the altar

where eternal bargains are struck
want love?
go down inside your destructible heart

8

In Almodóvar's film
we go for truth to the prostitutes' field
to find past and future

elegant   beaten-up and knifed
sex without gender
preyed-on and preying

transactions   zones of play
the circling drivers
in search of their desires

theater of love   Ninth Circle
there are so many teachers
here   no fire can shrink them

Do you understand?   you could get your face
slashed in such a place
Do you think this is a movie?

9

She says: I gave my name and it was taken
I no longer have my name
I gave my word and it was broken

My words are learning
to walk on crutches
through traffic

without stammering
My name is a prisoner
who will not name names

She says: I gave my tongue
to love   and this
makes it hard to speak

She says: When my life depended
on one of two
opposite terms

I dared mix beauty with courage
they were my lovers
together they were tortured

10

Sick of my own old poems   caught
on rainshower Fifth Avenue
in a bookstore

I reach to a shelf
and there you are   Pier Paolo
speaking to Gramsci's ashes

in the old encircling rhyme
Vivo nel non volere
del tramontato dopoguerra:

                       amando
il mondo che odio . . .
that vernacular voice
intimately political

and that was how you died
so I clasp my book to my heart
as the shop closes

II

Under the blackened dull-metal corners
of the small espresso pot
a jet flares blue

a smell tinctures the room
—some sniff or prescience of
a life that actually could be

lived   a grain of hope
a bite of bitter chocolate in the subway
to pull on our senses

without them we're prey
to the failed will
its science of despair

12

How I hate it when you ascribe to me
a "woman's vision"
cozy with coffeepots   drawn curtains

or   leaning in black leather dress
over your chair
black fingernail tracing your lines

overspent Sibyl drifting in a bottle

How I've hated speaking "as a woman"
for mere continuation
when the broken is what I saw

As a woman   do I love
and hate?   as a woman
do I munch my bitter chocolate underground?

Yes.   No.   You too
sexed as you are   hating
this whole thing   you keep on   it remaking

13

Where the novice pulls the guide
across frozen air
where the guide suddenly grips   the shoulder

of the novice   where the moss is golden
the sky sponged with pink at sunset
where the urine of reindeer barely vanished

stings the air like a sharp herb
where the throat of the clear-cut opens
across the surrendered forest

I'm most difficultly
with you   I lead
and I follow

our shadows   reindeer-huge
slip onto the map
of chance and purpose   figures

on the broken crust
exchanging places   bites to eat
a glance

2000

Four Short Poems

1

(driving home from Robin Blaser's reading)

The moon
is not romantic. No. It's
a fact of life and still
we aren't inured. You would think, it reflects
the waves not draws them. So
I'd compel you as I
have been compelled by you. On the coast road
between drafts of fog
that face (and yes, it is
expressioned) breaking in and out
doth speak to us
as he did in his courtliness
and operatic mystery.

2

We're not yet out of the everglades
   of the last century
      our body parts are still there

though we would have our minds careen and swoop
   over the new ocean
      with a wild surmise

the bloody strings
   tangled and stuck between
      become our lyre

3

Beethoven's "Appassionata" played on a parlor grand piano
in a small California town by a boy from Prague
here for a month to learn American
This is not "The Work of Art in the Age of Mechanical
    Reproduction"
This is one who startles the neighbors with his owning
of the transmissible heritage one evening
then for the whole month droops over the Internet.

4

From the new crudities, from the old
apartheid spraying ruin on revolution,
back to Du Bois of Great Barrington and Africa

or Kafka of the intransmissible
tradition
the stolen secrets in the cleft

reside   and this, beloved poets
is where our hearts, livers and lights still
dwell unbeknownst and vital

for Elizabeth Willis and for Peter Gizzi

2000

Rauschenberg's Bed

How a bed once dressed with a kindly quilt becomes
unsleepable site of anarchy   What body holes expressed
their exaltation loathing exhaustion
what horse of night has pawed those sheets
what talk under the blanket raveled
what clitoris lain very still in her own subversion
what traveler homeward reached for familiar bedding
and felt stiff tatters under his fingers
How a bed is horizontal yet this is vertical
inarticulate liquids spent from a spectral pillow

How on a summer night someone drives out on the roads
while another one lies ice-packed in dreams of freezing

Sometimes this bed has eyes, sometimes breasts
sometimes eking forth from its laden springs
pity compassion pity again for all they have worn and borne
Sometimes it howls for penis sometimes vagina sometimes
for the nether hole the everywhere

How the children sleep and wake
the children   sleep awake upstairs

How on a single night the driver of roads comes back
into the sweat-cold bed of the dreamer

leans toward what's there for warmth
human limbs   human crust

2000

Waiting for You at the Mystery Spot

I sat down facing the steep place where
tours clambered upward and others straggled down, the redwoods
    outstanding all
A family, East Asian, holding a picnic at their van:
"We are always hungry," the older sister said laughing, "and we
    always bring our food"
Roses clambered a rough fence in the slanting sun that speared
    the redwoods
We'd gone into the gift shop while waiting for your tour
found Davy Crockett coonskin caps, deerskin coin purses
scorpions embedded in plastic, MYSTERY SPOT bumper stickers
and postcards of men you wouldn't be left alone with
a moment if you could help it, illustrating
the Mystery Spot and its tricks with gravity and horizon
Your tour was called and you started upward.   I went back
to my redwood bench
                 "The *mystai* streamed"
                                  toward the

  mystery

But if anything up there was occult
nothing at ground level was: tiny beings flashing around
in the sun secure knowing their people were nearby
grandfathers, aunts, elder brothers or sisters, parents and loved
    friends
You could see how it was when each tour was called and gathered
    itself
who rode on what shoulders, ran alongside, held hands
the languages all different, English the least of these
I sat listening to voices watching the miraculous migration
of sunshafts through the redwoods   the great spears folding up

into letters from the sun deposited through dark green slots
each one saying
                    I love you but
I must draw away   Believe, I will return

Then: happiness! your particular figures
in the descending crowd: Anne, Jacob, Charlie!
Anne with her sandals off
in late day warmth and odor and odd wonder

2000

Ends of the Earth

All that can be unknown is stored in the black screen of a broken
    television set.
Coarse-frosted karst crumbling as foam, eel eyes piercing the
    rivers.
Dark or light, leaving or landfall, male or female demarcations
    dissolve
into the O of time and solitude. I found here: no inter/
ruption to a version of earth so abandoned and abandoning
I read it my own acedia lashed by the winds
questing shredmeal toward the Great Plains, that ocean. My fear.

Call it Galisteo but that's not the name of what happened here.

If indoors in an eyeflash (perhaps) I caught the gazer of spaces
lighting the two wax candles in black iron holders
against the white wall after work and after dark
but never saw the hand

how inhale the faint mist of another's gazing, pacing, dozing
words muttered aloud in utter silence, gesture unaware
thought that has suffered and borne itself to the ends of the earth
web agitating between my life and another's?
Other whose bed I have shared but never at once together?

2000

The School
Among the Ruins

Centaur's Requiem

Your hooves drawn together underbelly
shoulders in mud   your mane
of wisp and soil deporting all the horse of you

your longhaired neck
eyes   jaw yes   and ears
unforgivably human on such a creature
unforgivably what you are
deposited in the grit-kicked field of a champion

tender neck and nostrils   teacher   water-lily suction-spot
what you were   marvelous   we could not stand

Night drops . an awaited storm
driving in to wreck your path
Foam on your hide like flowers
where you fell   or fall   desire

2001

Equinox

Time split like a fruit between dark and light
and a usual fog drags
over this landfall
I've walked September end to end
barefoot room to room
carrying in hand a knife well honed for cutting stem or root
                              or wick   eyes open
to abalone shells   memorial candle flames
split lemons   roses laid
                    along charring logs   Gorgeous things
: : dull acres of developed land as we had named it: Nowhere
wetland   burnt garbage looming at its heart
gunmetal thicket   midnightblue blood and
                    tricking masks   I thought I knew
history was not a novel

So can I say it was not I   listed as Innocence
betrayed you   serving (and protesting always)
the motives of my government
thinking we'd scratch out a place
where poetry   old subversive shape
grew out of Nowhere   here?
where skin could lie on skin
a place "outside the limits"

                    Can say I was mistaken?

To be so bruised: in the soft organs   skeins of consciousness
Over and over have let it be
damage to others   crushing of the animate core
that tone-deaf cutloose ego swarming the world

so bruised: heart   spleen   long inflamed ribbons of the guts
the spine's vertical necklace swaying

Have let it swarm
through us   let it happen
as it must, inmost

but before this: long before this   those other eyes
frontally exposed themselves and spoke

2001

Tell Me

1

Tell me, why way toward dawn the body
close to a body familiar as itself
chills—tell me, is this the hour

remembered if outlived

as freezing—no, don't tell me

Dreams spiral birdwinged overhead
a peculiar hour   the silver mirror-frame's
quick laugh the caught light-lattice on the wall
as a truck drives off before dawn
headlights on

Not wanting
to write this up   for the public   not wanting
to write it down   in secret

just to lie here in this cold story
feeling it   trying to feel it through

2

Blink and smoke, flicking with absent nail

at the mica bar

where she refills without asking
Crouch into your raingarb   this will be a night
unauthorized shock troops are abroad

this will be a night
the face-ghosts lean

over the banister

declaring the old stories all
froze like beards or frozen margaritas
all the new stories taste of lukewarm
margaritas, lukewarm kisses

3

From whence I draw this: *harrowed in defeats of language*
in history to my barest marrow
This: one syllable then another
gropes upward
one stroke laid on another
sound from one throat then another
never in the making
making beauty or sense

always mis-taken, draft, roughed-in
only to be struck out
is blurt is roughed-up
hot   keeps body
in leaden hour
simmering

2001

The School Among the Ruins

Beirut.Baghdad.Sarajevo.Bethlehem.Kabul. Not of course here.

1

Teaching the first lesson and the last
—great falling light of summer will you last
longer than schooltime?
When children flow
in columns at the doors
BOYS GIRLS and the busy teachers

open or close high windows
with hooked poles   drawing darkgreen shades

closets unlocked, locked
questions unasked, asked, when

love of the fresh impeccable
sharp-pencilled   yes
order without cruelty

a street on earth   neither heaven nor hell
busy with commerce and worship
young teachers walking to school

fresh bread and early-open foodstalls

2

When the offensive rocks the sky when nightglare
misconstrues day and night when lived-in
rooms from the upper city
tumble cratering lower streets

cornices of olden ornament   human debris
when fear vacuums out the streets

When the whole town flinches
blood on the undersole thickening to glass

Whoever crosses   hunched   knees bent   a contested zone
knows why she does this suicidal thing

School's now in session day and night
children sleep
in the classrooms   teachers rolled close

3

How the good teacher loved
his school   the students
the lunchroom with fresh sandwiches

lemonade and milk
the classroom   glass cages
of moss and turtles
teaching responsibility

A morning breaks without bread or fresh-poured milk
parents or lesson plans

diarrhea first question of the day
children shivering   it's September
Second question: where is my mother?

4

One: I don't know where your mother
is   Two: I don't know
why they are trying to hurt us
Three: or the latitude and longitude
of their hatred   Four: I don't know if we
hate them as much   I think there's more toilet paper
in the supply closet   I'm going to break it open

Today this is your lesson:
write as clearly as you can
your name   home street   and number
down on this page
No you can't go home yet
but you aren't lost
this is our school

I'm not sure what we'll eat
we'll look for healthy roots and greens
searching for water though the pipes are broken

5

There's a young cat sticking
her head through window bars
she's hungry like us
but can feed on mice
her bronze erupting fur
speaks of a life already wild

her golden eyes
don't give quarter   She'll teach us   Let's call her
Sister
when we get milk we'll give her some

6

I've told you, let's try to sleep in this funny camp
All night pitiless pilotless things go shrieking
above us to somewhere

Don't let your faces turn to stone
Don't stop asking me why
Let's pay attention to our cat   she needs us

Maybe tomorrow the bakers can fix their ovens

7

"We sang them to naps   told stories   made
shadow-animals with our hands

wiped human debris off boots and coats
sat learning by heart the names
some were too young to write
some had forgotten how"

2001

This Evening Let's

not talk

about my country   How
I'm from an optimistic culture

that speaks louder than my passport
Don't double-agent-contra my

invincible innocence   I've
got my own

suspicions   Let's
order retsina

cracked olives and bread
I've got questions of my own but

let's give a little
let's let a little be

If *friendship is not a tragedy*
if it's a mercy

we can be merciful
if it's just escape

we're neither of us running
why otherwise be here

Too many reasons not
to waste a rainy evening

in a backroom of bouzouki
and kitchen Greek

I've got questions of my own but
let's let it be a little

There's a beat in my head
song of my country

called Happiness, U.S.A.
Drowns out bouzouki

drowns out world and fusion
with its *Get—get—get*

into your happiness before
happiness pulls away

hangs a left along the piney shore
weaves a hand at you—"one I adore"—

Don't be proud, run hard for that
enchantment boat

tear up the shore if you must but
get into your happiness because

before
and otherwise
it's going to pull away

So tell me later
what I know already

and what I don't get
yet   save for another day

Tell me this time
what you are going through

travelling the Metropolitan
Express

break out of that style
give me your smile
awhile

2001

There Is No One Story and One Story Only

The engineer's story of hauling coal
to Davenport for the cement factory, sitting on the bluffs
between runs looking for whales, hauling concrete
back to Gilroy, he and his wife renewing vows
in the glass chapel in Arkansas after 25 years
The flight attendant's story murmured
to the flight steward in the dark galley
of her fifth-month loss of nerve
about carrying the baby she'd seen on the screen
The story of the forensic medical team's
small plane landing on an Alaska icefield
of the body in the bag they had to drag
over the ice like the whole life of that body
The story of the man driving
600 miles to be with a friend in another country   seeming
easy when leaving but afterward
writing in a letter difficult truths
Of the friend watching him leave remembering
the story of her body
with his once and the stories of their children
made with other people and how his mind went on
pressing hers like a body
There is the story of the mind's
temperature neither cold nor celibate
Ardent   The story of
not one thing only.

2002

Usonian Journals 2000

[*Usonian:* the term used by Frank Lloyd Wright for his prairie-inspired architecture. Here, *of the United States of North America*.]

Citizen/Alien/Night/Mare

A country I was born and lived in undergoes rapid and flagrant change. I return here as a stranger. In fact I've lived here all along. At a certain point I realized I was no longer connected along any continuous strand to the nature of the change. I can't find my passport. Nobody asks me to show it.

Day/Job/Mare

. . . to lunch with K., USonian but recently from a British university. Described as "our Marxist." Dark and pretty, already she's got half the department classified: *She's crazy . . . He's carrying the chip of race on his shoulder . . . she's here because* he *is, isn't she? . . . He's not likely to make it through . . .* Ask her about current Brit. labor scene; she talks about the influence of the industrial revolution on Victorian prose. My aim: get clear of this, find another day job.

As we left the dark publike restaurant the street—ordinary enough couple of blocks between a parking lot and an office complex—broke into spitting, popping sounds and sudden running. I held back against the wall, she beside me. Something happened then everything. A man's voice screamed, then whined: a police siren starting up seemed miles away but then right there. I didn't see any blood. We ran in different directions, she toward, I away from, the police.

Document Window

Could I just show what's happening. Not that shooting, civil disturbance, whatever it was. I'd like you to see how differently we're all moving, how the time allowed to let things become known grows shorter and shorter, how quickly things and people get replaced. How interchangeable it all could get to seem. *Could get to seem . . .* the kind of phrase we use now, avoiding the verb *to be. There's a sense in which,* we say, dismissing other senses.

Rimbaud called for the rational derangement of all the senses in the name of poetry. Marx: capitalism deranges all the senses save the sense of property.

Keeping my back against unimportant walls I moved out of range of the confusion, away from the protection of the police. Having seen nothing I could swear to I felt at peace with my default. I would, at least, not be engaged in some mess not my own.

This is what I mean though: how differently we move now, rapidly deciding what is and isn't ours. Indifferently.

Voices

Wreathed around the entrance to a shopping mall, a student dining hall, don't pause for a word, or to articulate an idea. What hangs a moment in the air is already dead: *That's history.*

The moment—Edwin Denby describes it—when a dancer, leaping, stands still in the air. Pause in conversation when time would stop, an idea hang suspended, then get taken up and carried on. (Then that other great style of conversation: everyone at once, each possessed with an idea.) This newer conversation: *I am here and talking, talking, here and talking . . .* Television the first great lesson: against silence. "I thought she'd never call and I went aaah! to my friend and she went give it a week, she'll call you all right and you did"—" And you went waowh! and I went, right, I went O.K., it's only I was clueless? so now can we grab something nearby, cause I'm due on in forty-five?"

A neighbor painting his garage yelling in cell phone from the driveway: voice that penetrates kitchen-window glass. "Fucking worst day of my fucking life, fucking wife left me for another man, both on coke and, you know? I don't CARE! thought it was only maryjane she was, do you KNOW the prison term for coke? Fucking dealer, leaves me for him because she's HOOKED and I'm supposed to CARE? Do they know what they'll GET?"

Private urgencies made public, not collective, speaker within a bubble. In the new restaurant: "Marty? Thought I'd never get through to you. We need to move quickly with SZ-02, there are hounds on the trail. Barney won't block you at all. Just give him what we talked about."

USonian speech. Men of the upwardly mobilizing class needing to sound boyish, an asset in all the newness of the new: upstart, startup, adventurist, pirate lad's nasal bravado in the male vocal cords. Voices of girls and women screeking to an excitable edge of brightness. In an excessively powerful country, grown women sound like girls without authority or experience. Male, female voices alike pitched fastforward commercial, one timbre, tempo, intonation.

Mirrors

Possible tones of the human voice, their own possible physical beauty—no recognition. The fish-eye lens bobbles faces back.

Bodies heavy with sad or enraged feminine or macho brooding mimic stand–up comics, celebrities; grimace, gesticulate. The nakedest generation of young USonians with little intuition of the human history of nakedness, luminous inventions of skin and musculature. Their surfaces needlepointed with conventionally outrageous emblems, what mirror to render justly their original beauty back to them?

You touched me in places so deep I wanted to ignore you.

Artworks (I)

Painting on a gallery wall: people dwelling on opposite sides of a pane of glass. None of their eyes exchanging looks. Yellow flashes off the rug in the room and from the orchard beyond Houses of people whose eyes do not meet.

White people doing and seeing no evil.

(Photograph of family reunion, eyes on the wide-lens camera unmeeting.) "In fact I've lived here all along."

That was them not us. We were at the time in the time of our displacement, being torn from a false integrity. We stared at the pictures in the gallery knowing they were not us, we were being driven further for something else and who knew how far and for how long and what we were to do.

Stranger

Isolation begins to form, moves in like fog on a clear afternoon. Arrives with the mail, leaves its messages on the phone machine. If you hadn't undergone this so often it could take you by surprise, but its rime-white structure is the simple blueprint of your displacement. You: who pride yourself on not giving in, keep discovering in dreams new rooms in an old house, drawing new plans: living with strangers, enough for all, wild tomato plants along the road, redness for hunger and thirst. (Unrest, too, in the house of dreams: the underworld lashing back.)

But this fog blanks echoes, blots reciprocal sounds. The padded cell of a moribund democracy, or just your individual case?

Artworks (II)

Early summer lunch with friends, talk rises: poetry, urban design and planning, film. Strands of interest and affection binding us differently around the table. If an uneasy political theme rears up—the meaning of a show of lynching photographs in New York, after Mapplethorpe's photos, of sociopathic evil inside the California prison industry—talk fades. Not a pause but: a suppression. No one is monitoring this conversation but us. We know the air is bad in here, maybe want not to push that knowledge, ask *what is to be done?* How to breathe? *What will suffice?* Draft new structures or simply be aware? If art is our only resistance, what does that make us? If we're collaborators, what's our offering to corruption—an aesthetic, anaesthetic, dye of silence, withdrawal, intellectual disgust?

This fade-out/suspension of conversation: a syndrome of the past decades? our companionate immune systems under siege, viral spread of social impotence producing social silence?

Imagine written language that walks away from human conversation. A written literature, back turned to oral traditions, estranged from music and body. So what might reanimate, rearticulate, becomes less and less available.

Incline

Dreamroad rising steeply uphill; David is driving. I see it turning into a perpendicular structure salvaged from a long metal billboard: we will have to traverse this at a ninety-degree angle, then at the top go over and down the other side. There are no exits. Around is the Mojave Desert: open space. D.'s car begins to lose momentum as the incline increases; he tries shifting into a lower gear and gunning the engine. There is no way off this incline now, we're forced into a situation we hadn't reckoned on—a road now become something that is no road, something designated as "commercial space." I suggest rolling (ourselves in) the car down the steep dusty shoulder into the desert below, and out. For both of us, the desert isn't vacancy or fear, its life, a million forms of witness. The fake road, its cruel deception, is what we have to abandon.

Mission Statement

The Organization for the Abolition of Cruelty has an air deployment with bases on every continent and on obscurer tracts of land. Airstrips and hangars have been constructed to accommodate large and small aircraft for reconnoiter and rescue missions whether on polar ice or in desert or rainforest conditions. Many types of craft are of course deployed to urban clusters. The mission of the Organization is not to the First, Third, or any other World. It is directed toward the investigation and abrogation of cruelty in every direction, including present and future extraterrestrial locations.

It is obvious that the destruction of despair is still our most urgent task. In this regard, we employ paramilitary methods with great care and watchfulness.

The personnel dedicated to this new program are responsible to the mission, not to any national body. We are apprised of all new technologies as soon as available. Hence we have a unique fusion of policy and technology, unique in that its purpose is the abolition of cruelty.

Ours is the first project of its kind to be fully empowered through the new paranational charters. In principle, it is now recognized that both agents and objects of cruelty must be rescued and transformed, and that they sometimes merge into each other.

<u>In response to your inquiry:</u> this is a complex operation. We have a wide range of specializations and concerns. Some are especially calibrated toward language

> *because of its known and unknown powers*
> > *to bind and to dissociate*
>
> *because of its capacity*
> > *to ostracize the speechless*
>
> *because of its capacity*
> > *to nourish self-deception*
>
> *because of its capacity*
> > *for rebirth and subversion*
>
> *because of the history*
> > *of torture*
> > > *against human speech*

2000–2002

Transparencies

That the meek word like the righteous word can bully
that an Israeli soldier interviewed years
after the first Intifada could mourn on camera
what under orders he did, saw done, did not refuse
that another leaving Beit Jala could scrawl
on a wall: *We are truely sorry for the mess we made*
is merely routine   word that would cancel deed
That human equals innocent and guilty
That we grasp for innocence whether or no
is elementary   That words can translate into broken bones
That the power to hurl words is a weapon
That the body can be a weapon
any child on playground knows   That asked your favorite word
                                        in a game
you always named a thing, a quality, *freedom* or *river*
(never a pronoun never *God* or *War*)
is taken for granted   That word and body
are all we have to lay on the line
That words are windowpanes in a ransacked hut, smeared
by time's dirty rains, we might argue
likewise that words are clear as glass till the sun strikes it blinding

But that in a dark windowpane you have seen your face
That when you wipe your glasses the text grows clearer
That the sound of crunching glass comes at the height of the
                                        wedding
That I can look through glass
into my neighbor's house
but not my neighbor's life
That glass is sometimes broken to save lives

That a word can be crushed like a goblet underfoot
is only what it seems, part question, part answer: how
you live it

2002

Ritual Acts

i

We are asking for books
No, not—but a list of books
to be given to young people
Well, to young poets
to guide them in their work
He gestures impatiently
They won't read he says
My time is precious
If they want to they'll find
whatever they need
I'm going for a walk after lunch
After that I lie down
Then and only then do I read the papers
Mornings are for work
the proofs of the second volume
—my trilogy, and he nods
And we too nod recognition

ii

The buses—packed
since the subways are forbidden
and the highways forsaken
so people bring everything on—
what they can't do without—
Air conditioners, sculpture
Double baskets of babies
Fruit platters, crematory urns
Sacks of laundry, of books
Inflated hearts, bass fiddles

Bridal gowns in plastic bags
Pet iguanas, oxygen tanks
The tablets of Moses

iii

After all—to have loved, wasn't that the object?
Love is the only thing in life
but then you can love too much
or the wrong way, you lose
yourself or you lose
the person
or you strangle each other
Maybe the object of love is
   to have loved
   greatly
   at one time or another
Like a cinema trailer
watched long ago

iv

You need to turn yourself around
face in another direction
She wrapped herself in a flag
soaked it in gasoline and lit a match
This is for the murdered babies
they say she said
Others heard
for the honor of my country
Others remember
the smell and how she screamed
Others say, This was just theater

v

This will not be a love scene
but an act between two humans
Now please let us see you
tenderly scoop his balls
into your hand
You will hold them
under your face
There will be tears on your face
That will be all
the director said
We will not see his face
He wants to do the scene
but not to show
his face

vi

A goat devouring a flowering plant
A child squeezing through a fence to school
A woman slicing an onion
A bare foot sticking out
A wash line tied to a torn–up tree
A dog's leg lifted at a standpipe
An old man kneeling to drink there
A hand on the remote

We would like to show but to not be obvious
except to the oblivious
We want to show ordinary life
We are dying to show it

2003

Alternating Current

Sometimes I'm back in that city
in its/   not my/   autumn
                    crossing a white bridge
over a dun-green river
eating shellfish with young poets
under the wrought-iron roof of the great market
drinking with the dead poet's friend
                    to music struck
from odd small instruments

walking arm in arm with the cinematographer
through the whitelight gardens of Villa Grimaldi
earth and air stretched
to splitting still
                    his question:
have you ever been in a place like this?

———•———

No bad dreams.   Night, the bed, the faint clockface.
No bad dreams.   Her arm or leg or hair.
No bad dreams.   A wheelchair unit screaming
off the block.   No bad dreams.   Pouches of blood: red cells,
plasma.   Not here.   No, none.   Not yet.

———•———

Take one, take two
—camera out of focus   delirium swims
across the lens   Don't get me wrong   I'm not
critiquing your direction
but I was there   saw what you didn't

take   the care
you didn't   first of yourself then
of the child   Don't get me wrong I'm on
your side but standing off
where it rains   not on the set where it's
not raining yet
take three

———•———

What's suffered in laughter   in aroused afternoons
in nightly yearlong back-to-back
wandering each others' nerves and pulses
O changing love that doesn't change

———•———

A deluxe blending machine
A chair with truth's coat of arms
A murderous code of manners
A silver cocktail reflecting a tiny severed hand
A small bird stuffed with print and roasted
A row of Lucite chessmen filled with shaving lotion
A bloodred valentine to power
A watered-silk innocence
A microwaved foie gras
A dry-ice carrier for conscience donations
A used set of satin sheets folded to go
A box at the opera of suffering
A fellowship at the villa, all expenses
A Caterpillar's tracks gashing the environment
A bad day for students of the environment
A breakdown of the blending machine
A rush to put it in order
A song in the chapel a speech a press release

———•———

As finally by wind or grass
   drive-ins
         where romance always was
  an after-dark phenomenon
                  lie crazed and still
   great panoramas lost to air
     this time this site of power shall pass
         and we remain or not but not remain
    as now we think we are

———•———

for J.J.

              When we are shaken out

when we are shaken out to the last vestige
when history is done with us
   when our late grains glitter
                salt swept into shadow
   indignant and importunate strife-fractured crystals
will it matter if our tenderness (our solidarity)
             abides in residue
  long as there's tenderness and solidarity

Could the tempos and attunements of my voice
  in a poem or yours   or yours and mine
in telephonic high hilarity
              cresting above some stupefied inanity
   be more than personal

(and—as you once said—what's wrong with that?)

2 0 0 2 – 2 0 0 3

Dislocations: Seven Scenarios

1

Still learning the word
"home"   or what it could mean
                              say, to relinquish

   a backdrop of Japanese maples turning
   color of rusted wheelbarrow bottom
   where the dahlia tubers were thrown

You must go live in the city now
over the subway though not on
                              its grating

must endure the foreign music
of the block party

finger in useless anger
the dangling cords of the window blind

2

In a vast dystopic space the small things
multiply

when all the pills run out the pain
grows more general

flies find the many eyes
quarrels thicken then
                    weaken

tiny mandibles of rumor open and close
blame has a name that will not be spoken

you grasp or share a clot of food
according to your nature
                    or your strength

love's ferocity snarls
from under the drenched blanket's hood

3

City and world: this infection drinks like a drinker
whatever it can

casual salutations first
little rivulets of thought

then wanting stronger stuff
sucks at the marrow of selves

the nurse's long knowledge of wounds
the rabbi's scroll of ethics
the young worker's defiance

only the solipsist seems intact
in her prewar building

4

For recalcitrancy of attitude
the surgeon is transferred
to the V.A. hospital   where poverty
is the administrator
of necessity and her
orders don't necessarily
get obeyed
because
the government
is paying
and the
used-to-be
warriors
are patients

5

Faces in the mesh: defiance or disdain
        remember Paul Nizan?
            You thought you were innocent if you said

"I love this woman and I want to live
        in accordance with my love"
            but you were beginning the revolution

maybe so, maybe not
        look at her now
            pale lips papery flesh

at your creased belly   wrinkled sac
        look at the scars
            reality's autographs

along your ribs across her haunches
look at the collarbone's reverberant line

    how in a body can defiance
       still embrace its likeness

6

Not to get up and go back to the drafting table
where failure crouches accusing
like the math test you bluffed and flunked
so early on
not to drag into the window's
cruel and truthful light   your blunder
not to start over

but to turn your back, saying
all anyway is compromise
impotence and collusion
from here on I will be no part of it

is one way could you afford it

7

Tonight someone will sleep in a stripped apartment
the last domestic traces, cup and towel
awaiting final disposal

—has ironed his shirt for travel
left an envelope for the cleaning woman
on the counter under the iron

internationalist turning toward home
three continents to cross   documents declarations
searches queues

and home no simple matter
of hearth or harbor
bleeding from internal wounds

he diagnosed   physician
without frontiers

2002

Wait

In paradise every
the desert wind is rising
third thought
in hell there are no thoughts
is of earth
sand screams against your government
issued tent   hell's noise
in your nostrils   crawl
into your ear-shell
wrap yourself in no-thought
wait   no place for the little lyric
wedding-ring glint the reason why
on earth
they never told you

2003

Screen Door

Metallic slam on a moonless night
A short visit and so we departed.
A short year with many long
                                 days
A long phone call with many   pauses.
                          It was gesture's code
we were used to using, we were
                                   awkward without it.

Over the phone: knocking heard
at a door in another country.
Here it's tonight: there tomorrow.
A vast world we used to think small.
That we knew everyone who mattered.

Firefly flicker.   Metallic slam.   A moonless night.   Too dark
                              for gesture.
But it was gesture's code we were used to.
                           Might need again.   Urgent
                         hold-off or beckon.

Fierce supplication. One finger pointing: "Thither."
Palms flung upward: "What now?"
Hand slicing the air or across the throat.
A long wave to the departing.

2003

Tendril

1

Why does the outstretched finger of home
probe the dark hotel room like a flashlight beam

on the traveller, half-packed, sitting on the bed
face in hands, wishing her bag emptied again at home

Why does the young security guard
pray to keep standing watch forever, never to fly

Why does he wish he were boarding
as the passengers file past him into the plane

What are they carrying in their bundles
what vanities, superstitions, little talismans

What have the authorities intercepted
who will get to keep it

2

Half-asleep in the dimmed cabin
she configures a gecko

aslant the overhead bin   tendrils of vine
curling up through the cabin floor

buried here in night as in a valley
remote from rescue

Unfound, confounded, vain, superstitious, whatever we were
before
now we are still, outstretched, curled, however we were

Unwatched the gecko, the inching of green
through the cracks in the fused imperious shell

3

Dreaming a womb's languor valleyed in death
among fellow strangers

she has merely slept through the night
a nose nearby rasps, everyone in fact is breathing

the gecko has dashed into some crevice
of her brain, the tendrils retract

orange juice is passed on trays
declarations filled out in the sudden dawn

4

She can't go on dreaming of mass death
this was not to have been her métier

she says to the mirror in the toilet
a bad light any way you judge yourself

and she's judge, prosecutor, witness, perpetrator
of her time

's conspiracies of the ignorant
with the ruthless   She's the one she's looking at

5

This confessional reeks of sweet antiseptic
and besides she's not confessing

her mind balks   craving wild onions
nostril-chill of eucalyptus

that seventh sense of what's missing
against what's supplied

She walks at thirty thousand feet into the cabin
sunrise crashing through the windows

Cut the harping she tells herself
You're human, porous like all the rest

6

She was to have sat in a vaulted
library   heavy scrolls wheeled to a desk

for sieving, sifting, translating
all morning   then a quick lunch   thick coffee

then light descending slowly
on earthen-colored texts

but that's a dream of dust
frail are thy tents   humanity

facing thy monologues of force
She must have fallen asleep reading

7

She must have fallen asleep reading
The woman who mopped the tiles

is deliquescent   a scarlet gel
her ligaments and lungs

her wrought brain   her belly's pulse
disrupt among others mangled there

the chief librarian the beggar
the man with the list of questions

the scrolls never to be translated
and the man who wheeled the scrolls

8

She had wanted to find meaning in the past but the future drove
a vagrant tank a rogue bulldozer

rearranging the past in a blip
coherence smashed into vestige

not for her even the thought
of her children's children picking up

one shard of tile then another laying
blue against green seeing words

in three scripts flowing through vines and flowers
guessing at what it was

the levantine debris
Not for her but still for someone?

2003

Telephone Ringing
in the Labyrinth

Voyage to the Denouement

A child's hand smears a wall   the reproof is bitter
    wall contrives to linger   child, punisher, gone in smoke
An artisan lays on hues: lemon, saffron, gold
    stare hard before you start covering the whole room
Inside the thigh a sweet mole   on the balding
    skull an irregular island   what comes next
After the burnt forests   silhouettes wade
    liquid hibiscus air
Velvet rubs down to scrim   iron utensils
    discolor unseasoned
Secret codes of skin and hair
    go dim   left from the light too long

Because my wish was to have things simpler
    than they were   memory too became
a smudge   sediment from a hand
    repeatedly lying on the same surface
Call it a willful optimism
    from when old ownerships unpeeled   curled out
into the still nameless   new imperium   Call it
    haplessness of a creature   not yet ready
for her world-citizen's papers
    (Across the schoolroom mural   bravely
small ships did under sail traverse great oceans)
    Rain rededicates the exhumed
African burial ground
    traffic lashes its edges
the city a scar a fragment floating
    on tidal dissolution
The opal on my finger
    fiercely flashed till the hour it started to crumble

2004

Calibrations

She tunes her guitar for Landstuhl
where she will sit on beds and sing
ballads from when Romany
roamed Spain

. . .

A prosthetic hand calibrates perfectly
the stem of a glass
or how to stroke a face
is this how far we have come
to make love easy

Ghost limbs go into spasm in the night
You come back from war with the body you have

. . .

What you can't bear
carry endure lift
you'll have to drag

it'll come with you the ghostlimb

the shadow   blind
echo of your body spectre of your soul

. . .

Let's not talk yet of making love
nor of ingenious devices
replacing touch

And this is not theoretical:
A poem with calipers to hold a heart
so it will want to go on beating

2004

Wallpaper

1

A room papered with clippings:
newsprint in bulging patches
none of them mentions our names
none from that history then   O red

kite snarled in a cloud
small plane melted in fog: no matter:
I worked to keep it current
and meaningful: a job of living I thought

history as wallpaper
urgently selected clipped and pasted
but the room itself   nowhere

gone the address   the house
golden-oak banisters zigzagging
upward, stained glass on the landings
streaked porcelain in the bathrooms

loose floorboards quitting in haste we pried
up to secrete the rash imagination
of a time to come

What we said then, our breath   remains
otherwhere: in me   in you

2

Sonata for Unaccompanied Minor
Fugitive Variations
discs we played over and over

on the one-armed phonograph
Childish we were in our adoration
of the dead composer

who'd ignored the weather signs
trying to cross the Andes
stupidly   I'd say now

and you'd agree   seasoned
as we are   working stretched
weeks   eating food bought

with ordinary grudging wages
keeping up with rent, utilities

a job of living as I said

3

Clocks are set back   quick dark
snow filters past my lashes
this is the common ground

white-crusted sidewalks   windshield wipers
licking, creaking
to and *fro   to* and *fro*

If the word gets out if the word
escapes if the word
flies if it dies
it has its way of coming back

The handwritings on the walls
are vast and coded

the music blizzards past

2004

In Plain Sight

My neighbor moving
in a doorframe   moment's
reach of her hand   then

withdrawn   As from some old
                    guilty pleasure

Smile etched like a scar
which must be borne
                    Smile
in a photograph taken against one's will

Her son up on a ladder stringing
along the gutter
electric icicles in a temperate zone

If the suffering hidden in plain sight
is of her past her future
or the thin-ice present where
we're balancing here
                    or how she sees it
I can't presume

. . . Ice-thin.   Cold and precarious
the land I live in and have argued not to leave
Cold on the verge of crease
                    crack without notice

ice-green disjuncture   treasoning us
to flounder cursing each other
Cold and grotesque the sex
the grimaces the grab

A privilege   you say
to live here   *A luxury*
Everyone still wants to come here!
You want a christmas card, a greeting
to tide us over
with pictures of the children

then you demand a valentine
an easterlily   anything for the grab
a mothersday menu   wedding invitation

It's not as in a museum that I
observe
and mark in every Face I meet

            under crazed surfaces
traces of feeling   locked in shadow

Not as in a museum of history
do I pace here   nor as one who in a show
of bland paintings shrugs and walks on   I gaze
through faces   not as an X-ray
                              nor

as paparazzo shooting
the compromised celebrity

nor archaeologist filming
the looted site
nor as the lover tearing out of its frame
the snapshot to be held to a flame

but as if a mirror
forced to reflect a room
                              the figures

standing   the figures crouching

2004

Behind the Motel

A man lies under a car half bare
a child plays bullfight with a torn cloth
hemlocks grieve in wraps of mist
a woman talks on the phone, looks in a mirror
fiddling with the metal pull of a drawer

She has seen her world wiped clean, the cloth
that wiped it disintegrate in mist
or dying breath on the skin of a mirror
She has felt her life close like a drawer
has awoken somewhere else, bare

He feels his skin as if it were mist
as if his face would show in no mirror
He needs some bolts he left in a vanished drawer
crawls out into the hemlocked world with his bare
hands, wipes his wrench on an oil-soaked cloth

stares at the woman talking into a mirror
who has shut the phone into the drawer
while over and over with a torn cloth
at the edge of hemlocks behind the bare
motel a child taunts a horned beast made from mist

2004

Archaic

Cold wit leaves me cold
this time of the world   Multifoliate disorders
straiten my gait   Minuets don't become me
Been wanting to get out   see the sights
but the exits are slick with people
going somewhere fast
every one with a shared past
and a mot juste   And me so out of step
with my late-night staircase inspirations   my
utopian slant

Still, I'm alive here
in this village drawn in a tightening noose
of ramps and cloverleafs
but the old directions I drew up
for you
are obsolete

Here's how
to get to me
I wrote
Don't misconstrue the distance
take along something for the road
everything might be closed
this isn't a modern place

You arrived starving at midnight
I gave you warmed-up food
poured tumblers of brandy
put on Les Barricades Mystérieuses
—the only jazz in the house

We talked for hours   of barricades
lesser and greater sorrows
ended up laughing in the thicksilver
birdstruck light

2005

Long After Stevens

A locomotive pushing through snow in the mountains
more modern than the will

to be modern   The mountain's profile
in undefiled snow disdains

definitions of poetry   It was always
indefinite, task and destruction

the laser eye of the poet   her blind eye
her moment-stricken eye   her unblinking eye

She had to get down from the blocked train
lick snow from bare cupped hands

taste what had soared into that air
—local cinders, steam of the fast machine

clear her palate with a breath   distinguish
through tumbling whiteness   figures

frozen   figures advancing
weapons at the ready
for the new password

She had to feel her tongue
freeze and burn at once

instrument searching, probing
toward a foreign tongue

2005

Rhyme

Walking by the fence but the house
    not there

going to the river but the
    river looking spare

bones of the river spread out
    everywhere

O tell me this is home

Crossing the bridge but
    some planks not there

looking at the shore but only
    getting back the glare

dare you trust the river when there's
    no water there

O tell me is this home

Getting into town seeing
    nobody I know

folks standing around
    nowhere to go

staring into the air like
    they saw a show

O tell me was this my home

Come to the railroad no train
    on the tracks

switchman in his shanty
    with a great big axe

so what happened here so what
    are the facts

So tell me where is my home

2005

Hubble Photographs: After Sappho

It should be the most desired sight of all
the person with whom you hope to live and die

walking into a room, turning to look at you, sight for sight
Should be yet I say there is something

more desirable: the ex-stasis of galaxies
so out from us there's no vocabulary

but mathematics and optics
equations letting sight pierce through time

into liberations, lacerations of light and dust
exposed like a body's cavity, violet green livid and venous,
    gorgeous

beyond good and evil as ever stained into dream
beyond remorse, disillusion, fear of death

or life, rage
for order, rage for destruction

—beyond this love which stirs
the air every time she walks into the room

These impersonae, however we call them
won't invade us as on movie screens

they are so old, so new, we are not to them
we look at them or don't from within the milky gauze

of our tilted gazing
but they don't look back and we cannot hurt them

for Jack Litewka

2005

This Is Not the Room

of polished tables lit with medalled
torsos bent toward microphones
where ears lean hands scribble
"working the dark side"

—glazed eye meeting frozen eye—

This is not the room where tears down carven
cheeks track rivulets in the scars
left by the gouging tool
where wood itself is weeping

where the ancient painted eye speaks to the living eye

This is the room
where truth scrubs around the pedestal of the toilet
flings her rag into the bucket
straightens up   spits at the mirror

2005

Unknown Quantity

Spring nights you pillow your head on a sack
of rich compost   Charcoal, your hair

sheds sparks through your muttered dreams
Deep is your sleep in the starless dark

and you wake in your live skin to show me
a tulip   Not the prizewinning Queen of the Night

furled in her jade wrappings
but the Prince of Darkness, the not-yet, the X

crouched in his pale bulb
held out in the palm of your hand

Shall we bury him wait and see what happens
will there be time for waiting and to see

2005

Tactile Value

from crush and splinter
death in the market

jeering robotic
dry-ice disrupt

to conjure this:
perishing
persistent script

scratched-up smeared
and torn

> *let hair, nail cuttings*
> *nourish the vine and fig tree*

> *let man, woman*
> *eat, be sheltered*

. . .

Marx the physician laid his ear
on the arhythmic heart

felt the belly
diagnosed the pain

did not precisely write
of lips roaming damp skin

hand plunged in hair   bed-laughter
mouth clasping mouth

   (what we light with this coalspark
   living instantly in us
   if it continue

2005–2006

Director's Notes

You don't want a harsh outcry here
not to violate the beauty yet
dawn unveiling ochre village
but to show coercion
within that beauty, endurance required
Begin with girl
pulling hand over hand on chain
only sound drag and creak
in time it becomes monotonous

then must begin sense of unease produced by monotony
repetitive motion, repetitive sound
resistance, irritation
increasing for the viewers
sense of what are they here for, anyway
dislike of the whole thing how boring to watch

(they aren't used to duration
this was a test)

Keep that dislike that boredom as a value
also as risk
so when bucket finally tinks at rim
they breathe a sigh, not so much relief
as finally grasping
what all this was for

dissolve as she dips from bucket

2005

Rereading *The Dead Lecturer*

Overthrow.   And make new.

An idea.   And we felt it.
A meaning.   And we caught it
as the dimensions spread, gathering
in pre-utopian basements   figured shadows
scrawled with smoke and music.
                                        Shed the dead hand,
let sound be sense.   A world
echoing everywhere, Fanon, Freire, thin pamphlets lining
raincoat pockets, poetry on walls, damp purple mimeos cranking
—the feeling of an idea.   An idea of feeling.

That love could be so resolute

And the past?   Overthrow of systems, forms
could not overthrow the past
                                nor our
                                        neglect of consequences.
Nor that cold will we misnamed.

There were consequences.   A world
repeating everywhere: the obliterations.
What's surreal, hyperreal, virtual,
what's poetry what's verse what's new.   What is
a political art.   If we
(who?) ever were conned
into mere definitions.

                    If we
              accept

(book of a soul contending

2005

Letters Censored
Shredded
Returned to Sender
or Judged Unfit to Send

Unless in quotation marks (for which see Notes on the Poems), the letter fragments are written by various imaginary persons.

"We must prevent this mind from functioning . . .": words of the prosecutor sentencing Antonio Gramsci to prison, June 2, 1928.

—Could you see me laboring over this
right arm in sling, typing left-handed with one finger—

{*On a scale of one to ten what is your pain today*}

. . .

—shall I measure the split atoms
of pleasure flying outward from the core—

. . .

—To think of her naked every day unfreezes me—

. . .

Banditry, rapes, burning the woods
"a kind of primitive class struggle
with no lasting or effective results"

—The bakers strike, the needleworkers strike, the mechanics strike,
the miners strike

the great machine coughs out the pieces and hurtles on—

. . .

—then there are days all thought comes down to sound:
Rust.   August.   Mattress.   Must.
Chains . . .

—when consciousness + sensation feels like/ = suffering—

. . .

—the people, yes, as yet unformed—deformed—no: disinformed—

. . .

—What's realistic fantasy?—Call it hope—

. . .

—heard your voice on the news tonight, its minor key
your old-fashioned mindfulness—could have loved you again—

. . .

—Autumn invades my body, anger
wrapped in forgiving sunlight, fear of the cold—

. . .

—Words gather like flies above this carcass of meaning—

. . .

"this void, this vacuum"

. . .

—You think you are helpless because you are empty-handed
of concepts that could become your strength—

. . .

—we're told it's almost over, but we see no sign of it yet—

. . .

"caught between a feeling of immense tenderness for you
which seems . . . a weakness
that could only be consoled
by an immediate physical caress . . ."

[*We must prevent this mind from functioning for twenty years*]

" . . . and these inadequate, cold and colorless words"

. . .

—What I meant to write, belov'd critic, then struck it out
thinking you might accuse me of
whatever you would:
I wanted a sensual materialism to utter pleasure

Something beyond a cry that could sound like a groan—

. . .

—Vocalizing forbidden syllables—

. . .

—our mythologies choke us, we have enthralled ourselves—

. . .

       [Writing like this for the censors
       but I won't hide behind words]

. . .

"my body cells revolve in unison
with the whole universe

    The cycle of the seasons, the progression of the solstices
    and equinoxes
    I feel them as flesh of my flesh
    and under the snow the first violets are already trembling
        In short, time has seemed to me a thing of flesh
        ever since space
        ceased to exist for me"

. . .

—History = bodies in time—

or, in your language:

$$H = \frac{T}{b}$$

. . .

—to think of the one asleep
in that field beside the chimney
of the burnt-out house
a thing of flesh, exhausted—

. . .

—this flash is all we know . . . . can we shut our eyes to it . . . ?—

. . .

—more and more I dread futility—

. . .

"The struggle, whose normal external expressions
have been choked,
attaches itself to the structure
of the old class like a destructive gangrene . . .
it takes on morbid forms of mysticism,
sensualism, moral indifference,
physical and psychic pathological depravations . . .
The old structure does not contain and is unable
to satisfy the new needs . . ."

. . .

—Trying to hold an inner focus while hoarse laughter
ricochets from the guardroom—

. . .

—*liquefaction* is a word I might use for how I would take you—

. . .

—the daunted river finally
undammed?—

       [*prevent this mind*]

2005

The University Reopens as the Floods Recede

Should blue air in its purity let you disdain
the stink of artificial pine

the gaunt architecture
of cheap political solutions

if there are philosophies to argue
the moment when you would

or wouldn't spring to shield
a friend's body or jump

into scummed waters after
a stranger caught submerging

or walk off to your parked
car your sandwich your possible orange

if theories rage or dance
about this if in the event   any

can be sure who did
or did not act on principle or impulse

and what's most virtuous

can we not be nodding smiling
taking down notes like this

and of all places
in a place like this

I'll work with you on this bad matter   I can
but won't give you the time of day

if you think it's hypothetical

2006

Draft #2006

i

Suppose we came back as ghosts asking the unasked questions.

(What were you there for? Why did you walk out? What would have made you stay? Why wouldn't you listen?)

—Couldn't you show us what you meant, can't we get it right this time? Can't you put it another way?—

(You were looking for openings where they'd been walled up—)

—But you were supposed to be our teacher—

(One-armed, I was trying to get you, one by one, out of that cellar.   It wasn't enough)

ii

Dreamfaces blurring horrorlands: border of poetry.

Ebb tide sucks out clinging rockpool creatures, no swimming back into sleep.

Clockface says too early, body prideful and humble shambles into another day, reclaiming itself piecemeal in private ritual acts.

Reassembling the anagram scattered nightly, rebuilding daily the sand city.

iii

What's concrete for me: from there I cast out further.

But need to be there. On the stone causeway. Baffled and obstinate.

Eyes probing the dusk. Foot-slippage possible.

iv

Sleeping that time at the philosopher's house.   Not lovers, friends from the past.

Music the vertex of our triangle.   Bach our hypotenuse strung between philosophy and poetry.

Sun loosening fog on the hillside, cantata spun on the turntable: *Wie schön leuchtet der Morgenstern.*

Feeling again, in our mid-forties, the old contrapuntal tension between our natures.   The future as if still open, like when we were classmates.

He'd met Heidegger in the Black Forest, corresponded with Foucault.   We talked about Wittgenstein.

I was on my way to meet the one who said *Philosophers have interpreted the world: the point is to change it.*

v

On a street known for beautiful shops she buys a piece of antique Japanese silk, a white porcelain egg.

Had abandoned her child, later went after him, found the
child had run away.

Hurt and angry, joined a group to chant through the pain.
They said, you must love yourself, give yourself gifts.

Whatever eases you someone says, lets you forgive yourself,
let go.

America, someone says.

Orphaning, orphaned here, don't even know it.

vi

Silent limousines meet jets descending over the Rockies.
Steam rooms, pure thick towels, vases of tuberose and jas-
mine, old vintages await the après-skiers.

Rooms of mahogany and leather, conversations open in
international code.   Thighs and buttocks to open later by
arrangement.

Out of sight, out of mind, she solitary wrestles a huge
duvet, resheathes heavy tasselled bolsters.   Bed after bed.
Nights, in her room, ices strained arms.   Rests her legs.

Elsewhere, in Andhra Pradesh, another farmer swallows
pesticide.

vii

Condemned, a clinic coughs up its detritus.

Emergency exit, gurneys lined double, mercy draining
down exhausted tubes.

Drills and cranes clearing way for the new premises.

As if I already stood at their unglazed windows, eyeing the distressed site through skeletal angles.

Tenant already of the disensoulment projects.

Had thought I deserved nothing better than these stark towers named for conglomerates?—a line of credit, a give-away?

viii

They asked me, is this time worse than another.

I said, for whom?

Wanted to show them something.   While I wrote on the chalkboard they drifted out. I turned back to an empty room.

Maybe I couldn't write fast enough. Maybe it was too soon.

ix

The sheer mass of the thing, its thereness, stuns thought. Since it exists, it must have existed.   Will exist.   It says so here.

Excruciating contempt for love.   For the strained fibre of common affections, mutual assistance

sifted up from landfill, closed tunnels, drought-sheared riverbeds, street beds named in old census books, choked under the expressway.

Teachers bricolating scattered schools of trust.   Rootlets
watered by fugitives.

Contraband packets, hummed messages.   Dreams of the
descendants, surfacing.

Hand reaching for its like exposes a scarred wrist.
Numerals.   A bracelet of rust.

In a desert observatory, under plaster dust, smashed lenses
left by the bombardments,

star maps crackle, unscrolling.

2006

Telephone Ringing in the Labyrinth

i

You who can be silent in twelve languages
trying to crease again in paling light
the map you unfurled that morning   if

you in your rearview mirror sighted me
rinsing a green glass bowl
by midsummer nightsun in, say, Reykjavík

if at that moment my hand slipped
and that bowl cracked to pieces
and one piece stared at me like a gibbous moon

if its convex reflection caught you walking
the slurried highway shoulder after the car broke down
if such refractions matter

ii

Well, I've held on   peninsula
to continent, climber
to rockface

Sensual peninsula attached so   stroked
by the tides' pensive and moody hands
Scaler into thin air

seen from below as weed or lichen
improvidently fastened
a mat of hair webbed in a bush

A bush ignited   then
consumed
Violent lithography

smolder's legacy on a boulder traced

iii

Image erupts from image
atlas from vagrancy
articulation from mammal howl

strangeness from repetition
even this   default location
surveyed again   one more poem

one more Troy or Tyre or burning tire
seared eyeball genitals
charred cradle

but a different turn   working
this passage of the labyrinth
as laboratory

I'd have entered, searched before
but that ball of thread   that clew
offering an exit choice was no gift at all

iv

I found you by design or
was it your design
or: we were drawn, we drew

Midway in this delicate
negotiation   telephone rings
(Don't stop! . . . they'll call again . . .)

Offstage the fabulous creature scrapes and shuffles
we breathe its heavy dander
I don't care how, if it dies   this is not the myth

No ex/interior: compressed
between my throat
and yours, hilarious oxygen

And, for the record, each did sign
our true names on the register
at the mouth of this hotel

v

I would have wanted to say it
without falling back
on words   Desired not

you so much as your life,
your prevailing   Not for me
but for furtherance   how

you would move
on the horizon   You, the person, you
the particle   fierce and furthering

2006

Tonight No Poetry
Will Serve

Waiting for Rain, for Music

Burn me some music   *Send my roots rain*   I'm swept
dry from inside   Hard winds rack my core

A struggle at the roots of the mind   Whoever said
it would go on and on like this

Straphanger swaying inside a runaway car
palming a notebook scribbled in

contraband calligraphy   against the war
poetry wages against itself

. . .

Once under a shed's eaves
thunder drumming membrane of afternoon
electric scissors slitting the air

thick drops spattering few and far
we could smell it then a long way off

But where's the rain coming to soak this soil

. . .

Burn me some music   There's a tune
"Neglect of Sorrow"
I've heard it hummed or strummed
my whole life long
in many a corridor

waiting for tomorrow
long after tomorrow
should've come

on many an ear it should have fallen
but the bands were playing so loud

2007

Reading the *Iliad* (As If) for the First Time

Lurid, garish, gash
rended creature struggles to rise, to
    run with dripping belly
Blood making everything more real
    pounds in the spearthruster's arm as in
the gunman's neck the offhand
moment—Now!—before he
    takes the bastards out

. . .

Splendor in black and ochre on a grecian urn
    Beauty as truth
The sea as background
    stricken with black long-oared ships
on shore chariots shields greaved muscled legs
    horses rearing   Beauty!   flesh before gangrene

. . .

Mind-shifting gods rush back and forth   Delusion
a daughter seized by the hair   swung out to bewilder men
Everything here is conflictual and is called man's fate

. . .

Ugly glory: open-eyed wounds
feed enormous flies
Hoofs slicken on bloodglaze

Horses turn away their heads
weeping equine tears
                        Beauty?
a wall with names of the fallen
from both sides   passionate objectivity

2009

Tonight No Poetry Will Serve

Saw you walking barefoot
taking a long look
at the new moon's eyelid

later spread
sleep-fallen, naked in your dark hair
asleep but not oblivious
of the unslept unsleeping
elsewhere

Tonight I think
no poetry
will serve

Syntax of rendition:

verb pilots the plane
adverb modifies action

verb force-feeds noun
submerges the subject
noun is choking
verb   disgraced   goes on doing

now diagram the sentence

2007

Scenes of Negotiation

Z: I hated that job but   You'd have taken it too if you'd had a family

Y: Pretty filthy and dangerous though wasn't it?

Z: Those years, one bad move, you were down on your knees begging for work

Zz: If you'd had a family! Who'd you think we were, just people standing around?

Yy: Filthy and dangerous like the streets I worked before you ever met me?

Zz: Those years you never looked at any of us. Staring into your own eyelids. Like you saw a light there. Can you see me now?

. . .

Hired guards shove metal barriers through plate glass, then prod the first line of protestors in through the fanged opening. Video and cellphone cameras devouring it all. Sucked in and blurted worldwide: "Peace" Rally Turns Violent

Protestors, a mixed bunch, end up in different holding cells where they won't see each other again

Being or doing: you're taken in for either, or both. Who you were born as, what or who you chose or became. Facing moral disorder head-on, some for the first time, on behalf of others. Delusion of inalienable rights. Others who've known the score all along

Some bailed-out go back to the scene. Some go home to sleep.
Others, it's months in solitary mouthing dialogues with nobody.
Imagining social presence. Fending off, getting ready for the
social absence called death

. . .

This isn't much more than a shed on two-by-fours over the water.
Uncaulked. Someone's romantic hideaway. We've been here awhile, like it
well enough. The tide retches over rocks below. Wind coming up now. We
liked it better when the others were still here. They went off in different
directions. Patrol boats gathered some in, we saw the lights and heard the
megaphones. Tomorrow I'll take the raggedy path up to the road, walk
into town, buy a stamp and mail this. Town is a mini-mart, church,
oyster-bar-dance-hall, fishing access, roadside cabins. Weekenders, locals,
we can blend in. They couldn't so well. We were trying to stay with the
one thing most people agree on. They said there was no such one thing
without everything else, you couldn't make it so simple

Have books, tapes here, and this typewriter voice telling you what I'm
telling you in the language we used to share. Everyone still sends love

. . .

There are no illusions at this table, she said to me

Room up under the roof. Men and women, a resistance cell   ?
I thought. Reaching hungrily for trays of folded bread, rice with
lentils, brown jugs of water and pale beer. Joking across the table
along with alertness, a kind of close mutual attention. One or two
picking on small stringed instruments taken down from a wall

I by many decades the oldest person there. However I was there

Meal finished, dishes rinsed under a tap, we climbed down a
kind of stair-ladder to the floor below. There were camouflage-
patterned outfits packed in cartons; each person shook out and put
on a pair of pants and a shirt, still creased from the packing. They
wore them like work clothes. Packed underneath were weapons

Thick silverblack hair, eyes seriously alive, hue from some ancient
kiln. The rest of them are in profile; that face of hers I see full focus

One by one they went out through a dim doorway to meet
whoever they'd been expecting. I write it down from memory.
Couldn't find the house later   yet

—*No illusions at this table.*   Spoken from her time back into
mine.   I'm the dreaming ghost, guest, waitress, watcher, wanting
the words to be true.

Whatever the weapons may come to mean

2009

From Sickbed Shores

From shores of sickness: skin of the globe stretches and snakes
out and in   room sound of the universe bearing
undulant wavelengths to an exhausted ear

(sick body in a sick country: can it get well?

what is it anyway to exist as
matter   to
*   matter?)*

All, all is remote from here: yachts carelessly veering
tanker's beak plunging into the strut of the bridge
slicked encircling waters

wired wrists   jerked-back heads
gagged mouths   flooded lungs

All, all remote and near

Wavelengths—
whose?   mine, theirs, ours   even

yours who haven't yet put in a word?

.   .   .

So remoteness glazes sickened skin   affliction of distance   so

strangely, easily, clinging like webs spread overnight
by creatures vanished
before we caught them at work

So: to bear this state, this caul which could be hell's
airborne anaesthetic, exemption from feeling   or
hell's pure and required definition:
—surrender
to un-belonging, being-for-itself-alone, runged
behind white curtains in an emergency cubicle, taking care of its
    own
condition

. . .

All is matter, of course, matter-of-course   You could have taken
courses in matter all along attending instead of cutting the class
You knew the telephone had wires, you could see them overhead
where sparrows sat and chattered together
you alongside a window somewhere phone in hand
listening to tears thickening a throat in a city somewhere else
you muttering back your faulty formulae
ear tuned to mute vibrations from an occupied zone:
an old, enraged silence still listening for your voice
                                    Did you then holding
the phone tongue your own lips finger your naked shoulder as
if you could liquefy touch into sound through wires   to lips or
    shoulders   lick

down an entire body in familiar mystery   irregardless laws of
    matter?

Hopeless imagination of signals not to be
received

. . .

From the shores of sickness you lie out on listless
waters with no boundaries   floodplain without horizon
dun skies mirroring its opaque face and nothing not

a water moccasin or floating shoe or tree root to stir interest
Somewhere else being the name of whatever once said your name
and you answered   now the only where is here   this dull
   floodplain
this body sheathed in indifference   sweat no longer letting the
   fever out
but coating it in oil   You could offer any soul-tricking oarsman
whatever coin you're still palming but there's a divide
between the shores of sickness and the legendary, purifying
river of death   You will have this tale to tell, you will have to live
to tell
this tale

2008

Axel Avákar

Axel Avákar

Axel: backstory

Axel, in thunder

I was there, Axel

Axel, darkly seen, in a glass house

[Axel Avákar: fictive poet, counter-muse, brother]

Axel Avákar

The I you know isn't me, you said, truthtelling liar
My roots are not my chains
And I to you: Whose hands have grown
through mine?   Owl-voiced I cried then: Who?

But yours was the one, the only eye assumed

Did we turn each other into liars?
holding hands with each others' chains?

At last we unhook, dissolve, secrete into islands
—neither a tender place—
yours surf-wrung, kelp-strung
mine locked in black ice on a mute lake

I dug my firepit, built a windbreak,
spread a sheepskin, zoned my telescope lens
to the far ledge of the Milky Way
lay down to sleep out the cold

Daybreak's liquid dreambook:
lines of a long poem pouring down a page
Had I come so far, did I fend so well
only to read your name there, Axel Avákar?

Axel: backstory

Steam from a melting glacier

your profile hovering
there   Axel as if we'd lain prone at fifteen
on my attic bedroom floor   elbow to elbow reading
in Baltimorean August-
blotted air

Axel I'm back to you
brother of strewn books   of late
hours drinking poetry scooped in both hands

Dreamt you into existence, did I, boy-
comrade who would love
                    everything I loved

Without my eyelash glittering piercing
sidewise in your eye
where would you have begun, Axel   how
would the wheel-spoke have whirled
your mind?   What word
stirred in your mouth without my
nipples' fierce erection?   our
twixt-and-between

                    Between us   yet
my part belonged to me
                    and when we parted

I left no part behind   I knew
how to make poetry happen

Back to you Axel through the crackling heavy
salvaged telephone

Axel, in thunder

Axel, the air's beaten
    like a drumhead here where it seldom thunders

dolphin
            lightning
                        leaps

over the bay   surfers flee

   crouching to trucks

climbers hanging
   from pitons in their night hammocks
     off the granite face

wait out an unforetold storm

while somewhere in all weathers you're
   crawling exposed   not by choice   extremist
hell-bent searching your soul

   —O my terrified   my obdurate
my wanderer   keep the trail

I was there, Axel

Pain made her conservative.
Where the matches touched her flesh, she wears a scar.
           —*"The Blue Ghazals"*

Pain taught her the language
root of *radical*

she walked on knives to gain a voice
fished the lake of lost

messages gulping up
from far below and long ago

needed both arms to haul them in
one arm was tied behind her

the other worked to get it free
it hurt itself because

work hurts   I was there Axel
with her in that boat

working alongside

and my decision was
to be in no other way

a woman

Axel, darkly seen, in a glass house

1

And could it be I saw you
under a roof of glass
in trance

could it be   was passing
by and would translate

too late the strained flicker
of your pupils   your
inert gait   the dark

garb of your reflection
in that translucent place

could be I might have
saved you   still
could   or would   ?

2

Laid my ear to your letter trying to hear
Tongue on your words to taste you there
Couldn't   read what you
                           had never written there

Played your message over
                           feeling bad
Played your message over it was all I had
To tell me what and wherefore
                           this is what it said:

I'm tired of you asking me why
I'm tired of words like the chatter of birds

Give me a pass, let me just get by

3

Back to back our shadows
stalk each other Axel but

not only yours and mine   Thickly lies
the impasto

scrape down far enough you get
the early brushwork   emblems

intimate detail

and scratched lines underneath
—a pictograph

one figure leaning forward
to speak or listen

one figure   backed away
unspeakable

(If that one moved—)

    but the I you knew who made

you once can't save you

my blood won't even match yours

4

"The dead" we say   as if speaking
of "the people" who

gave up on making history
simply to get through

Something dense and null   groan
without echo   underground

and owl-voiced I cry Who
are these dead these people these

lovers who if ever did
listen no longer answer

: *We* :

5

Called in to the dead: *why didn't you write?*
What should I have asked you?

—what would have been the true
unlocking code

if all of them failed—
I've questioned the Book of Questions

studied gyres of steam
twisting from a hot cup
in a cold sunbeam

turned the cards over   lifted the spider's foot
from the mangled hexagon

netted the beaked eel from the river's mouth
asked   and let it go

2007–2008

Ballade of the Poverties

There's the poverty of the cockroach kingdom and the rusted
    toilet bowl
The poverty of to steal food for the first time
The poverty of to mouth a penis for a paycheck
The poverty of sweet charity ladling
Soup for the poor who must always be there for that
There's poverty of theory poverty of swollen belly shamed
Poverty of the diploma or ballot that goes nowhere
Princes of predation let me tell you
There are poverties and there are poverties

There's the poverty of cheap luggage bursted open at immigration
Poverty of the turned head averted eye
The poverty of bored sex of tormented sex
The poverty of the bounced check poverty of the dumpster dive
The poverty of the pawned horn of the smashed reading glasses
The poverty pushing the sheeted gurney the poverty cleaning up
    the puke
The poverty of the pavement artist the poverty passed out on
    pavement
Princes of finance you who have not lain there
There are poverties and there are poverties

There is the poverty of hand-to-mouth and door-to-door
And the poverty of stories patched up to sell there
There's the poverty of the child thumbing the Interstate
And the poverty of the bride enlisting for war
There is the poverty of stones fisted in pocket
And the poverty of the village bulldozed to rubble
There's the poverty of coming home not as you left it
And the poverty of how would you ever end it

Princes of weaponry who have not ever tasted war
There are poverties and there are poverties

There's the poverty of wages wired for the funeral you
Can't get to the poverty of bodies lying unburied
There's the poverty of labor offered silently on the curb
The poverty of the no-contact prison visit
There's the poverty of yard-sale scrapings spread
And rejected the poverty of eviction, wedding bed out on street
Prince let me tell you who will never learn through words
There are poverties and there are poverties

You who travel by private jet like a housefly
Buzzing with the other flies of plundered poverties
Princes and courtiers who will never learn through words
Here's a mirror you can look into: take it: it's yours.

for James and Arlene Scully

2009

Emergency Clinic

Caustic implacable
poem   unto and contra:

I do not soothe minor
injuries   I do
not offer   I require
                        close history
of the case   apprentice-
ship in past and fresh catastrophe

The skin too quickly scabbed
mutters for my debriding

For every bandaged wound
I'll scrape another   open

I won't smile
                    while wiping
your tears
            I do not give
simplehearted   love and nor
allow you simply love me

if you accept   regardless
this will be different

Iodine-dark
poem walking to and fro all night

un–gainly
unreconciled

unto and contra

2008

Confrontations

It's not new, this condition, just for awhile
        kept deep
in the cortex of things imagined

Now the imagination comes of age

I see ourselves, full-lipped, blood-flushed
in cold air, still conflicted, still
        embraced

boarding the uncharter'd bus of vanishment

backward glances over and done
afterimages
swirl and dissolve along a shoal of footprints

Simple ghouls flitter already among our leavings
fixing labels in their strange language
                                        But
        up to now we're not debris
(only to their fascinated eyes)

2009

Circum/Stances

A crime of nostalgia
—is it—to say

the "objective conditions"
seemed a favoring wind

and we younger then
                    —objective fact—

also a kind of subjectivity

Sails unwrapped to the breeze
no chart

• • •

Slowly repetitiously to prise
up the leaden lid where the forensic
evidence was sealed

cross-section of a slave ship
diagram of a humiliated
mind   high-resolution image
of a shredded lung

color slides of refugee camps

Elsewhere
            (in some calm room far from pain)
bedsprings   a trunk empty
but for a scorched
                    length of electrical cord

how these got here from where
what would have beheld

Migrant assemblage: in its aura
immense details writhe, uprise

. . .

To imagine what   Become
present thén

within the monster
nerveless and giggling

(our familiar   our kin)
who did the scutwork

To differentiate
the common hell
the coils inside the brain

. . .

Scratchy cassette ribbon
history's lamentation song:

> Gone, friend I tore at
> time after time
> in anger
>
> gone, love I could
> time upon time
> nor live nor leave

gone, city
of spies and squatters
tongues and genitals

All violence is not equal

(I write this
with a clawed hand

2008

Winterface

i. hers

Mute it utters ravage   guernican
mouth in bleak December

Busted-up lines of Poe:

   —each separate dying ember
   wreaks its ghost upon the floor

January moon-mouth
phosphorescence purged in dark to
swallow up the gone

Too soon

Dawn, twilight, wailing
newsprint, breakfast, trains

all must run their inter-
ruptured course

—So was the girl moving too fast   she was moving fast
across an icy web

Was ice a mirror   well the mirror was icy

And did she see herself in there

ii. his

Someone writes asking about your use
of Bayesian inference

in the history of slavery

What flares now from our burnt-up
furniture

You left your stricken briefcase here
no annotations

phantom frequencies stammer
trying to fathom

how it was inside alone where you were dying

2009

Quarto

1

Call me Sebastian, arrows sticking all over
The map of my battlefields.   Marathon.
Wounded Knee.   Vicksburg.   Jericho.
Battle of the Overpass.
Victories turned inside out
But no surrender

Cemeteries of remorse
The beaten champion sobbing
Ghosts move in to shield his tears

2

No one writes lyric on a battlefield
On a map stuck with arrows
But I think I can do it if I just lurk
In my tent pretending to
Refeather my arrows

I'll be right there! I yell
When they come with their crossbows and white phosphorus
To recruit me

Crouching over my drafts
Lest they find me out
And shoot me

3

Press your cheek against my medals, listen through them to my heart
Doctor, can you see me if I'm naked?

Spent longer in this place than in the war
No one comes but rarely and I don't know what for

Went to that desert as many did before
Farewell and believing and hope not to die

Hope not to die and what was the life
Did we think was awaiting after

Lay down your stethoscope back off on your skills
Doctor can you see me when I'm naked?

4

I'll tell you about the mermaid
Sheds swimmable tail   Gets legs for dancing
Sings like the sea with a choked throat
Knives straight up her spine
Lancing every step
There is a price
There is a price
For every gift
And all advice

2009

Black Locket

It lies in "the way of seeing the world": in the technical sacredness of seeing that world.

—Pier Paolo Pasolini, *of his film* Accatone

The ornament hung from my neck is a black locket
with a chain barely felt for years   clasp I couldn't open
Inside: photographs of the condemned
                                        Two
mystery planets
invaded from within

. . .

Pitcher of ice water thrown in a punched-in face
Eyes burnt back in their sockets
Negative archaeology

. . .

Driving the blind curve trapped in the blind alley
my blind spot blots the blinding
beauty of your face

. . .

I hear the colors of your voice

2009

Generosity

Death, goodlooking as only a skeleton can get
(good looks of keen intelligence)
sits poised at the typewriter, her locale, her pedestal
two books, one called *Raging Beauty*
another *Lettera Amorosa*, on this table
of drafts arguments letters
Her fine bony fingers go on calmly typing
the years at her turquoise-blue machine
(I say her but who knows death's gender
as in life there are possible variations)
Anyway he or she sat on your desk in Tucson
in the apartment where you lived then and fed me
champagne, frybread, hominy soup and gave me
her or him   Later at the 7-Eleven we bought
a plastic sack of cotton to pack Death safe for travel
vagabond poet who can work anywhere
now here and of course still working
but startled by something or someone
turns her head   fingers lifted in midair

for Joy Harjo

2009

Powers of Recuperation

i

A woman of the citizen party—*what's that*—
is writing history backward

her body   the chair she sits in
to be abandoned   repossessed

The old, crusading, raping, civil, great, phony, holy, world,
    second world, third world,
    cold, dirty, lost, on drugs,

infectious, maiming, class
war lives on

A done matter she might have thought
ever undone though   plucked

from before her birthyear
and that hyphen coming after

She's old, old, the incendiary
woman

endless beginner

whose warped wraps you shall find in graves
and behind glass   plundered

ii

Streets empty now   citizen rises   shrugging off
her figured shirt   pulls on her dark generic garment   sheds
identity inklings   watch, rings, ear studs
now to pocket her flashlight   her tiny magnet
shut down heater   finger a sleeping cat
lock inner, outer door   insert
key in crevice   listen once twice
to the breath of the neighborhood
take temperature of the signs   a bird
scuffling   a frost settling

*. . . you left that meeting around two a.m.   I thought
someone should walk with you*

Didn't think then I needed that

years ravel out   and now

who'd be protecting whom

I left the key in the old place
in case

iii

Spooky those streets of minds
shuttered against shatter

articulate those walls
pronouncing rage and need

fuck the cops   come jesus
blow me again

Citizen walking catwise
close to the walls

heat of her lungs leaving
its trace upon the air

fingers her tiny magnet
which for the purpose of drawing

particles together will have to do
when as they say the chips are down

iv

Citizen at riverbank   seven bridges
Ministers-in-exile with their aides
limb to limb dreaming underneath

conspiring by definition

Bridges   trajectories arched
in shelter   rendezvous

two banks to every river   two directions
to every bridge
twenty-eight chances

every built thing has its unmeant purpose

v

Every built thing with its unmeant
meaning   unmet purpose

every unbuilt thing

child squatting   civil
engineer   devising

by kerosene flare   in mud
possible tunnels

carves in cornmeal mush   irrigation
canals by index finger

all new learning looks at first
like chaos

the tiny magnet throbs
in citizen's pocket

vi

Bends under the arc walks bent listening for chords and codes
bat-radar-pitched or twanging
off rubber bands and wires tin-can telephony

to scribble testimony by fingernail and echo
her documentary alphabet still evolving

Walks up on the bridge   windwhipped   roof and trajectory
shuddering under her catpaw tread
one of seven

built things holds her suspended
between desolation

and the massive figure on unrest's verge
pondering the unbuilt city

cheek on hand and glowing eyes and
skirted knees apart

2007

New and Unpublished Poems

Itinerary

i.

Burnt by lightning   nevertheless
she'll walk this terra infinita

lashes singed on her third eye
searching definite shadows   for an indefinite future

Old shed-boards beaten silvery hang
askew as sheltering
some delicate indefensible existence

Long grasses shiver in a vanished doorway's draft
a place of origins   as yet unclosured and unclaimed

Writing cursive instructions on abounding air

If you arrive with ripe pears, bring a sharpened knife
Bring cyanide with the honeycomb

       call before you come

ii.

Let the face of the bay be violet   black the tumbled torn
kelp necklaces strewn alongshore

Stealthily over time arrives the chokehold
stifling ocean's guttural chorales
               a tangle
of tattered plastic rags

iii.

In a physical world the great poverty would be
to live insensate   shuttered against the fresh

slash of urine on a wall
low-tidal rumor of a river's yellowed mouth
a tumor-ridden face asleep on a subway train

What would it mean to not possess
a permeable skin
explicit veil to wander in

iv.

A cracked shell crumbles.
Sun moon and salt dissect the faint
last grains

An electrical impulse zings
out   ricochets
in meta-galactic orbits

a streak of nervous energy rejoins the crucible
where origins and endings meld

There was this honey-laden question mark
this thread extracted from the open
throat of existence—Lick it clean!
—let it evaporate—

2011

For the Young Anarchists

Whatever we hunger for
we're not seagulls, to drop things
smash on the rocks   hurtling beak-down
Think instead the oysterman's
gauging eyes, torqued wrist
hand sliding the knife into
and away from the valve hinge—
astuteness honed through
generations to extract
the meat   Cut out it can slip
through your fingers   Kicked in the sand
forget it   Only every so often will
diver rise up from stalking grounds
lifting this creature into daylight and
everyone standing around
shrinks   or think they want some   We've
fumbled at this before   trammeled
in fury, in hunger   Begin there, yes
—only fury knowing its ground
has staying power—
Then go dead calm remembering
what this operation calls for—
eye, hand, mind   Don't
listen to chatter, ignore all yells
of haphazard instruction   And
when you taste it don't
get too elated   There'll be grit
to swallow   Or spit to the side

2010

Fragments of an Opera

Scene One: Ales, Sardinia, 19——

Child's voice (Antonio):

from this beam

the doctors think

I can hang straight

in this har

ness dang

ling

dai

ly

grow how

I

should be

Explicator's voice:

Village doctor on a southern island
Treating one of seven
Children of a
Father in prison
For smalltime
Pecuniary
Crimes, maybe
Framed

Mother's
Heroic measures:
Knee presses, releases
Presses again the lever
Of a machine

Fingers push
Cloth
Under the needle

A woman stitches
Years months weeks days pass
In this way

Six children
Run and scream
Antonio must hang
From a beam

Recitativo: Neurosurgeon's voice:

It would have been a kind of traction.   Who knows how
it might have been done differently, elsewhere, in another
era of medical intervention?   Another country?   Other
family?   It was a kind of childhood.   Perhaps rickets?   spina
bifida?   scoliosis?

Explicator's voice:

A kind of mind
That would address
Duress
Outward in larger terms

A mind inhaling exigency
From first breath
Knows poverty
Of mind
As death

Whose body must
Find its own mind

Recitativo: Prosecutor's voice: from the future:

We must prevent this mind from functioning for twenty years.

Scene Two: Turin, Northern Italy

Industrialist's voice:

Turin, Turin makes tractors for FIAT
Makes armored cars and planes
We're making, we're taking,
We're raising our goals
We can use immigrants
We can use women
Illiterate peasants from the South
There's a war out there
A World War and it's buying
Who's crying?

Liberté

Ankles shackled
metalled and islanded
holding aloft a mirror, feral
lipstick, eye-liner
                              She's
a celebrity   a star attraction

A glare effacing
the French Revolution's
risen juices   vintage taste

the Paris Commune's
fierce inscriptions
lost in translation

2011

Teethsucking Bird

Doves bleat, crows repeat
ancient scandals
mockingbird's flown to mock
some otherwhere

Listen, that teethsucking bird's
back up on the telephone wire
talking times and customs
naming the dead to the half-alive
hardship to lyric and back again
to the open road of the toll-taker's
booth at the last exit
to skateboarding boys of body bags
to the breaker of hearts of the old-age motel
to the would-be weird of the scalded woman's
escarpment of a face

And this is the now the then the gone
the means and ends the far and near
the news we hear
from the teethsucking bird

2010

Undesigned

i.

It wasn't as if our lives depended on it—
a torrential cloudburst scattering
mirrors of light :: sunset's prismatics
in a Tucson parking lot
then the desert's mute inscrutable
way of going on
but it was like that between us :: those
moments of confrontation caught in dread
of time's long requirements

. . .

What's more dreadful than safety
you're told your life depends on
a helmet through whose eyeholes
your gun is seeing
only what guns can see

—a mask that wove itself without your
having designed it

ii.

On video :: a man exploding
about being sick for no reason
though he knows he knows the reason
:: a video that will travel
around the world
while the man sickens and sickens

. . .

You say we live in freedom
Have you watched the ceiling overhead
descending like Poe's pendulum
moving down slow and soundless
lower and closer for longer
than we'd thought

The last word in freedom
The first word

2011

Suspended Lines

Scrape a toxic field with a broken hoe

Found legacies turn up in splinters   blood-codes, secret sharings

Cracks of light in a sky intent on rain

    Reading our words from a time
    when to write a line was to know it true

    Today your voice :: *you can make from this*

One-string / blue / speaking / guitar

suspended here

2011

Tracings

This chair delivered yesterday

built for a large heavy man

left me from his estate

lies sidewise legs upturned

He would sit in the chair spooked by his own thoughts

He would say to himself *As the fabric shrinks*

the pattern changes

and forget to write it

He would want to say *The drug that ekes out*

life disenlivens life

I would see words float in the mirror

behind his heaped desk

as thought were smoke

.   .   .

The friends I can trust are those who will let me have my death
—traced on a rafter salvaged
from a house marked for demolition

Sky's a mottled marble slab
webs drift off a railing
There were voices here
once, a defiance that still doesn't falter
Imagine a mind overhearing language
split open, uncodified as
yet or never
Imagine a mind sprung open to music
—not the pitiless worm of a tune that won't let you forget it
but a scoreless haunting

2011

From Strata

1

Under this blue
immune unfissured autumn
urbs et orbis   pivot and axis   thrashing

upthrust from strata
deep under : silences
pressed each against

another : sharpened flints
pulverized coral   stoneware crumblings
rusted musket muzzles

chips of China-trade
porcelain   shackled bone
no death unchained

Here at eye-level the new
news new season new
moment's momentary flare :

floodlit abstractions
root-riven   scrambling
for adulation

Yes, we lived here long and hard
on surfaces stunned by the wrecking ball
where time's thought's creature only

and when all's fallen   even
our remnant renegade selves
—let this too sleep in strata :

the nerve-ends of my footsole
still crave your touch as when
my earlobes glowed between

your quiet teeth

2

Say a pen must write underground   underwater   so be it

   The students gather at the site :

   Come over here and look at this
   Looks like writing   yes   that's how they did it   thought it

   into marks they thought
   would outlast them

   it would take patience to do that   Anyone
                              recognize the script?

   Could it be music?   a manifesto?

3

Rescuers back off   hands lifted open as in guilt
for the ancestors no one is rescued from :

curated galleried faces staring
off   from behind long-stiffened bandages

but who would meet those lookaway eyes
maybe they're metal   blind reflectors

maybe only who choose to look can see :
thought finding itself in act

violet olive brush strokes speaking of flesh
leaps diagonals pauses : a long conversation

with others living and dead
palpable and strange

4

Viscous stealth, brutal calm : subterfugal, churning
encrypted in tar   sending expendable

bodies to underworlds unseen   until
catastrophe blows apart

the premises   a spectacle hits
the TV channels   then in a blink

a dense cloth wipes history clean :

but never in beds never to warm again
with the pulsing of arrival   shudder of wordless welcome

the body heat of breadwinners and lovers

5

My hands under your buttocks   your fingers numbering my ribs
how a bow scrapes, a string holds the after-pluck

astonishing variations   hours, bodies without boundaries

Back into that erotic autumn I search my way defiant

through passages of long neglect

6

Throw the handwritten scraps of paper
into the toilet bowl

to work their way spiraling down
the open gullet of advanced barbarism

So : if you thought no good came from any of this
not the resistance nor its penalties

not our younger moments nor the continuing on
then, I say, trash the evidence

So : a scrap of paper   a loved bitter scrawl
swirls under into the confluence

of bodily waste and wasted bodies :
—a shred   absorbed, belonging

7

Weathers drag down and claw up the will :
yellowdust wind   asphalt fog   a green slash
of aurora borealis   or :

a surveillance helicopter's high-intensity beam
impaling solitudes   ransacking solidarities

In the end no pleas no bargains :

it's your own humanity you'll have to drag
over and over, piece by piece
                page after page
                        out of the dark

2010—2011

Endpapers

i.

If the road's a frayed ribbon strung through dunes
continually drifting over
if the night grew green as sun and moon
changed faces and the sea became
its own unlit unlikely sound
consider yourself lucky to have come
this far   Consider yourself
a trombone blowing unheard
tones   a bass string plucked or locked
down by a hand its face articulated
in shadow, pressed against
a chain-link fence   Consider yourself
inside or outside, where-
ever you were when knotted steel
stopped you short   You can't flow through
as music or
as air

ii.

What holds what binds is breath   is
primal vision in a cloud's eye
is gauze around a wounded head
is bearing a downed comrade out beyond
the numerology of vital signs
into predictless space

iii.

The signature to a life requires
the search for a method
rejection of posturing
trust in the witnesses
a vial of invisible ink
a sheet of paper held steady
after the end-stroke
above a deciphering flame

2011

Notes on the Poems

Your Native Land, Your Life

SOURCES

The phrase "an end to suffering" was evoked by a sentence in Nadine Gordimer's *Burger's Daughter*: "No one knows where the end of suffering will begin."

NORTH AMERICAN TIME: IX

Julia de Burgos (1914–1953), Puerto Rican poet and revolutionary who died on the streets of New York City.

DREAMS BEFORE WAKING

"Hasta tu país cambió. Lo has cambiado tú mismo" ("Even your country has changed. You yourself have changed it"). These lines, from Morejón's "Elogio de la Dialéctica," and Georgina Herrera's poem "Como Presentación, Como Disculpa" can be found in Margaret Randall, ed., *Breaking the Silences: Twentieth Century Poetry by Cuban Women* (1982). Pulp Press, 3868 MPO, Vancouver, Canada V6B 3Z3.

ONE KIND OF TERROR: A LOVE POEM: 6

"Now you have touched the women, you have struck a rock, you have dislodged a boulder, you will be crushed." Freedom song sung by African women in mass demonstration in Pretoria, 1956, in which 20,000 women gathered to protest the issue of passes to women. See Hilda Bernstein, *For Their Triumphs and for Their Tears*, International Defence and Aid Fund for Southern Africa, 1975.

YOM KIPPUR 1984

The epigraph and quoted lines from Robinson Jeffers come from *The Women at Point Sur and Other Poems* (New York: Liveright, 1977).

CONTRADICTIONS: 16

See Elizabeth Bishop, *The Complete Poems 1927–1979* (New York: Farrar, Straus & Giroux, 1983), p. 173.

CONTRADICTIONS: 26

See Cynthia Ozick, *Art and Ardor* (New York: Farrar, Straus & Giroux, 1984), p. 255: "the glorious So What: the life-cry."

CONTRADICTIONS: 27

Ding Ling, leading Chinese novelist and major literary figure in the Revolutionary government under Mao. Exiled in 1957 for writing too critically and independently. Imprisoned as a counter-revolutionary in 1970; cleared of all charges in 1976 at the end of the Cultural Revolution.

Time's Power

SLEEPWALKING   NEXT TO DEATH

Title and opening words from "Slaapwandelen (naast de dood)" by Chr. J. van Geel, Dutch poet and painter. For the original and my translation, see Adrienne Rich, *Necessities of Life* (New York: Norton, 1966).

HARPERS FERRY

In 1859, the white abolitionist John Brown rented a farm near Harpers Ferry, Virginia (now West Virginia), as a base for slave insurrections. On October 16 of that year, he and his men raided and captured the federal arsenal, but found their escape blocked by local militia; the U.S. marines then seized the arsenal. Ten of Brown's men were killed in this conflict, and Brown himself was later tried and hanged. Harriet Tubman (1820–1913), Black anti-slavery activist and strategist, led more than 300 people from slavery to freedom via the Underground Railroad. She was known as "General Moses." Though in contact with John Brown, she withdrew from participation before the raid. Tubman never actually came to Harpers Ferry; her appearance in this poem is a fiction.

LIVING MEMORY

"it was pick and shovel work . . .": quoted from *Wally Hunt's Vermont* (Brownington, Vt.: Orleans County Historical Society, 1983).

An Atlas of the Difficult World

AN ATLAS OF THE DIFFICULT WORLD: V

"over the chained bay waters." From Hart Crane, "To Brooklyn Bridge," in *The Poems of Hart Crane*, ed. Marc Simon (New York and London: Liveright, 1989; poem originally published in 1930). "There are roads to take when you think of your country." From Muriel Rukeyser, *U.S. I* (New York: Covici Friede, 1938); see also Muriel Rukeyser, *The Collected Poems* (New York: McGraw-Hill, 1978). "I don't want to know how he tracked them." On May 13, 1988, Stephen Roy Carr shot and killed Rebecca Wight, one of two lesbians camping on the Appalachian Trail in Pennsylvania. Her lover, Claudia Brenner, suffered five bullet wounds. She dragged herself two miles along the trail to a road, where she flagged a car to take her to the police. In October of that year, Carr was found guilty of first-degree murder and sentenced to life in prison without parole. During the legal proceedings, it became clear that Carr had attacked the women because they were lesbians. See *Gay Community News* (August 7 and November 11, 1988).

AN ATLAS OF THE DIFFICULT WORLD: VI

"Hatred of England smouldering like a turf-fire." See Nella Braddy, *Anne Sullivan Macy: The Story behind Helen Keller* (Garden

City, N.Y.: Doubleday, Doran & Company, 1933), p. 13. "Meat three times a day." See Frank Murray, "The Irish and Afro-Americans in U.S. History," *Freedomways: A Quarterly Review of the Freedom Movement* 22, no. 1 (1982): 22.

AN ATLAS OF THE DIFFICULT WORLD: X

The passages in italics are quoted from *Soledad Brother: The Prison Letters of George Jackson* (New York: Bantam, 1970), pp. 24, 26, 93, 245

TATTERED KADDISH

"The Reapers of the Field are the Comrades, masters of this wisdom, because *Malkhut* is called the Apple Field, and She grows sprouts of secrets and new meanings of Torah. Those who constantly create new interpretations of Torah are the ones who reap Her" (Moses Cordovero, Or ha-Hammah on Zohar III, 106a). See Barry W. Holtz, ed., *Back to the Sources: Reading the Classic Jewish Texts* (New York: Summit, 1984), p. 305.

FOR A FRIEND IN TRAVAIL

"The love of our neighbor in all its fullness simply means being able to say to him 'What are you going through?'" Simone Weil, *Waiting for God* (New York: Putnam, 1951), p. 115.

Dark Fields of the Republic

WHAT KIND OF TIMES ARE THESE

The title is from Bertolt Brecht's poem "An Die Nachgeborenen" ("For Those Born Later"): *What kind of times are these / When it's almost a crime to talk about trees / Because it means keeping still about so many evil deeds?* (For the complete poem, in a different translation, see John Willett and Ralph Manheim, eds., *Bertolt Brecht, Poems 1913–1956* [New York: Methuen, 1976], pp. 318–320.)

"our country moving closer to its own truth and dread . . ." echoes Osip Mandelstam's 1921 poem that begins *I was washing outside in the darkness* and ends *The earth's moving closer to truth and to dread.* (Clarence Brown and W. S. Merwin, trans., *Osip Mandelstam: Selected Poems* [New York: Atheneum, 1974], p. 40.) Mandelstam was forbidden to publish, then exiled and sentenced to five years of hard labor for a poem caricaturing Stalin; he died in a transit camp in 1938.

"To be human, said Rosa . . .": Rosa Luxemburg (1871–1919) was a Polish-born middle-class Jew. Early in her abbreviated life she entered the currents of European socialist revolutionary thinking and action. She became one of the most influential and controversial figures in the social-democratic movements of Eastern Europe and Germany. Besides her political essays, she left hundreds of vivid letters to friends and comrades. Imprisoned during World War I for her strongly internationalist and anticapitalist beliefs, she was murdered in Berlin in 1919 by right-wing soldiers, with the passive collusion of a faction from her own party. Her body was thrown into a canal. On December 28, 1916, from prison, she wrote a New Year letter to friends she feared were both backsliding and complaining: "Then see to it that you remain a *Mensch!* [Yiddish/German for human being] . . . Being a *Mensch* means happily throwing one's life 'on fate's great scale' if necessary, but, at the same time, enjoying every bright day and every beautiful cloud. Oh, I can't write you a prescription for being a *Mensch.* I only know how one is a *Mensch*, and you used to know it too when we went walking for a few hours in the Südende fields with the sunset's red light falling on the wheat. The world is so beautiful even with all its horrors." *The Letters of Rosa Luxemburg*, ed., trans. and with an intro. by Stephen Eric Bronner (Atlantic Highlands, N.J.: Humanities Press, 1993), p. 173.

CALLE VISIÓN

Calle Visión is the name of a road in the southwestern United States—literally, "Vision Street."

"that tells the coming of the railroad." "With the coming of the railroad, new materials and pictorial designs and motifs, including trains themselves, appeared in Navaho weaving (ca. 1880)." (From the Museum of Indian Arts and Culture, Museum of New Mexico, Santa Fe.)

"a place not to live but to die in." See Sir Thomas Browne, *Religio Medici* (1635): "For the World, I count it not an Inn, but an Hospital; and a place not to live, but to dye in." (*Religio Medici and Other Writings by Sir Thomas Browne* [London: Everyman's Library, J. M. Dent, 1947], p. 83.)

"Have you ever worked around metal? . . ." From a questionnaire filled out before undergoing a magnetic resonance imaging (MRI) scan.

"The world is falling down . . . ." From the song "The World Is Falling Down," composed by Abbey Lincoln, sung by her on the Verve recording of the same title, 1990 (Moseka Music BMI).

"And the fire shall try . . . ." I Corinthians 3:13: "Every man's work shall be made manifest . . . and the fire shall try every man's work of what sort it is." Used by Studs Terkel as an epigraph to his *Working* (New York: Pantheon, 1974).

REVERSION

This poem is for Nina Menkes and her film *The Great Sadness of Zohara*.

THEN OR NOW

This sequence of poems derives in part from Hannah Arendt and Karl Jaspers, *Correspondence 1926–1969*, ed. Lotte and Hans Saner, trans. Robert and Rita Kimbel (New York: Harcourt Brace Jovanovich, 1992). While reading these letters, I had been reflecting on concepts of "guilt" and "innocence" among artists and intellectuals like myself in the United States. The poems owe much also to the continuing pressure of events.

SIX NARRATIVES

The narratives are spoken by different voices.

"Vigil for boy of responding kisses, . . ." See Walt Whitman, "Vigil strange I kept on the field one night," in *The Essential Whit-*

man, selected and ed. Galway Kinnell (New York: Ecco Press, 1987,) pp. 123–124.

Inscriptions

"I need to live each day through . . . ." These two lines are quoted from an earlier poem of mine ("8/8/68: I") in "Ghazals (Homage to Ghalib)"; see above.

"When shall we learn, what should be clear as day, . . . ?" These two lines are from W. H. Auden's "Canzone," in *The Collected Poetry of W. H. Auden* (New York: Random House, 1945), p. 161.

"Medbh's postcard from Belfast." I thank the Northern Irish poet Medbh McGuckian for permission to quote her words from a postcard received in August 1994.

"suffused / by what it works in, 'like the dyer's hand.' " I had written "suffused," later began looking up the line I was quoting from memory: was it Coleridge? Keats? Shakespeare? My friend Barbara Gelpi confirmed it was Shakespeare, in his Sonnet 111: *Thence comes it that my name receives a brand / And almost thence my nature is subdued / To what it works in, like the dyer's hand.* I have kept "suffused" here because to feel *suffused* by the materials that one has perforce to work in is not necessarily to be *subdued*, though some might think so.

Midnight Salvage

Char

Italicized phrases and some images from *Leaves of Hypnos*, the journal kept in 1942–1943 by the poet René Char while he was a commander in the French Resistance, and from some of Char's poems. I have drawn on both Jackson Mathews's and Cid Corman's translations of Char's journal in integrating his words into my poem. Char joined the Surrealist movement late and broke with it prior to World War II. It was André Breton who said, "The simplest surrealist act consists of going down into the street, revolver in hand, and shooting at random."

MODOTTI

Tina Modotti (1896–1942): photographer, political activist, revolutionary. Her most significant artistic work was done in Mexico in the 1920s, including a study of the typewriter belonging to her lover, the Cuban revolutionary Julio Antonio Mella. Framed for his murder by the fascists in 1929, she was expelled from Mexico in 1930. After some years of political activity in Berlin, the Soviet Union, and Spain, she returned incognito to Mexico, where she died in 1942. In my search for Modotti I had to follow clues she left; I did not want to iconize her but to imagine critically the traps and opportunities of her life and choices.

CAMINO REAL

"Can you afford not to make / the magical study / which happiness is?" From Charles Olson, "Variations Done for Gerald Van der Wiele," in *Charles Olson, Selected Poems*, ed. Robert Creeley (Berkeley: University of California Press, 1997), p. 83.

"George Oppen to June Degnan: . . ." See George Oppen, *The Selected Letters of George Oppen*, ed. Rachel Blau DuPlessis (Durham, N.C.: Duke University Press, 1990), p. 212.

Fox

MESSAGES

Blaise Pascal (1623–1662): *Le silence éternel de ces espaces m'affraye.* (The eternal silence of these infinite spaces frightens me). See *Pensées of Blaise Pascal*, trans. W. F. Trotter, Everyman's Library no. 874 (London: Dent, 1948), p. 61.

NOCTILUCENT CLOUDS

"Several times in the last few months, observers in the lower 48 have seen 'noctilucent clouds,' which develop about 50 miles above the earth's surface—clouds so high that they reflect the sun's rays long after nightfall. . . . [G]lobal warming seems to be driving them toward the equator. . . . In retrospect it will be clear."

Bill McKibben, "Indifferent to a Planet in Pain," *New York Times*, Saturday, 4 September 1999, sec. A.

"Usonian": The term used by Frank Lloyd Wright for his prairie-inspired American architecture.

Terza Rima: 3

Vivo nel non volare . . . : "I live in the failed will / of the post-war time / loving the world I hate"—Pier Paolo Pasolini, "Le Ceneri di Gramsci," in Lawrence R. Smith, ed. and trans., *The New Italian Poetry, 1945 to the Present* (Berkeley: University of California Press, 1981), pp. 80–81. See also Pier Paolo Pasolini, *Poems*, selected and trans. Norman MacAfee and Luciano Martinengo (London: John Calder, 1982), pp. 10–11.

Waiting for You at the Mystery Spot

"The *mystai* streamed toward [the Telestrion]." C. Kerényi, *Eleusis*, trans. Ralph Manheim, Bollingen series 65, vol. 4 (New York: Bollingen Foundation/Pantheon, 1967), p. 82.

The School Among the Ruins

Tell Me

"remembered if outlived / as freezing." Emily Dickinson, *The Complete Poems*, ed. Thomas H. Johnson (Boston: Little, Brown, 1960), no. 341.

"harrowed in defeats of language." Michael Heller, "Sag Harbor, Whitman, As If An Ode," in *Wordflow: New and Selected Poems* (Jersey City, N.J.: Talisman House, 1997), p. 129.

"in history to my barest marrow." *Black Salt: Poems by Édouard Glissant*, trans. Betsy Wing (Ann Arbor: University of Michigan Press, 1998), p. 33.

This Evening Let's

"friendship is not a tragedy." See June Jordan, "Civil Wars" (1980), in *Some of Us Did Not Die: New and Selected Essays* (New York: Basic Books, 2002), p. 267.

TRANSPARENCIES

"we are truely sorry . . .": Clyde Haberman, "Palestinians Reclaim Their Town after Israelis Withdraw," *New York Times*, August 31, 2001, p. A6.

ALTERNATING CURRENT

The Villa Grimaldi outside Santiago, formerly a military officers' club, was converted to a detention and torture facility during the Pinochet regime in Chile. It is now a memorial park honoring the victims of torture.

DISLOCATIONS: SEVEN SCENARIOS: 5

"You thought you were innocent . . .": See Paul Nizan, *Aden Arabie* (New York: Monthly Review Press, 1968), p. 131.

Telephone Ringing in the Labyrinth

CALIBRATIONS

Landstuhl: American military hospital in Germany.

"You go to war with the army you have." U.S. Secretary of Defense Donald Rumsfeld, December 2004.

HUBBLE PHOTOGRAPHS: AFTER SAPPHO

For Sappho, see *Greek Lyric*, I: *Sappho, Alcaeus*, trans. David A. Campbell, Loeb Classical Library 142 (Cambridge, Mass.: Harvard University Press, 1982–), fragment 16, pp. 66–67: "Some say a host of cavalry, others of infantry, and others of ships, is the most beautiful thing on the black earth, but I say it is whatsoever a person loves. . . . I would rather see her lovely walk and the bright sparkle of her face than the Lydians' chariots and armed infantry."

THIS IS NOT THE ROOM

U.S. Vice President Richard Cheney, on NBC's *Meet the Press*, September 16, 2001: "we also have to work, though, sort of, the dark side . . . use any means at our disposal, basically, to achieve our objective."

REREADING *The Dead Lecturer*

See LeRoi Jones (Amiri Baraka), *The Dead Lecturer: Poems* (New York: Grove, 1967).

LETTERS CENSORED, SHREDDED, RETURNED TO SENDER OR JUDGED UNFIT TO SEND

Passages in quotes are for *Giuseppe Fiori, Antonio Gramsci: Life of a Revolutionary*, trans. Tom Nairn (New York: Verso, 1990), pp. 31, 239; Antonio Gramsci, *Prison Letters*, ed. and trans. Hamish Henderson (London: Pluto Press, 1996), p. 135; and *Antonio Gramsci, Prison Notebooks,* ed. Joseph A. Buttigeig, trans. Joseph A. Buttigeig and Antonio Callari, 2 vols. (New York: Columbia University Press, 1992), I, p. 213.

DRAFT #2006: VI

"Out of sight, out of mind." See Carolyn Jones, "Battle of the Beds," *San Francisco Chronicle*, December 19, 2005, p. A-1.

Tonight No Poetry Will Serve

WAITING FOR RAIN, FOR MUSIC

"*Send my roots rain.*" Gerard Manley Hopkins, *Gerard Manley Hopkins: Selections, 1986,* ed. Catherine Phillips, The Oxford Authors (New York: Oxford University Press, 1986), p. 183.

"*A struggle at the roots of the mind.*" Raymond Williams, *Marxism and Literature* (Oxford, Eng.: Oxford University Press, 1977), p. 212.

READING THE *ILIAD* (AS IF) FOR THE FIRST TIME

"For those dreamers who considered that force, thanks to progress, would soon be a thing of the past, the *Iliad* could appear as an historical document; for others, whose powers of recognition are more acute and who perceive force, today as yesterday, at the very center of human history, the *Iliad* is the purest and the loveliest of mirrors": Simone Weil, *The Iliad; or, The Poem of Force*, (1940), trans. Mary McCarthy (Wallingford, Pa.: Pendle Hill, 1956), p. 3.

"Delusion / a daughter." See Homer, *The Iliad*, trans. Rich-mond Lattimore (Chicago: University of Chicago Press, 1951), pp. 394–395, bk. 19, lines 91–130.

"Horses turn away their heads / weeping." Homer, pp. 365–366, bk. 17, lines 426–440.

I WAS THERE, AXEL

"The Blue Ghazals." See Adrienne Rich, *The Will to Change* (New York: Norton, 1971), p. 24.

BALLADE OF THE POVERTIES

This revival of an old form owes inspiration to François Villon, *The Poems of François Villon*, ed. and trans. Galway Kinnell (Boston: Houghton Mifflin, 1977).

BLACK LOCKET

"*It lies in 'the way of seeing the world'* . . .": Laura Betti, ed., *Pier Paolo Pasolini: A Future Life* (Italy: Associazione "Fondo Pier Paolo Pasolini," 1989), pp. 19–20.

GENEROSITY

The books mentioned are James Scully, *Raging Beauty: Selected Poems* (Washington, D.C.: Azul Editions, 1994), and René Char, *Lettera Amorosa* (Paris: Gallimard, 1953), with illustrations by Georges Braque and Jean Arp.

POWERS OF RECUPERATION

"the massive figure on unrest's verge." See *Melencolia I*, a 1514 engraving by Albrecht Dürer. The "I" is thought to refer to "Melen-colia Imaginativa," one of three types of melancholy described by Heinrich Cornelius Agrippa (1486–1535).

Acknowledgments

Some of the new poems included appeared in the following print and online journals:

Xcp: Cross-Cultural Poetics: "For the Young Anarchists"
Red Wheelbarrow: "Teethsucking Bird"
Monthly Review: An Independent Socialist Magazine: "Liberté"
Granta: "Endpapers"
Tin House: "From Strata"
Paris Review: "Itinerary"
A Public Space: "Tracings"
Kweli Journal: "Undesigned," "Suspended Lines"

Index of Titles
and First Lines